TIMPSON'S ENGLISH ECCENTRICS

CONTRIBUTORS

AUTHOR
John Timpson O.B.E.

RESEARCHERS
Jan Tavinor
Paula Granados
Sue Winston

EDITOR
Paula Granados

DESIGNER
Geoff Staff

PHOTOGRAPHERS
John Brooks
Neil Jinkerson
Charles Nicholas

ILLUSTRATOR
Ryz Hajdul

BUST OF EDWIN JEHOSOPHAT ODELL, SAVAGE CLUB, LONDON.

CHARLES WATERTON'S UNIVERSAL SUNDIAL, WALTON HALL, WEST YORKSHIRE.

THE DYED DOVES OF FARINGDON HOUSE, BERKSHIRE.

TIMPSON'S ENGLISH ECCENTRICS
Designed and produced by Parke Sutton Publishing Limited, Norwich
for Jarrold Publishing, Norwich

First published 1991 by Jarrold Publishing
Paperback edition 1994

ISBN 0-7117-0559-3 hardback ISBN 0-7117-0683-2 paperback

Printed in Belgium

TIMPSON'S ENGLISH ECCENTRICS

JOHN TIMPSON

CONTENTS

Viscount Petersham, who invented the Petersham Coat.

John Bigg – The Dinton Hermit.

INTRODUCTION

I suppose my first encounter with English eccentrics en masse was during my early years on 'Today', when the programme did not take itself quite so seriously for quite so much of the time. I always found it a relief to escape for a few minutes from erudite economists and garrulous generals – let alone all those plausible politicians – to have a chat with the clairvoyant chip shop owner from Wigan who knew what a customer was going to order from the colour of his car, or the Doncaster businessman who drove to his office in a mechanical digger because vandals kept taking bits off his Rolls Royce. I was quite enchanted by the seventy-four-year-old Norfolk lady who climbed the Himalayas spurning any kind of transport, four-wheeled or four-legged, accompanied only by sherpas who all addressed her as 'Mummy'; I was less enchanted by the gourmet who brought some of his spiders into the studio – and ate them.

There was the RAF sergeant who somehow played 'Rule Britannia' by hitting himself on the head with a nine-inch spanner – it was something to do with how wide he opened his mouth. He was surpassed only by the man in Portsmouth who played tunes by cupping his hand under his armpit and pumping his arm up and down. It was unfortunate that our line to Portsmouth got crossed with the line to another studio, where an eminent statesman was waiting to address us on the state of the nation; he seemed a little disconcerted when the first question from London was: 'Before we start the interview, would you mind playing us a tune under your armpit?'

No doubt that hapless politician thought it was the interviewer who was being eccentric. And this is the problem with defining just what eccentricity is. Something which fifty years ago would have seemed very odd indeed – a two-piece swimsuit, watching hours of snooker on television, diet books in the bestseller list – is commonplace today; what may seem very odd today – baggy football shorts, a man offering his seat to a lady, interviewers being polite to politicians – would be perfectly normal then. And what may seem eccentric to me could seem entirely natural to you. But I think the characters in this book would seem eccentric to most of us in any age – and on the whole, endearingly so.

If one were looking for the archetypal English eccentric, I suppose a strong candidate would be Colonel Charles de Laet Waldo Sibthorp, whose name alone should earn him a place in these pages. Colonel Sibthorp was MP for Lincoln from 1826 until his death in 1855, and in those thirty years, as one commentator put it: 'he set a standard of reaction, nationalism and xenophobia unrivalled in parliamentary history'.

He considered that any change in the English way of life was a change for the worse, and the arrival of the railways was the worst change of all. 'They are run by public frauds and private robbers whose nefarious schemes will collapse, and the old and happy mode of travelling the turnpike roads, in chaises, carriages and stages, will be restored.' He did in fact succeed in preventing the Great Northern Railway from taking its main line through Lincoln, to the despair of its more enterprising citizens. But his greatest loathing was reserved for foreigners – 'it would take ninety-nine foreigners to make one thorough good Englishman' – and he fought against the 1851 Great Exhibition because it would attract hordes of spies and foreign ragamuffins. His detestation of foreigners did not exclude Prince Albert, and one of his rare parliamentary successes was to get the Prince Consort's allowance reduced by nearly half. Again his constituents paid the penalty: Queen Victoria was so incensed she vowed never to visit the city while Sibthorp was its MP.

Yet such is the good-humoured attitude of the English to our great eccentrics that the good burghers of Lincoln re-elected their bizarre Member time after time. Punch *absolutely revelled in 'our gallant Colonel', as they called him, and his bushy black whiskers, his quizzing glass and his out-dated tailcoat and high boots featured in countless cartoons. Even his fellow MPs, exasperated as they were by his preposterous utterances and obstructive tactics – he constantly divided the House to vote against his minority of one – still seemed to tolerate his antics with remarkable patience. Those he lambasted in his speeches – which meant just about everybody – seemed quite resigned to being accused of anything from 'apostasy, hypocrisy and perfidy' to 'treachery, expediency and pusillanimous tergiversation'. It was only old Sibthorp, they reflected – and in* Hansard *his speeches were peppered, not with cries of protest or counter-accusation, but just the oft-repeated word, 'Laughter'.*

These days our politicians are a less colourful lot, and more's the pity. We have to look outside Parliament for these larger than life eccentrics, but when we find them we still appreciate them. I need only mention Jeffery Bernard, Low Life correspondent of the Spectator, *whose attitude to women would seem very reminiscent of Colonel Sibthorp's attitude to foreigners. His worst moment, I understand, was when they started serving drinks to women in El Vino's. I once interviewed him on the subject of office parties, and he was particularly virulent about those which overflowed into his pub – which he normally used as an office. 'Suddenly the place is filled with these Christmas idiots. There are the silly*

A DANGEROUS CHARACTER.

Policeman Sibthorp. "COME, IT'S HIGH TIME YOU WERE TAKEN TO THE HOUSE; YOU'VE DONE QUITE MISCHIEF ENOUGH."

little girls who drink Cointreau, then a light ale and a snowball, and round it off with a glass of sherry. They usually end up in tears, being sick, and probably pregnant.'

His distaste in this instance was not confined to the women. 'With them are the "young executives" with their Mexican moustaches and their aluminium attaché cases, filled with copies of Yachting Monthly *and* Motor Sport, *thinking they've got tremendous style because just once a year they say: "Have a drink, and make it a* **large one**" *– as if there's anything less than a large one.'*

You may think that Mr Bernard would make himself a trifle unpopular with this sort of outburst. On the contrary, it led to him being immortalised by Keith Waterhouse in one of the most successful West End productions of recent years, as the English public demonstrated its delight for a genuine English eccentric.

There are about 120 more in this book. I have divided them into different groups: eccentric animal-lovers, eccentric clergy, eccentric recluses, and so on. By a happy chance – well, not entirely – even the initial letters of the chapter titles add up to eccentricity. But many of these characters were difficult to classify under any particular heading, and you may well consider that my choice in some cases is, yes, eccentric. Wherever they pop up, I hope you will enjoy meeting them, if only at second hand, as much as I did when I first discovered them.

I may have had some gentle fun with them, but I hope I have never mocked them, because however bizarre their behaviour may have seemed to others, I am sure they considered it entirely normal themselves. As far as they are concerned, it is the rest of us who are the eccentrics. And who can be certain they are wrong?

John Timpson O.B.E.

PERFORMANCE OF OUR FRIEND SIBBY IN THE LOBBY OF THE HOUSE OF COMMONS, AFTER THE DECISION TO PULL DOWN THE CRYSTAL PALACE.

ECCENTIMENTALS

love me, love my rat
– or whatever

The English have always been eccentric about animals. What other country would have a 'Royal' Society for the Prevention of Cruelty to Animals, but only a 'National' Society for the Prevention of Cruelty to Children? And what other country would spend millions trying to keep human sewage away from its beaches, but merely tut-tut when they are extensively fouled by pet dogs? Indeed it is dogs we are mostly dotty about, with cats a close second, but the devotion of English eccentrics can extend to pigs, and cows, and sheep, and rats.

Rats? Most certainly. Not just the smaller rodents, the white mice and gerbils and lemmings – though keeping a lemming has an eccentric quality all its own. We had a pair of them in our household at one time, rejoicing in the improbable names of Robert and Margaret. I always wanted to let them loose on the table to see if they would take a flying leap to destruction, but my small son, whose pets they were, refused to chance it. They did occasionally escape from his bedroom, but always stopped half-way down the stairs. His theory was that, having got that far, they decided the jump from each stair wasn't sufficiently challenging, so they gave up in disgust.

I was never quite sure why he gave them such unlemming-like names, but I know it seemed quite logical at the time. Thus animals make eccentrics of us all. But even my devoted lemming-owner would have baulked – I hope – at full-size rats, which I reckon are the most unlovable creatures to invade the domestic scene.

Not so SIR THOMAS BARRETT-LENNARD, squire of Belhus in Essex from 1857 until his death in 1918 at the age of ninety-two. His workers were instructed to keep a fresh bowl of water in the corn rick for the rats, and his servants were ordered not to harm any that entered the house. The servants were not too happy about this, though no doubt the rats were delighted. A Mrs Duligal, who was a maid at Belhus, recalled many years later: 'The worst trouble was the rats. They were so big – they were as big as cats, and as tame as tame could be. Sir Thomas wouldn't let them be killed, so everything had to be put under cover or it was all eaten up. The noise they made was like people running up and down the corridor. Sometimes you could hear chairs moving – they must have been everywhere'.

SIR THOMAS BARRETT-LENNARD, WHOSE LOVE FOR ANIMALS EXTENDED EVEN TO RATS – HIS WORKERS WERE INSTRUCTED TO KEEP A FRESH BOWL OF DRINKING WATER IN THE CORN RICK FOR THEIR BENEFIT. THE HOUSE WAS FULL OF THEM TOO – 'AS BIG AS CATS, AND AS TAME AS TAME COULD BE'.

Sir Thomas was equally solicitous about the rooks, which everybody else considered a pest, and about his deer, which he was very reluctant to have killed for venison. He was appalled by ill-treatment of animals of any variety, and the *Grays & Tilbury*

Gazette recorded how, in his later years, he came upon a butcher mistreating his pony. 'He bade the brute desist, and upon receiving a cheeky reply to "mind his own business", Sir Thomas whipped off his coat in a moment, and before the astonished butcher knew where he was, he was the recipient of a tremendous hiding at the hands of the old gentleman, who to his surprise knew something of the art of fisticuffs.'

As well as being handy with his fists, Sir Thomas was a great runner. On muddy days, when he considered the land was too heavy for a horse to pull his carriage with him inside it, he would run alongside to save it the effort. He was a great rider too, with an expert knowledge of horseflesh, and for a time he kept the South Essex Foxhounds, but his love of animals extended to foxes also, and while the hunt took out the hounds he went steeplechasing instead.

In his later years Sir Thomas became somewhat eccentric over his clothes as well, wearing the shabbiest he could find. He liked to tell how he once opened his park gates for a visitor and was given a shilling tip. This little quirk about old clothes led to an interesting encounter with a policeman when he was walking home across the fields from Brentwood mental hospital, where he was Chairman of the Essex Asylums Committee. He was

Belhus, the splendid Essex home of Sir Thomas Barrett-Lennard and his dogs, cats, horses — and rats. His kindness to animals extended to humans too; he frequently answered the front door to save his butler the trouble. He liked to wear the shabbiest of clothes, and visitors were often startled into thinking they were being welcomed to this magnificent mansion by a tramp.

scrambling out of a hedge when the policeman grabbed him and asked where he had come from.

'Brentwood lunatic asylum,' said Sir Thomas.

'I knew it!' cried the policeman, and marched him back there again . . .

Of all the animals that Sir Thomas cared for, his greatest passion was for his dogs – not only the hounds and pointers that he bred, but the pet ones that shared his house with the rats. Whenever one died, it was placed in a coffin and accorded a full-scale funeral in the grounds, with a footman bearing the dear departed and Sir Thomas leading the procession in a long white robe. As the coffin was lowered into the grave in his private canine cemetery, Sir Thomas read prayers from the Anglican burial service.

ALL THAT REMAINS OF SIR THOMAS BARRETT-LENNARD'S HOME AT BELHUS – NOW SURROUNDED BY A GOLF COURSE. THE HORSES, DOGS, CATS AND RATS HAVE BEEN REPLACED BY BIRDIES, EAGLES AND THE OCCASIONAL ALBATROSS.

This rather excessive sentimentality over dogs was not unusual among the aristocracy, and Sir Thomas was not the only one to accord them full posthumous honours. For instance, in 1916 a Pekinese called Che Foo – Wuzzy to his friends – was commemorated by its owner, the then DUCHESS OF BEDFORD, by a bronze effigy slumbering on top of a stone plinth in the grounds of Woburn Abbey, under a wrought iron dome set on Corinthian pillars. The plinth bears one of those verses which is guaranteed to make animal-haters of us all. It reads, if you can bear it:

When the body that lived at your single will,
When the whisper of welcome is still (how still),
When the spirit that answered your every mood
Is gone — wherever it goes — for good.
You will discover how much you care
And will give your heart to a dog to tear . . .

I believe it goes on, but you have borne enough. As for Che Foo himself, immortalised in these tear-jerking lines, I think Ogden Nash summed it up admirably: 'A dog's best friend,' he wrote, 'is its illiteracy'. He makes a good point too about another popular pet:

The trouble with a kitten is
That
It eventually becomes a cat . . .

The elaborate monument to the Duchess of Bedford's favourite Pekinese.

But before I leave dogs, I cannot omit the most eccentric aristocratic dog-lover of them all, **Francis Henry Egerton**, the eighth Earl of Bridgewater, who did not just honour his dogs with fancy tributes when they were dead, he treated them most extravagantly while they were alive, entertaining them to dinner dressed in the height of fashion — and that was the dogs, not the Earl. The little dears sat on chairs in all their finery, with handmade leather shoes on their feet and linen napkins round their necks, and a footman stationed behind each dog to tend to its needs. The Earl maintained that they behaved themselves as well as any gentleman, 'with decency and decorum', but if one of them did put a paw wrong it was stripped of its fine clothes, put into servants' livery, and sent to eat in the kitchen for a week.

A doggy dinner is served at the Earl of Bridgewater's. Animal crackers, perhaps?

The Earl preferred living in France to the splendid family mansion, Ashridge House in Hertfordshire, and frequently drove through Paris in his ornate carriage adorned with the Bridgewater crest outside and half a dozen dogs on silk cushions inside. The Parisians doubtless assumed that all Englishmen behaved this way and thought nothing of it, even when he left the carriage and walked in the rain in the Bois de Boulogne with an umbrella protecting, not him, but the dogs . . .

Two aspects of Ashridge House in Hertfordshire, where the eighth Earl of Bridgewater entertained his dogs to dinner. The horses, one assumes, were not invited.

What he did miss about English life, apparently, was hunting, and he would stage miniature hunts in his Paris garden, wearing hunting pink and riding behind imported English hounds, with an imported English huntsman, in pursuit of an imported English fox. Again the locals accepted that this was quite natural behaviour for an Englishman, but I understand they did baulk at another little fancy of his, installing pigeons and partridges with clipped wings in his garden so he could shoot them in comfort.

Lord Bridgewater's eccentricities, like Sir Thomas Barrett-Lennard's, spread from his animals to his own attire, but in a different direction. He had a passion for footwear, and wore a different pair of shoes on each day of the year. Each night his boots were placed beside those he had worn the day before, until he had rows and rows of them, all in the right order and all in the same state as when he took them off. Thus he could not only calculate the date by adding them all up, but he could also work out what the weather had been like on any particular day, from the amount of mud or dust on that pair of boots. A diary would have

Francis Henry Egerton, eighth Earl of Bridgewater and eccentric animal-lover.

The magnificent chapel at Ashridge House. In spite of having such a splendid family mansion in Hertfordshire he much preferred living in France, where they no doubt assumed that his odd little ways were merely normal behaviour for the English aristocracy.

been simpler, and taken up less space, but it all seemed perfectly logical to the Earl.

Perhaps not surprisingly he never married, and when he died in 1829 the title became extinct. Among bibliophiles his name is still remembered for the Egerton manuscripts he left to the British Museum, but I shall remember him for those doggy dinner parties and the phrase which they may have inspired: 'done up like a dog's dinner'.

As a footnote to the story of Lord Bridgewater, it is perhaps worth recording the very conversational identity disc that FREDERICK, PRINCE OF WALES put on the pet dog given to him by Alexander Pope. Normally it would just be a name and address, but this well-bred little aristocrat had the message engraved on his collar: 'I am his Highness' dog at Kew; pray tell me, sir, whose dog are you?'

Enough of dogs and other orthodox pets. How about a household containing an albino hedgehog, a duck with no webbing between its toes, a three-toed sloth and a Brazilian toad? These were all the pets of CHARLES WATERTON of Walton Hall in West Yorkshire, notable nineteenth-century naturalist, traveller, explorer – and eccentric animal-lover. He was fond of all kinds

WALTON HALL, THE WEST YORKSHIRE HOME OF CHARLES WATERTON, RENOWNED NATURALIST AND FRIEND OF ANYTHING THAT WALKED, FLEW OR SLITHERED. HE TURNED THE GROUNDS INTO ENGLAND'S FIRST NATURE RESERVE – COMMENDABLY 'GREEN' THESE DAYS, BUT QUITE ECCENTRIC AT THE TIME.

An unfinished water-colour depicting Charles Waterton re-enacting his intrepid crocodile-ride in the grounds of Walton Hall, with his other animal friends looking on.

of animals, with the notable exception, unlike Sir Thomas, of brown rats, which he detested. But snakes, toads, vampire bats, crocodiles – he doted on them all.

He also had his own methods of coping with them. When his native guides in Guiana had difficulty in capturing a large boa constrictor, he solved the problem by removing his braces and tying them round the snake's jaws; and he once captured a crocodile, Tarzan-style, by jumping on its back, hanging on to its front legs, and staying astride it until it was exhausted. He commented afterwards that it had been much the same as riding to hounds.

Mr Waterton was not quite so successful with a vampire bat that he captured and kept in his bedroom, in the hope it would bite him and he could record the effect. He slept with one bare foot hanging out of the blankets for bait, but the bat ignored the foot and bit his Indian servant instead. He was at least able to record the servant's reactions – or those parts that were fit to print.

When he gave up his travels and moved into Walton Hall in the 1820s he fenced off a large area of the estate to create a bird and animal sanctuary. It was the first of its kind, and considered very eccentric at the time; these days it would just be called 'diversification'. He continued to devote all his time to his furry friends; the live ones on the estate he kept observation on – often from the upper branches of a tree – and the dead ones he stuffed, sometimes in the most unlikely forms. He liked to join up the limbs and bodies of different species and

A more orthodox portrait – except for the stuffed bird and the bodyless cat. From Cheshire, perhaps?

Two of Charles Waterton's curious creations, made from bits of different animals and birds. 'John Bull and the National Debt', a porcupine with an almost human face weighed down by monetary devils (above). The Nondescript, not a newly-discovered species but made by Waterton from the skin of a howler monkey (right).

place the bizarre results around the house to unnerve his guests.

One of these creations was just the head of a bearded man, but made from the skin of a howler monkey. He called it The Nondescript, and liked to spread sensational stories about it. First he pretended it was a new species of wild animal, and when that failed to impress, he said it was modelled on a customs officer he had fallen foul of at Liverpool Docks. The locals preferred to believe it was the head of some weird native he had murdered on his travels, which he had had mounted like a hunting trophy. Whatever story was current at the time, the The Nondescript was guaranteed to give visitors a nasty turn when they suddenly came upon it at the top of the staircase.

An ardent Catholic, Waterton created a bird he called Noctifer by combining parts of an eagle owl with a bittern, and explained it was 'the Spirit of the Dark Ages, unknown in England before the Reformation'; while a monkey with horns and a sinister expression was described as 'Martin Luther after his fall'.

His eccentricity over animals extended to imitating their behaviour. His guests not only had to put up with his strange stuffed exhibits, but also with Waterton himself, hiding in the hallway on all fours when they arrived, and nipping them in the shin as they hung up their coats. It did not stop there. In front of one bewildered dinner party he followed up the cheese and biscuits by dissecting a gorilla on the dining-room table.

Newcomers visiting Walton Hall for the first time got a foretaste of what they were in for as soon as they reached the front door. It had two knockers, both cast in the shape of human faces, and a friend described them thus: 'One face represents mirth, and the other misery. The former is immovably fixed to the door, so when you have wound up your feelings to give a smart rap-tap-tap, and are suddenly and unexpectedly disappointed by not being able to raise the knocker, this face seems to grin with intense delight'. By the time you have used the genuine knocker, and then been greeted by your host sinking his teeth into your calf, I suppose a stuffed head on the staircase and a half-dissected gorilla on the dining-table must seem quite run of the mill . . .

THE WEIRD DOOR KNOCKERS AT WALTON HALL; ONLY THE MISERABLE ONE WORKED.

There is no denying, however, that Charles Waterton's eccentric approach to the animal world was enormously effective. At London Zoo they probably still talk about his encounter with an orang-utan that had just arrived from Borneo and was in a very bad temper indeed. Waterton asked to enter the cage to soothe him, believing that the beast was just feeling lonely. Fortunately he was right. The orang-utan greeted him literally with open arms, they hugged like old friends, and spent some time together, inspecting each other's anatomy in traditional orang-utan style. When they eventually parted it was with obvious regret on both sides.

Waterton's colourful life had its sad side. After the early death of his wife he refused to sleep in a bed, and for the next thirty-five years spent his nights lying on the floor wrapped in a cloak, with a block of wood for a pillow. He rose at 3.30 am, spent an hour in his private chapel, then started his day's work, always breakfasting on dry toast and watercress with a cup of milkless weak tea. But this frugal life seemed to keep him uncommonly fit. He was still climbing trees when he was eighty, and his death in 1865 at the age of eighty-three was not through illness but the result of a fall. At his own request he was buried between two large oaks in his park-cum-nature-reserve; there is a charming local legend that flights of birds followed his coffin to the grave.

About the time that Waterton was born, another Yorkshireman was already making a name for himself as an eccentric

The birthplace of Jemmy Hirst, who started his eccentric career with animals while still at school, teaching his headmaster's pig to jump hurdles. In later years he went hunting on his pet bull, but his attempt to train pigs as foxhounds was a failure — their squealing was too much for the huntsmen, let alone the fox.

animal-lover, but James Hirst of Rawcliffe was a very different character, and interested in very different animals. Like Waterton he did go in for curious house pets; he had an otter and a tame fox, and a not-so-tame bear called Nicholas which mauled him badly in one encounter. But he concentrated mainly on bulls, pigs and mules. He always rode a bull at the local hunt, he tried to train pigs as hounds, and he had four Andalusian mules to draw a weird wickerwork carriage which he designed himself.

None of Jemmy Hirst's activities was in the cause of conservation or research, like Charles Waterton's. They were purely for his own entertainment, though they provided a fair amount of entertainment for spectators as well. But he did share Waterton's inclination to play practical jokes involving his animals; and fortunately, like Waterton, he had very tolerant friends – both men were extremely popular in their own circles.

Jemmy was not so popular with his masters at school, where his eccentricity over animals was already developing. In 1746, at the age of eight, he was sent to a boarding school at Pontefract, where he made an immediate enemy of the headmaster by removing the lenses from the spectacles he had left on the desk. But this was only a preliminary skirmish; Jemmy created much more of an impression when he started riding the headmaster's pig. An anonymous biographer wrote: 'He had just got the old sow to jump over a stick about a foot high, and was practising this novel equestrian feat after school hours one night, when who should come into the yard but the principal himself, bringing a horsewhip with him'.

Jemmy got a thrashing and was put on bread and water, 'yet was in no wise deterred from mounting his swinish charger in future whenever he had the opportunity'. He had many more beatings before he left school, but this merely seemed to encourage him. By the time he was twenty-five he had transferred his attention from sows to bulls, and managed to break in a young bull called Jupiter, with such success that he regularly rode

THE COUNTESS OF MOUNT EDGCUMBE in her grand mansion in Cornwall, and MR WILLIAM KEYTE in his modest cottage in Gloucestershire, could have had little in common except for one idiosyncrasy — they were both devoted to an unlikely pet. In the case of the Countess it was a pig, in Mr Keyte's it was a trout.

It is not clear why her ladyship formed such a close association with a pig, but it would be nice to think it had something to do with the family coat of arms, which includes three boars' heads, or the family crest, which is an entire boar complete with ferocious fangs at one end and curly tail at the other. But however it came about, Cupid the pig was Lady Emma's constant companion at all her social engagements and even on her long journeys from Cornwall to London.

When it died in 1789 it was buried beneath an obelisk in the gardens of Mount Edgcumbe, and Lady Emma's son, the second Earl, composed the inscription for it: 'Porco Fiddissimo cupidini, Hic Tumulus inscribitur', which I suppose means roughly: 'Here lies Cupid, a jolly nice pig'.

One of the Countess' friends, the writer John Wolcott, did rather better. He wrote what he called a 'consolatory stanza' for her ladyship which perhaps puts her bereavement more in perspective:

O dry that tear so round and big,
Nor waste in sighs your precious wind
Death only takes a single pig —
Your lord and son are still behind.

William Keyte's trout did not actually travel about with him, but undoubtedly there was a close bond between them. He trained it to rise to the surface and take food from his hand, and thanks to his loving care it survived for a remarkable twenty years in his garden at Fish Cottage, Blockley. Surprisingly he never seems to have given it a name; it was just known as 'The Old Trout'. When it died in 1855, again it was the owner's son who composed the epitaph. Keyte junior did not run to Latin epigrams; his message was simple and direct:

Under the soil the old fish do lie,
Twenty years he lived, and then did die.
He was so tame you understand,
He would come and eat out of your hand.

him to hounds. His extraordinary mount became a familiar sight at local meets; the hunt permitted him to join them for his sheer entertainment value. It was not only the bull that distinguished him from the other riders; his hunting gear consisted of a lambswool hat with a brim nine feet in circumference, a red jacket with blue sleeves, a multi-coloured waistcoat made from his tailor's spare clippings, equally dazzling breeches and yellow boots.

Needless to say, some of the riders tried to make fun of him, but he was easily their match. One youngster insisted on addressing him as Joseph, saying that must be his name because he had a coat of many colours. 'Young fellow,' said Jemmy, 'thou shouldn't never be too ready to take things by their first appearance, for on first sight of thee I took thee to be a gentleman.'

When Jemmy tried his hand at training pigs to act as hounds, perhaps remembering his exploits with the headmaster's sow, it turned out that their continual grunting was too off-putting for the huntsmen, let alone the fox. So he turned his hand to inventions. He produced a windmill for cutting up turnips, which actually worked, and a pair of feathered wings to fly with, which didn't. Then he devoted the best part of a year to building a wickerwork carriage, rather like an up-ended cradle on a pair of wheels.

At first he used the versatile Jupiter to pull it; later he made an enlarged version and harnessed it to four Andalusian mules. But whatever animals were in the shafts, it was Jemmy Hirst and

JEMMY HIRST'S HUNTING GEAR WAS AS ECCENTRIC AS HIS MOUNT — ENORMOUS LAMBSWOOL HAT, RED AND BLUE JACKET, MULTI-COLOURED WAISTCOAT AND BREECHES, AND YELLOW BOOTS. THE SIGHT OF JEMMY ON HIS BULL JUPITER MUST HAVE BEEN ALMOST AS UNNERVING FOR HIS FELLOW HUNTSMEN AS IT UNDOUBTEDLY WAS FOR THE FOX.

the carriage which made the impact on other road users — even more so when he attached a sail to it and travelled by wind power instead of bull power or mule power. On his first excursion into Pontefract a puff of wind caught him amidships and blew the carriage into a draper's window. Jemmy climbed out of the shattered window, righted the overturned carriage and proceeded to the nearest tavern, where he bought a barrel of ale to celebrate his survival. This proved so popular with the locals that they insisted on drawing his carriage themselves until he reached the outskirts of the town, safely out of range of any more shop windows. Then he set sail again and had a safe journey home.

Jemmy's exploits with his animals and his curious carriage reached the ear of George III, who was so intrigued he instructed a chamberlain to invite him to court. Jemmy's reply was fairly typical. 'What does his Majesty wish to see me for? I'm nothing related to him, and I owe him nothing that I know of. I suspect thou has been telling him what queer clothes I wear, and suchlike. Well, thou may tell his Majesty that I am very busy just now, training an otter to fish, but I'll contrive to come in the course of a month or two.'

The King took this uncommonly well, and in due course Jemmy drove to London in his wicker carriage, drawn by the four mules and wearing his multi-coloured hunting gear with the enormous broad brimmed hat. The journey took three days, and he was greeted with delighted amusement all the way, not least on his arrival in London. When he reached the court and was shown into the royal presence, instead of kneeling and kissing the King's hand he shook it warmly, said he was glad to meet such a plain and homely old gentleman, and he'd be happy to see him at Rawcliffe any time he cared to come.

Anyone else might have finished up in the Tower, but it is a measure of the true eccentric that he caused no offence. In fact the King took to him greatly, and asked to inspect his famous carriage. Jemmy showed him the clock he had invented for it which measured the distance he had travelled (the original carriage clock?) and also drew attention to the container he had installed for carrying wine, which was conspicuously empty. The King took the hint, and had it filled from the royal cellars.

As Jemmy was leaving, one of the court commented loudly on the size of his hat: 'It is three times as big as need be'. It gave Jemmy the

ANOTHER OF JEMMY HIRST'S LITTLE ECCENTRICITIES — HE PRODUCED AN IMITATION FIVE-POUND NOTE WHICH WAS ACTUALLY MADE OUT FOR FIVE HALFPENCE AND ISSUED BY HIS NON-EXISTENT BANK OF RAWCLIFFE. THE NOTE'S ONLY GENUINE FEATURE WAS THE ILLUSTRATION OF HIS WICKERWORK CARRIAGE, WHICH HE ALSO DESIGNED HIMSELF.

A commemorative mug showing Jemmy Hirst's bull Jupiter and his wickerwork carriage.

chance for one of his crushing one-liners. 'I'll tell thee what, young fellow, if people never made use of any more than they just required, his Majesty would not require thy attendance, for what good thou canst do.' Applause, and exit stage left.

Mr Hirst, you will have gathered, was anything but a morbid man – he enjoyed life enormously. But this did not prevent him from making his own eccentric arrangements for his demise. He made himself a coffin for his eventual occupation – and to make good use of it in the meantime he stood it on end in his sitting-room, fitted it with glass doors instead of a lid, and used it as a drinks cabinet. He was so taken with this style of furniture that he had another one made, this time rather larger with trick doors and a bell inside. He persuaded his visitors to enter it, whereupon the doors closed and locked automatically. The bell was installed in case somebody got trapped inside when he was not present – but he made them wait for up to half an hour before releasing them, and then extracted a forfeit for their inquisitiveness.

Jemmy Hirst was ninety when the drinks cabinet was at last required for its original use. His final journey was as bizarre as any that he made in his lifetime. In his will he asked that twelve old maids should carry him to the grave, led by a Scottish bagpiper and a fiddler. The vicar objected to so much musical accompaniment – not the bagpipes, surprisingly, but the fiddle – and the piper had to play solo. There also had to be a compromise over the twelve old maids, since only two could be found who were able to swear they were virgins. The ten vacancies were filled by broadminded widows.

Jemmy had one final eccentric gesture to make from the grave. One of his bequests, to a local lawyer, was just a short length of rope. His will made it quite clear why: 'I give to John Bingley a small rope which we call a falce line – suchlike things are used with unfortunate people at the gallows at York and other places – for his roguish and rascally villainous scandalous deceiving behaviour to me for carrying on a law suit against my mind and orders which cost me £250 . . . I also wish and desire a copy of this to be put up in some public place in Rawcliffe on Feast Monday in August every year, so long as the said John Bingley shall live. I promised him I would leave him something at my death, and I always had a great liking to be as good as my word'.

No doubt John Bingley was roguish and rascally enough to find some way of preventing this annual humiliation, but well done Jemmy, it was worth a try . . .

COMPETICENTRICS

taking sport to extremes

Some forms of sport have always struck me as eccentric in themselves. Jogging, for instance. What an astonishingly tedious activity, panting along the pavements wearing ridiculous clothes and an agonised expression, causing embarrassment to passers-by as they get a whiff of all that sweat, and possibly doing more harm than good to the actual jogger – at best bruised heels, at worst a heart attack. Does anybody actually enjoy it, I wonder? God loves a cheerful giver, but He might be even more impressed by a cheerful-looking jogger.

Then there is fishing. I can understand the delights of whiling away an afternoon on a sunlit river bank, the scent of wild flowers wafting on the breeze, the water rippling peacefully at one's feet. But just as Mark Twain dismissed golf with his immortal 'Why spoil a good walk?', why spoil a good sit by impaling maggots on hooks in order to impale fish on the maggots? It is an odd enough occupation in fine weather; in a heavy rainstorm or a biting gale, when the experience is almost as unpleasant for the fishermen as for the unfortunate fish they catch, it must surely enter the realms of eccentricity.

Yet some anglers go to even greater extremes. Take THOMAS BIRCH, for instance, who led a fairly mundane working life as a librarian at the British Museum, but in his spare time was a quite fanatical fisherman. He had the ingenious idea of deceiving the fish by disguising himself as a tree, and he devised an elaborate costume which concealed him inside an imitation tree-trunk with his arms sticking out as branches. The fishing rod was covered by a spray of blossom. This sort of get-up is not unknown in pantomime, and even Shakespeare disguised one of his characters as a wall, but among the eighteenth-century fishing fraternity it was regarded as distinctly odd, and Thomas Birch, although fancying himself as Thomas *the* Birch, took such a ribbing from his colleagues that he

GONE FISHING . . . THOMAS BIRCH DISGUISED HIMSELF AS A TREE TO CONFUSE THE FISH, BUT ONLY CONFUSED THE LOCAL RAMBLERS.

had to give it up – but not before he had caused considerable alarm to unsuspecting passers-by. Nobody seems to have recorded whether he actually caught any fish.

Fifty years later his idea was taken up, in somewhat modified form, by SIR HUMPHREY DAVY, distinguished scientist, inventor of the coalminers' Davy Lamp, and enthusiastic angler. He liked to disguise himself, not quite as a tree, but as some form of natural greenery. He wore a green coat, green trousers and a green hat. As one of his contemporaries observed: 'Davy flattered himself he resembled vegetable life as closely as it was possible to do'. He was also a keen shot, and here he took the opposite theory when selecting his dress. Apparently not trusting the eyesight nor the accuracy of his fellow sportsmen, he always tried to be as conspicuous as possible, to insure against being shot by mistake. He particularly favoured a bright red broad-brimmed hat, which must have effectively deterred the birds as well as the bullets.

The sport which seemed to attract the strangest characters, however, was neither shooting nor fishing, but hunting. In the eighteenth and nineteenth centuries the hunting fields of England were bespattered with pink-clad eccentrics. The uneatable was pursued, not so much by the unspeakable as by the absolutely incredible. Such a man was GEORGE OSBALDESTON, so devoted to hunting that he was popularly known as 'The Squire of All England'. He maintained that any week in which he did not spend six days in the saddle was a week wasted, and his feats of sporting endurance, both on and off the hunting field, became legendary.

GEORGE OSBALDESTON, WHOSE ENTHUSIASM FOR HUNTING EARNED HIM THE TITLE OF 'SQUIRE OF ALL ENGLAND'. ANY WEEK IN WHICH HE FAILED TO SPEND SIX DAYS IN THE SADDLE WAS A WEEK WASTED.

Osbaldeston was born in 1787, and was already hunting by the time he went to Oxford. He became a Master of Hounds while he was still an undergraduate – it was just a matter of buying a pack from the Earl of Jersey – and he went hunting three days a week until he left university early, without bothering to take a degree, in order to devote more time to the sport. At the age of twenty-five, probably to his own surprise, he found himself in Parliament, but never spent enough time there to make a speech. Instead, if he was not on the hunting field as Master of the Pytchley, he was shooting in Norfolk, or racing at Newmarket, or gambling almost anywhere.

If there had been a Guinness Book of Records in the early nineteenth century, George Osbaldeston would have monopolised it. He was reputed to have killed a hundred birds with a hundred shots, to have put forty bullets from a pistol through the ace of diamonds at thirty yards, to have played billiards for fifty hours non-stop, and in one all-night card session to have gambled £100 a trick and £1,000 a rubber. But his most spectacular feats were in the saddle. He rode so tirelessly that he exhausted his hounds, so he bought mastiffs instead which he thought had more stamina, but they were outridden too. His riding culminated in a remarkable race against time in 1831, when he bet that he could ride two hundred miles in ten hours, round and round the four-mile course at Newmarket. Somebody offered him better odds if he could do it in only nine, and Osbaldeston could not resist the challenge.

Various writers have chronicled how he arrived at Newmarket in the early hours, a diminutive figure just over five feet tall, resplendent in a purple silk shirt, white riding breeches and black velvet cap. He had a bad limp from a hunting accident which had put him on crutches for a year, and at the age of forty-four some thought he was past his prime. Nevertheless he

Having ridden two hundred miles round and round the Newmarket racetrack in a record eight hours forty-two minutes, Osbaldeston celebrated with a hot bath at the Rutland Arms Hotel.

completed the two hundred miles in eight hours and forty-two minutes, using a series of twenty-seven horses and stopping only once to partake of a partridge and a brandy-and-water. And as soon as the timekeeper told him he had beaten the clock he got back in the saddle and galloped off to the Rutland Arms in Newmarket for a hot bath . . .

So Osbaldeston won that bet, but he lost a great many others, and eventually squandered the entire family fortune. He ended his days living on an allowance in St John's Wood, still a hero to the general public though not so popular among those who knew a little more about him. As an amateur rider, for instance, he used to crowd his professional opponents on the rails at Newmarket so they could not use their whips, knowing that the stewards, all fellow members of the gentry, would not penalise him. He could also be very unpleasant to anyone who got in the way of his hunting; if the League Against Cruel Sports had existed in those days, he would undoubtedly have done them a mischief.

But there is one creditable story about his inexhaustible energy as a rider, and the eccentric way he put it to use. At a ball in Lincoln he noticed that a very attractive lady was snubbed by another woman whom she tried to compliment on the fine orchid she was wearing. Osbaldeston decided to avenge her. He discovered that the orchid was grown in a private conservatory twenty-five miles away, and forthwith he leapt on his horse and galloped off to acquire a better one. The mission involved four hours of hard riding and some late-night wheeler-dealing at the conservatory, but he reappeared in the ballroom mudstained and somewhat sweaty, presented an even rarer orchid to the astonished young lady, and danced with her until dawn . . .

George Osbaldeston was just one of the nineteenth-century hunting fraternity who combined endurance with eccentricity. One Master, a MR TAILBY, was over seventy when his horse threw him and fell on top of him; he lay unattended for several hours with a broken thigh. But as soon as it mended he was back in the saddle again, and was still riding when he was over eighty. The Cheshire Hunt may remember a huntsman called JOE MAIDEN, who broke his hip once and leg twice, but still hunted six days a week with one stirrup half the length of the other. And for really spectacular eccentricity both on and off the field it is difficult to beat JACK MYTTON, Squire of Halston in Shropshire and a contemporary of Osbaldeston, though perhaps it is as well they never met – it would have been a most exhausting encounter.

Mytton has been called the Evel Knievel of his time, but he went much further than jumping motorbikes over rows of buses. He fought dogs and bears with his teeth, he drove his carriage over tollgates (or at least attempted to), he went duck-hunting in winter in his nightshirt, and he chased rats cross frozen ponds on his skates. He once bet a friend that he could give him a fifteen-minute start and still out-ride him home, then won comfortably by taking a short cut through a lake, still seated in the saddle, regardless of the fact that he could not swim and if he had been thrown in the water he would probably have drowned.

Even his horse, called Baronet, was something of an eccentric, a one-eyed animal which had been Jack Mytton's charger when he was serving in the Hussars, and adapted itself to the hunting field so ably that it could jump nearly thirty feet across water. During bad weather Mytton would knock on a cottage door and ask if Baronet could dry off by the fire – and since the cottage probably belonged to him anyway he was rarely refused. With another of his horses, called Sportsman, he tried a different method of warming it up on a chilly day; he plied it with an entire bottle of port. Soon afterwards, perhaps predictably, Sportsman dropped dead – though no doubt with a smile on his face.

There were many similarities between Mytton and George Osbaldeston. Both came from good county families and inherited substantial fortunes, both had unmemorable academic careers (Mytton was expelled from every school he attended), and both lost all their money – Osbaldeston mostly on gambling and Mytton mostly on drink. Some estimate that he got through five bottles of port a day, others put the figure at eight (not counting what he gave to his horse), and if the port ran out it was said that eau-de-Cologne or lavender water would do. Both men were Masters of hunts, but while Osbaldeston was considered the best breeder of hounds of his day, Mytton had no interest in his pack, and when times grew hard he sold them for the price of their skins. They were so ill-trained that even his own huntsman observed that they would chase anything 'from a helephant down'.

But where Mytton did excel was in sheer extravagance. His wardrobe contained 150 pairs of riding breeches, 700 pairs of boots, over 1,000 hats and nearly 3,000 shirts. Yet when he went shooting his standard dress, even in the coldest weather, was a light jacket, linen trousers, silk stockings and boots as flimsy as dancing shoes, which only lasted a couple of days. In the excite-

'NEVER BEEN OVERTURNED IN A GIG? WHAT A DAMNED SLOW FELLOW YOU MUST HAVE BEEN ALL YOUR LIFE!' AND THAT WAS WHEN JACK MYTTON DROVE INTO A RABBIT HOLE . . .

ment of the chase he would often cast off what few clothes he was wearing to chase ducks naked through the marshes.

He drove a gig with as much abandon as Boadicea drove her chariot, and the effects were nearly as disastrous. He liked to drive into rabbit holes at high speed to see if the gig would turn over – and it invariably did. The experience came in useful when a nervous passenger complained about his reckless speed. 'Have you ever been overturned in a gig?' asked Mytton, and the passenger confessed he had not. 'Then what a damned slow fellow you must have been all your life,' cried Mytton, and promptly turned it over. Amazingly, they both escaped unhurt.

Like Osbaldeston, Mytton had a short way with any of the 'lower orders' who hampered his progress, but being rather larger than Osbaldeston he was quite prepared to settle matters with his fists. When a burly Welsh miner tried to head off his hounds he challenged him to fisticuffs and fought twenty gruelling rounds until the miner gave in. Then he congratulated the man on his performance and gave him half a sovereign.

Not all his eccentric escapades ended so happily. He decided to enliven a dinner party by riding a bear into the dining-room, but the bear had a poor sense of humour and declined to join in the fun. Instead it sank its teeth into Mytton's calf, and a doctor

Two more of Mytton's eccentric escapades: riding a bear into the dining-room among his guests, and setting fire to his own night-shirt to cure an attack of hiccups. In the first case he got badly bitten; in the second he was badly burned — but it did cure his hiccups.

had to be called. Mytton seems to have borne no ill will; he may well have given the bear half a sovereign too.

It took him only fifteen years to gamble away the family estate in Shropshire, lose the Parliamentary seat which the Myttons had held for generations, and dispose of his inheritance. He died in a debtor's prison when he was only thirty-eight. But even in his final days he had one more eccentric card to play. When he had a violent attack of hiccups he decided he needed a

shock to cure it – and set fire to his own night-shirt. His friends arrived in time to save his life, but he suffered appalling burns. His only comment: 'Well, the hiccups is gone, by God!'

I confess to a sneaking admiration for Jack Mytton, and certainly his hunting companions and other acquaintances admired him too; more than 3,000 of them attended his funeral. His more commendable qualities, of daring combined with good-natured eccentricity, were continued in the hunting field by a rather more famous Master, HUGH CECIL LOWTHER, fifth Earl of Lonsdale. His fame is associated more with boxing than hunting, through his sponsorship of the Lonsdale Belt, but he was a great rider to hounds too, Master at various times of the Cottesmore, the Quorn and the Woodland Pytchley, and he is credited with one of the biggest jumps in the history of fox-hunting, thirty-two feet, which Jack Mytton's Baronet never quite achieved.

Lord Lonsdale did not go in for riding bears into dining-rooms or overturning gigs in rabbit holes, but in other ways he was just as larger than life. With his fresh gardenia each morning and his six-inch cigar, he was once described as 'almost an emperor and not quite a gentleman' – though not, I imagine, to his face. He was more popularly known as 'The Yellow Earl', because of the yellow livery he designed for his servants and vehicles. It applied also in his gardens: the wheelbarrows were

THE SPORTING LORD LONSDALE WAS CALLED 'THE YELLOW EARL' BECAUSE OF HIS YELLOW CARRIAGES, YELLOW SERVANTS' LIVERY, EVEN YELLOW WHEELBARROWS IN HIS GARDEN. HE ALSO HAPPENED TO BE PRESIDENT OF THE AA . . .

The Yellow Earl himself.

yellow and so were the gardeners' cardigans. The Earl was President of the Automobile Association at the time, and many people maintain that the AA's yellow livery was his idea too. More probably it was chosen because it is easy for drivers to spot, but it's a nice theory.

The Yellow Earl understandably disliked his nickname, even though it was not as uncomplimentary as it would be today, and preferred to be called Lordy. This was how he was addressed on the hunting field, where he showed all the dash and daring of Osbaldeston and Mytton, with a little more irascibility thrown in. He was inclined to lash out at his fellow riders, let alone the 'lower orders', if they got in his way, and his horses fared rather worse. When a new hunter which had cost him £500 refused to jump, he ordered his groom to shoot it. The groom did not do so immediately, thinking that Lordy would remember what it cost and relent. He assumed that was why his Lordship came to the stables that evening and asked if the horse had been shot yet. 'No, m'lord,' said the groom, no doubt with some relief. 'Then shoot it,' said Lordy. And he did.

Lord Lonsdale came to a happier end than Mytton, or Osbaldeston. He was appointed a Knight of the Garter and his Barleythorpe Stud in Leicestershire became renowned for its thoroughbred stock. He continued hunting as Master of the Cottesmore until he was in his sixties, and he was eighty-seven when he died at Barleythorpe in 1944.

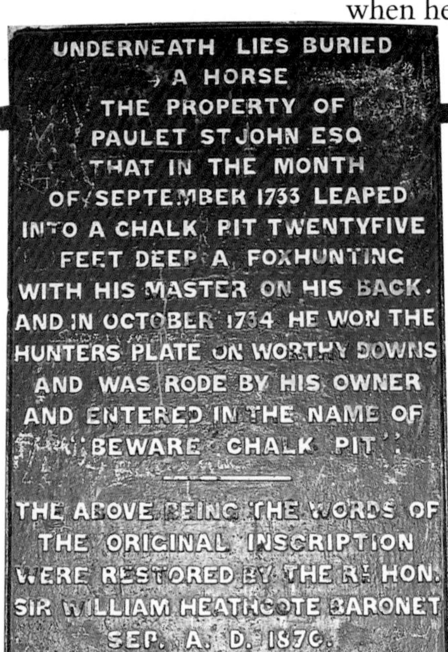

The epitaph on the monument to Paulet St John's oddly named hunter, 'Beware Chalk Pit' — it also explains how he earned the name.

Few hunting folk could be as ruthless with their horses as Lord Lonsdale, but few would go to such an opposite extreme as Paulet St John, who was so devoted to his mount that he erected a massive monument to it on a hillside near Winchester. The monument is as remarkable as the horse's name, 'Beware Chalk Pit', which it earned when it saved its master's life on the hunting field in 1733. They came upon a chalk pit too late to avoid it, and the horse leapt into it and landed safely, twenty-five feet below, with his master still on his back. Mr St John was so proud of his horse's feat that he erected the monument to commemorate it for all time, after 'Beware Chalk Pit' had leapt into the Last Great Chalk Pit in the Sky. The original plaque recounting the story had to be restored in 1870, but the monument itself, a lofty pyramid with porches on three sides, stands there still, a reminder not only of the prowess of the horse but also of the unusual character who rode it.

Adeline, Lady Cardigan, still held balls at which she appeared in a mantilla and layered skirts (left) when she was in her seventies. One of her ball gowns still survives today (above).

While most of the larger than life figures on the hunting field were men, they had a kindred spirit in Lady Cardigan, later the Comtesse de Lancastre, an eccentric Victorian lady who outraged society, not least the Queen, by living openly with Lord Cardigan for a year before they were married. She smoked openly too, which was nearly as bad, and she liked to go cycling in red military trousers and a leopard skin cape. But she was also devoted to hunting, and when she was too old to ride she still attended the meets wearing full hunting dress. She would emerge from her carriage, apparently eager to mount her hunter. Discovering it was not there, she would complain loudly that the stupid groom must have taken it to the wrong meet. Honour satisfied, she was able to settle back in the carriage and follow the hunt in comfort.

By now in her seventies, Lady Cardigan's behaviour away from the hunting field was just as unconventional. She would hold balls at which she appeared in a mantilla and layered skirts, and danced wild Spanish fandangos with castanets clicking. She would stroll in Hyde Park wearing a Louis XVI coat, a three-cornered hat over a curly blonde wig, and trailing her leopard skin cape. And she kept a coffin in the house for several years before her death, so she could lie in it to test it for size and comfort. When she did eventually occupy it permanently, life in London society must have been that much duller . . .

In the eighteenth and nineteenth centuries hunting was very much a rich man's sport, so it was hardly surprising that most of the hunting eccentrics came from the aristocracy. Wrestling was much less fashionable, which makes **Sir Thomas Parkyns** a much rarer character. The Wrestling Baronet, as he was known, was completely devoted to the sport, and apart from indulging in it himself he employed two professional wrestlers at his Nottinghamshire home, Bunny Hall, and organised regular wrestling contests for which he gave a cocked hat as a prize. The Hall was specially designed to accommodate these bouts, and he also gave

Bunny Hall, the home of Sir Thomas Parkyns, 'The Wrestling Baronet'. With its semi-circular roof surmounted by a square tower, he designed it to accommodate wrestling contests.

THE MEMORIAL TO SIR THOMAS PARKYNS IN BUNNY CHURCH. 'THE WRESTLING BARONET' LIES PROSTRATE, THROWN BY A PUGNACIOUS-LOOKING 'TIME'.

it a rather odd tower surmounting an enormous semi-circular roof. He built most of Bunny village too, on rather more orthodox lines, but when he came to design his own memorial in Bunny Church his passion for the wrestling ring took over. His tomb features a pugnacious little figure in typical wrestling stance, clad only in a loincloth and a large pair of wings. It looms over another prostrate figure, and an hourglass lying beside it illustrates the inscription:

> *That Time at length did throw him it is plain,*
> *Who lives in hopes that he should rise again.*

One might have thought, incidentally, that living in a place called Bunny, Sir Thomas would be more interested in shooting than wrestling, but in fact there is no connection with rabbits. The name comes from an old English word meaning 'reed' or 'rush', and there was indeed some boggy marshland near the village.

While wrestling was an unusual sport for a gentleman like Sir Thomas at the start of the eighteenth century, ballooning was just as unusual a sport for a lady at the start of the twentieth. MARY ELIZABETH COVE, known as Lily, must have been considered a trifle eccentric to take up ballooning in the first place, but she added a further touch of quirkiness by combining it with parachuting – on a professional basis. She was trained by her employer, one Captain Bidmead, billed as 'the hero of 400 balloon ascents and 83 parachute descents'. On the other 327 flights presumably he thought better of it.

Captain Bidmead had had some unpleasant experiences when he did jump. Once he fell eighty feet onto a roof, which fortunately was a sloping one so the impact was not quite so painful. On another occasion his parachute remained attached to the

Before the days of sponsorship the main excuse for idiotic sporting events was a wager. True gamblers would bet on almost anything, and if there was nothing actually happening to bet on, they invented it. Such a gambler was GEORGE HANGER, later Baron Coleraine, who by the age of twenty-two had fought three duels, married a gypsy, reached the rank of colonel and been wounded in the American War of Independence. At this stage he decided to retire from such hazardous pursuits and devote himself, as one writer put it, to 'drinking, gambling, racing and whoring' – but mostly gambling.

Inevitably he lost his fortune and spent eighteen months in a debtor's prison, but he emerged a reformed character, and to the astonishment and disdain of his aristocratic friends he went into business as a coal merchant. In due course most of his gambling escapades were forgotten, but one of his unlikely sporting promotions has lived on in the record books. Not content with conventional horse-racing, he staged a contest between twenty geese and twenty turkeys over a ten-mile course; not so much the Sport of Kings as the Sport of Cooks.

I have read of the stamina of geese being walked from Norfolk to London, and having seen the ungainliness of their opponents, I would have put my money on the geese. Typically, the eccentric Colonel Hanger put £500 on the turkeys. For once I would have been right – the turkeys turned out to be a load of old gobblers, and dropped out of the race after three miles. I hope that at least he enjoyed eating the losers – even at £25 a bird . . .

Lily Cove, intrepid lady balloonist at the turn of the century, in full flight. But alas, as a parachutist, her luck ran out. Her tombstone is in Haworth churchyard.

balloon, suspending him below it for several miles. When it neared the ground he was dragged across two fields, through a canal, and finally into a hedge. However, neither of these crash landings was as tragic as the fate that befell Lily Cove at Haworth Gala in Yorkshire on 11 June, 1906.

Lily had learned her jumping technique by sharing a double parachute with the captain, and she had completed some twenty successful solo drops by the time she performed at Haworth, so she had, as it were, got the hang of it. Captain Bidmead checked all the parachute fastenings before she took off, and at seven o'clock in the evening the balloon went up. Lily was wearing a white blouse, black knee-length trousers and, of course, the parachute. At 700 feet she made the jump. The crowd saw her part company with the balloon – and then, alas, she parted company with the parachute.

Nobody ever discovered how it happened. Captain Bidmead's theory was that she was drifting towards a reservoir, wanted to avoid it because she couldn't swim, and thinking she was close enough to the ground she detached the parachute. But it was much too great a drop for her to survive. When rescuers reached her she was unconscious, and bleeding from the nose and mouth. The first to arrive, a Mr Cowling Heaton, addressed her with more crispness than sympathy. 'My good woman,' he exhorted her, 'if you can speak, do!' Lily could not, and didn't. She died before a doctor arrived.

Lily Cove is buried in Haworth churchyard. Visitors are probably less interested in her than in those other Haworth ladies, the Brontés, but their eye may be caught by her unusual gravestone, which commemorates not only her, but the sport which caused her death. Above her name there is carved a balloon.

If she were alive these days, no doubt Lily would be into the sponsored parachute-jumping business. It is one of the many unlikely 'sports' which people indulge in to make money for charity. Three-legged climbs up mountains, pram and bedstead races, marathon tiddly-wink matches – once they would have been considered eccentric, today they are an accepted part of the sponsorship scene, in which the performers get the limelight, the charity gets the money, and friends, relatives, office colleagues and innocent passers-by get the bill. Eccentric sports are no longer for eccentrics, they are just for raising money; but I make an exception of JOHN SLATER, whose eccentricity is not entirely financial.

Mr Slater, it is safe to say, has led a varied life. In his fifty-odd years he has been a Royal Marine bandsman, a lorry-driver, a steward on a luxury yacht, an insurance broker, a waiter, a salesman and a painter and decorator. He has lived with down-and-outs in London to find out their problems, and at the other extreme he lived in a remote cave in the Western Highlands, his only visitor being the rising tide. He apparently runs some sort of company, since he appointed one of his dogs as a director.

All this, I would say, qualifies him as an eccentric. I can forgive him therefore for offering to spend six months in a cage at London Zoo to raise funds for conserving the Giant Panda, a stunt only slightly more commendable than the Revd Harold Davidson's sojourn with Freddie the lion in Skegness, reported in the next chapter. And I must reluctantly admire the stamina he showed in order to get into the record book, by walking from Land's End to John O'Groats in bare feet, wearing nothing but striped pyjamas. He was accompanied by a dog which, to compensate for his own frugality in footwear, wore two pairs of home-made suede bootees. It was surely the name of the dog which underlines why John Salter undertook this eccentric sporting feat. It was called Guinness.

CLERICCENTRICS
quirkiness is next
to godliness

The clergy seem particularly prone to eccentricity, perhaps because they feel that anyone who is expected to wear his collar the wrong way round is entitled to other odd habits as well. Some limit themselves to curious clothing to go with their curious collars, some have curious ways of conducting services, some keep curious pets or adopt curious forms of transport. I can think of only one who combined all these eccentricities – and pretended to be a mermaid as well.

THE HUT BUILT BY THE VICAR OF MORWENSTOW ON THE CORNISH CLIFFS. HE RETIRED THERE IN HIS SEA-BOOTS AND FISHERMAN'S JERSEY TO MEDITATE — AND TO WATCH FOR SHIPWRECKS.

Admittedly the mermaid episode occurred before ROBERT HAWKER was ordained. Each night for a week he perched on a rock just off the coast at Bude, wearing only a wig made of seaweed and an oilskin wrapped round his legs, and wailing plaintively to the moon, to the great mystification of the crowds on the beach. They were mystified even more by the farewell performance, when the 'mermaid' sang the National Anthem before disappearing for ever.

But it was after his appointment as Vicar of Morwenstow in 1835 that Hawker's eccentricity came into its own. He discarded the standard cassock, and wore either a fisherman's jersey and sea-boots to go and sit in a hut he built on the cliffs, or a yellow blanket with a hole in it for his head – an exact replica, he liked to maintain, of the garb worn by early Cornish saints – in which he toured his parish, riding a mule and accompanied by his pet pig. He took his other pets into church with him, a small dog which sat on the altar steps and a covey of cats which sat almost anywhere, though one was excommunicated for catching a mouse during the sermon.

He conducted his services wearing red gloves, for no obvious reason. At weddings he would unnerve the bridegroom

THE REVD ROBERT HAWKER, VICAR OF MORWENSTOW, AND THE VICARAGE HE BUILT FOR HIMSELF, WITH CHIMNEYS IN THE SHAPE OF HIS FAVOURITE CHURCH TOWERS.

by throwing the ring in the air before handing it to him, and at baptisms, though he restrained himself from doing the same thing with the baby, he would march up and down the aisle waving it aloft and bellowing: 'We receive this child into the congregation of Christ's flock' – a procedure which is not unknown these days in our more charismatic Anglican churches, but in the early nineteenth century was thought very strange indeed.

The church itself was strewn with all manner of Hawker litter: driftwood, candle-ends, expiring wild flowers, disintegrating prayer-books, discarded poems. A fussy young curate was once ill-advised enough to sweep it all up and take it to the vicarage in a wheelbarrow. Hawker demolished him with a memorable one-liner.

'Complete the pile by sitting on top,' he said coldly, 'and we'll see the whole lot speedily got rid of.'

Incidentally the vicarage itself still bears the eccentric Hawker touch. Its chimneys are replicas of his favourite church towers, except for the kitchen chimney which is shaped like his mother's tomb . . .

But let us be fair. The Revd Robert Hawker was courageous as well as eccentric; he helped to rescue many a shipwrecked mariner from the rocks below his church. He revived the life of the parish too, and his parishioners' initial astonishment gradually turned into respect. And not all his poems were discarded on the church floor – one of his lines is still familiar: 'Shall Trelawny die?'

THE VICAR OF MORWENSTOW MAKING HIS PARISH VISITS ON HIS MULE, DRESSED IN A YELLOW BLANKET WITH A HOLE FOR HIS HEAD, AND ACCOMPANIED BY HIS PET PIG.

If Cornwall were not so far from Essex I might have suspected that the Vicar of Morwenstow acquired some of his eccentric inspiration from the REVD FRANCIS WARING, Vicar of Heybridge near Maldon, who died just before Mr Hawker took up his duties. Mr Waring also had a distinctive style for his services; he got through them at a tremendous speed, allowing no time for the usual responses, and reducing his sermons to a couple of crisp sentences. He then ran down the aisle, jumped on his horse, and galloped off to take two more services, just as briskly, in his other churches.

He also shared Robert Hawker's eccentric tastes in dress. He designed his own vestments, with curious hats to match, and once startled his bishop by wearing scarlet breeches and white stockings at a formal gathering of clergy. When the bishop gently drew attention to the inappropriateness of his attire the vicar, quite unabashed, offered him a visiting card and replied cheerfully: 'My

The Revd Francis Waring's church at Heybridge, and the graveyard where he is buried. He took his services at tremendous speed, allowing no time for the usual responses and reducing his sermons to a couple of crisp sentences. His congregation may well have been the envy of neighbouring parishes.

Lord, that you should condescend to notice my breeches is an honour I did not expect. Do let me recommend my tailor to you'.

It was this irreverent approach to authority which endeared him to his parishioners. His most notable riposte was made to the pompous and unpopular Mayor of Maldon, a Mr Bugg, whose

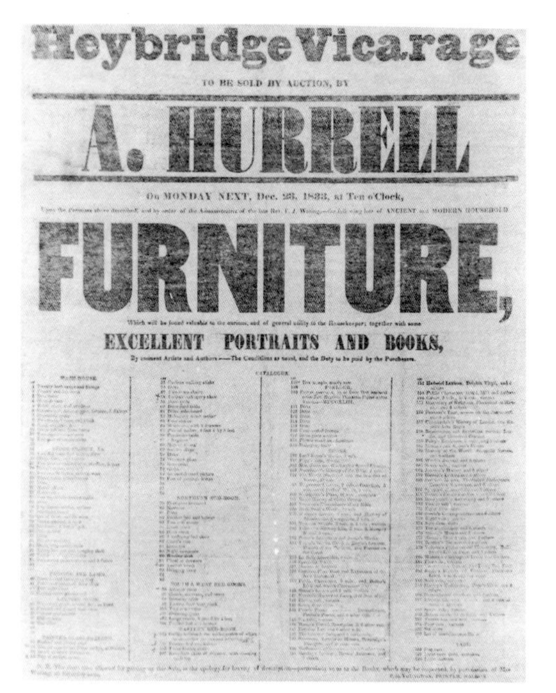

THE LOTS AT THE VICARAGE AUCTION, AFTER FRANCIS WARING'S DEATH, REFLECTED HIS TASTE FOR THE UNUSUAL. THEY RANGED FROM 'CURIOUS WALKING-STICKS' TO 'GOTHIC BEDSTEAD, THE WORKMANSHIP OF WHICH IS ALTOGETHER CURIOUS AND BEAUTIFUL'.

bulging jowls had earned him the nickname of Bulldog Bugg. He was unwise enough to make some slighting comment to Francis Waring at a public dinner. The vicar beamed back at him – and barked.

Waring's other similarity to Robert Hawker was the eccentric design of his vicarage. Instead of tower-shaped chimneys he gave it a mock-medieval front door studded with spikes and nails, and insisted on having a corridor through the middle of the house, even though the main fireplaces already occupied that space. As a result the passage had to be made so narrow that it was impossible for two people to pass in it, and the vicar himself, a man of considerable girth, had to edge along it sideways. He also designed his own rather basic furniture; there were logs to sit on instead of chairs, his children ate from a trough, and he and his wife slept in a king-size wicker cradle which swung from the ceiling. His final touch was to devise a different bird-call for each member of his family. Thus instead of calling them by name, he just whistled . . .

The whistling, barking, swinging Vicar of Heybridge died in 1833 and was widely mourned, not least at the Old Ship Inn at Maldon where he had been a frequent customer. He could be seen most evenings walking back home from the inn, wearing his distinctive yellow scarf, pepper-and-salt coat and black pantaloons, and carrying a teapot. It contained, needless to say, not tea but a pint of ale to drink with his supper.

Another eccentric churchman of the nineteenth century, JOHN FITZGERALD, belonged to an eccentric Suffolk family. 'FitzGeralds are all mad, but John is the maddest of the family, for he does not know it,' said someone who ought to know – his brother Edward – translator of the *Rubaiyat* and pretty odd himself. He wandered around Woodbridge wearing an extremely tall hat which he tied on his head with a handkerchief, a grey plaid shawl in winter and barefoot in summer with his boots slung on a stick. But brother John, a fervent evangelical lay preacher, was far more flamboyant in his foibles.

He too was inclined to remove his boots, and sometimes his stockings as well, not because of the hot weather but to allow him greater freedom while delivering his sermons. When he really got

going he took off other articles of clothing also, though as one of his congregation very fairly observed, 'he never exceeds the limits of decency'. While he was giving his address he was inclined to stand on one leg for considerable periods, perhaps to concentrate his mind, and in order to emphasise a point he would wave a lighted candle at his congregation, to the considerable discomfort of the wax-bespattered occupants of the front pews.

One would imagine that a John FitzGerald sermon was one of the big attractions of church life in the 1850s, if only for their entertainment value, but they had one great drawback – they were inordinately long. Not just an hour, but two or three. He also had a slight speech impediment which made him hiss and whistle while he was talking, most disconcerting for those not used to it. The hissing and whistling was not confined to his own sermons; they occurred while he was listening to anyone else's. The same applied to his practice of shedding clothes. His neighbour at one service recorded: 'To my surprise, when the preacher entered the pulpit, Mr FitzGerald began to undress. He did nothing worse, however, than remove his boots and stockings and a few other minor articles of attire, and empty the contents of his pockets onto the cushions of the seat, after which he seemed comfortable and to thoroughly enjoy the service – though he unwittingly whistled now and again'.

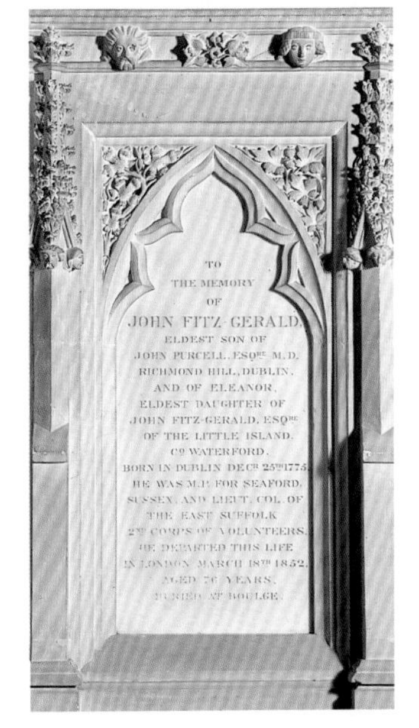

JOHN FITZGERALD'S CHAPEL AT BOULGE HALL, AND HIS MEMORIAL TABLET.

In spite of, or perhaps because of, his eccentricities FitzGerald drew large crowds to listen to his tirades against drink, slavery and Roman Catholics, in the chapel he built for himself near his Suffolk home, Boulge Hall. The regulars no doubt learned to bring a packed lunch as well. The real unfortunates were the visiting speakers whom he introduced; his introductions were liable to last as long as his sermons.

Edward FitzGerald was on the whole very tolerant of his brother's idiosyncrasies, but even he became exasperated at times by what he generously referred to as John's indecisiveness, but which, if John had been my brother, I would have called bloody-

At Boulge Hall, John FitzGerald's handsome house in Suffolk, there was a clock in every room, but he always rang for a servant to tell him the time.

mindedness. He used to say that when John made an appointment 'DV', it did not mean 'God willing' but 'if I happen to be in the humour'. The only time he could be certain his brother would visit him was when he said it was impossible to do so. And he once told a friend, 'John is a man one could really love - two and three quarter miles off!'

It must have been even more unsettling for his servants. Even though there was a clock in every room at Boulge Hall, he would always ring for a servant to tell him the time. After making a visit he would often ignore his own carriage awaiting him outside and hire another instead, leaving his groom to drive the empty one back. He was just as likely to ignore the hired coach too, and have both of them follow behind as he walked home. It was almost worse for the coachman when he did decide to travel in it. First he would complain that he was driving too slowly, then when he went faster he cried: 'Do you mean to break our necks?' Yes, definitely bloody-minded . . .

JOHN FITZGERALD'S MAUSOLEUM.

But like so many religious eccentrics, there was a generous side to FitzGerald too. At Boulge Hall he fitted out one room like a shop, stocked with household goods and clothing – not to be sold, but to be given away to the needy. He donated thousands of pounds to charity, particularly to help miners – his father's mine had to be closed because of flooding, putting many hundreds out of work. But while he was kind to the poor, he had little time for the rich if they had not been to university. It is recorded that when any such ill-educated aristocrat attempted to shake his hand, his response would simply be two fingers. Which was not quite as rude as it sounds – he did not raise the fingers, merely offered them in a half-handshake. But no doubt he made his point.

WILLIAM HUNTINGTON, the eighteenth-century 'Coal-heaver Preacher', would have given FitzGerald short shrift if he had shown any sign of whistling or hissing during his sermons. When any sound from the congregation disturbed him he would shout: 'Silence that noisy numskull!' or perhaps, 'Wake that snoring sinner!' or indeed, 'Turn out that drunken dog!' He did not actually heave coal at the offender, as his nickname might suggest, but I am sure he would not have hesitated if a lump had come to hand.

WILLIAM HUNTINGTON, KNOWN AS THE 'COAL-HEAVER PREACHER', HERE PORTRAYED IN A MORE INTELLECTUAL POSE.

Huntington was in fact a coal-heaver before becoming a full-time preacher, and in his more penurious days he continued heaving coal between sermons to earn a few extra shillings. Then he found a less energetic way of making ends meet; he decided to rely for his income on 'the inexhaustible Bank of Heaven'.

'I have found God's promises to be the Christian's banknotes,' he told his flock. And sure enough, it worked. If he prayed publicly for a new coat, someone gave him a coat. If he prayed for a ham, a ham duly appeared. He even prayed for a pair of breeches, and an anonymous donor made a pair for him, which turned out to fit exactly. As Huntington observed, 'God guided his hand to cut, because He perfectly knows my size'.

This demonstrated, he claimed, the amazing power of prayer, but his critics suggested that all it demonstrated was the amazing gullibility of his congregations. Huntington explained that 'I use my prayers as gunners use their swivels, turning them every day, as various cases required'. One sceptic put it rather differently. 'He let the specific object of his prayers and their general tendency always be understood, where a word to the unwise was sufficient. He began to want a horse, then to wish, and lastly to pray for one; and before the day was over he was presented with a horse, which had been purchased for him by subscription.'

Whether it was a genuine response to prayer or a touch of moral blackmail, Huntington never had to lift a coal-sack again. In due course he acquired a country house, a fully-stocked farm, and not just one horse but a coach and pair, and he lived in this style, on the generosity of his flock, for several years. It was a far cry from his days as William Hunt, the son of a farm labourer at Cranbrook in Kent, who became an errand boy, a gunmaker's apprentice, a sawyer's pitman, a hearse-driver and, of course, a coal-heaver before getting involved in a scandal with the local tailor's

The Jireh Chapel near Lewes, where the 'Coal-heaver Preacher' is buried. It was built by one of his disciples, Jenkin Jenkins, and Huntington awarded him the initials 'WA', which appear on a tablet at the chapel. They actually just stand for 'Welsh Ambassador'.

daughter and leaving the area under the assumed name of Huntington.

Then came his conversion. He adopted the initials SS, standing for Sinner Saved, because as he said, 'I have no DD, for want of cash, and no MA, for want of learning'. His preaching and his praying proved so effective that the 'Bank of Heaven' built a chapel for him in London, as well as keeping him provided for personally. The 'Bank' did not, alas, provide fire insurance when the chapel burned down, but Huntington seems to have had no difficulty in raising enough credit to build a new one. This time he showed more foresight and invested the freehold in himself, which meant he could stop drawing on his 'Heavenly Bank' account and live comfortably on the pew rents.

'The Coal-heaver Preacher', as caricatured by one of his critics. The inscription on his tomb at the Jireh Chapel portrays him more kindly — but then he probably wrote it himself.

Although his coal-heaving days were long since gone, they were not forgotten by his critics. One produced a singularly unflattering portrait with the inscription:

> *He might pass, as far as appearances go, for a convict, but he looks too conceited. The vitality and strength of his constitution are fearful to behold, and it is certain that he looks better fitted for coal-heaving than religious oratory.*

However, Huntington was no more bashful about his coal-heaving than he was about his oratory. At the Jireh Chapel near Lewes in Sussex his tomb — which looks not unlike an enormous coal-bunker — bears the epitaph which it is assumed he wrote himself:

> *Here lies the Coal-heaver, beloved of his God*
> *but abhorred of men. The Omniscient Judge*
> *at the Grand Assize shall ratify and confirm*
> *this to the confusion of many thousands,*
> *for England and its metropolis shall know*
> *that there hath been a Prophet among them.*

Again his critics took a rather different view — and devised a rather different epitaph:

Here lies WH, once a heaver of coals, but he left his employ and turned saver of souls. And he changed for the better too, fifty times o'er, for instead of a coal cart he kept coach-and-four . . .

In spite of attacks like this, his followers remained devoted to him, and when his effects were put up for auction they paid handsomely for any memento. His spectacle case sold for seven guineas and an old armchair fetched sixty. But even here the sceptics could not leave him alone. One of them wrote: 'Many other articles fetched equally high prices, so anxious were his besotted admirers to obtain some precious memorial of that most artful fanatic'.

Artful fanatic, or inspired eccentric? It's a thin line . . .

Huntington died in 1813, and a few years later another notable figure with unorthodox views launched himself on the preaching circuit. ROBERT AITKEN was ordained into the Church of England, but got along much better with the Methodists and, in due course, became a Methodist lay preacher, though he always claimed that he remained an Anglican clergyman. He built a Methodist chapel on his estate in the Isle of Man, which he said was 'open to every child of God, provided he does not disturb the

EYRETON CASTLE ON THE ISLE OF MAN, BUILT AS A METHODIST BOARDING SCHOOL BY THE REVD ROBERT AITKEN – A CHURCH OF ENGLAND CLERIC.

congregation with peculiarities of doctrine' – which I suppose meant any doctrine that did not coincide with his own.

This situation not surprisingly irritated his bishop, and may well have confused the Methodists, but in due course he clarified his position by moving to 'the neighbouring island of Britain', as Manxmen like to call it, and founding his own group, the Christian Society. He became an itinerant preacher, either among his own followers or in Methodist chapels, then after eight years he caused further confusion by deciding to rejoin the Church of England.

EYRETON CASTLE IN ITS HEYDAY, WITH ITS ASSORTED TOWERS AND BATTLEMENTS. ONE GATHERS THAT ROBERT AITKEN DESIGNED IT AS HE WENT ALONG.

Normally this would have involved three years' suspension from any form of preaching before re-admission, which to a man like Aitken would have been slightly worse than purgatory, but it seems the rules were waived in his case and his Christian Society chapel in Liverpool was licensed as the Church of St John the Evangelist. His devoted followers must have found it difficult to keep up with all these changes, but he was such a splendid preacher, whatever denomination he happened to belong to at the time, that he brought about thousands of conversions and was rated the greatest revivalist of his time. The *Dictionary of National Biography* observes drily: 'His untiring zeal and sympathy concealed his rashness of judgment'.

But it was not only the variations in his theological thinking which marked him out from the average parson. He also went in

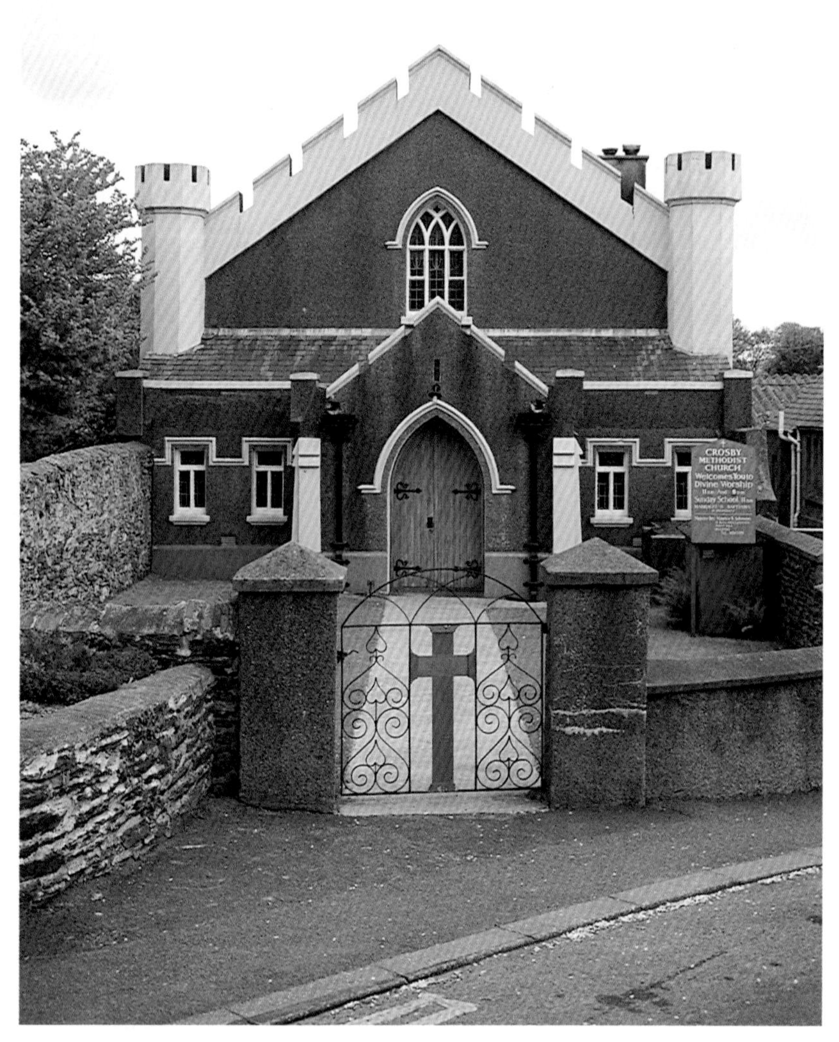

The Methodist Chapel which Aitken built at Crosby during his Methodism period — though he always claimed that he remained an Anglican clergyman. His congregations must have had some difficulty in keeping up with his denominational detours.

for designing buildings, starting with that chapel on his Manx estate. The estate originally had the good local name of Ballyemin, but he renamed it Eyreton after his wife's mother, Elizabeth Eyre. It would be nice to think that this was the affectionate gesture of a devoted son-in-law, but more likely it was because she put up the money for him to buy it. It has been called Eyreton ever since, and in addition to the chapel, which is still in use, there is also his other creation, Eyreton Castle.

In 1833, just after he had built the chapel, Aitken had one of his change-of-course periods. Before coming to the Isle of Man he had been a schoolteacher near Sunderland. He decided to go back to teaching again, and just as he had built his own chapel to preach in, so he built his own school to teach in. The result was

Eyreton Castle, which he designed as he went along. He gave it two massive round towers and one square one, joined by castellated walls, and occupying a frontage of thirty yards.

This was to be a Methodist boarding school, where the boys would spend two hours in prayer and Bible study each day as well as eight hours of lessons. Its motto would be 'Holiness to the Lord'. But having drawn up the syllabus and published the prospectus, which included arrangements for shipping pupils from 'the neighbouring island of Britain', and set the fees at between £22 and £30 a year, Aitken got itchy feet again and set off on his peregrinations on the mainland. According to the local directory there was still a school at Eyreton Castle twelve years later, but by then he had founded and finished his Christian Society, rejoined the Church of England, and was somewhere in the North doing what he was best at – preaching.

THE REVD ROBERT AITKEN IN HIS LATER YEARS — VENERABLE, BUT STILL PREACHING.

His first wife had died young and his second one preferred Cornwall to the Isle of Man, so this was where the roving preacher finished up. She persuaded him to take a living at Pendeen, a tiny village on the south-west tip of Cornwall near St Just. What may have decided him was that Pendeen had no church, which gave him a chance to go back into the design business and build one himself. He based it on the cathedral at Iona, but having built it he spent much of his time away from it, travelling around the country on revivalist and temperance crusades. At last, in his seventies, he finally hung up his hat and settled down in the vicarage at Pendeen. And yes – he built it himself.

The REVD MORGAN JONES of Blewbury in Berkshire did not have a well-to-do mother-in-law like Robert Aitken, nor indeed did he get many dividends from William Huntington's 'Bank of Heaven'. He also lacked the good fortune to be born an Englishman, so technically he does not qualify for these pages, but he spent forty-three years of his life as vicar of an English country parish, and he was eccentric to the point of paranoia, so I feel it is worth stretching a point.

Morgan Jones was in fact Welsh, as you might have expected, but his eccentricity was entirely English. He was, in a word, a miser. Yet his parishioners were very fond of him; indeed, such is the eccentric way in which the English regard their eccentrics, they were rather proud of him. When a stranger enquired of

The Revd Morgan Jones' church at Blewbury, and the postcard commemorating his bizarre overcoat, which he wore throughout his forty-three years in the parish.

a friend on the way back from church in Blewbury why he had raised his hat to an old beggar in the street, the friend took some delight in telling him that the 'old beggar' was in fact the parson who had just taken the service.

Actually Morgan Jones did manage to look reasonably respectable in his vestments; it was when he changed into mufti that his miserliness became apparent. Throughout all his forty-three years in Blewbury he wore the same overcoat, the same hat, and even the same shirt. The coat was the most remark-

MORGAN JONES' OVERCOAT IS STILL PRESERVED IN A GLASS CASE. FIRST HE TURNED IT INSIDE-OUT, THEN HE CUT OFF THE TAILS TO USE AS PATCHES, MISSING BUTTONS WERE REPLACED BY STRING, AND HOLES WERE MENDED WITH ANY THREAD HE COULD SCROUNGE.

able garment in this ensemble. According to contemporary reports it was already much the worse for wear when he arrived in Blewbury from Ashton Keynes in 1781. At that stage it was in the form of a surtout, a clerical frock-coat with long tails. He adapted it first by turning it inside out, as the lining was rather less tattered than the outer cloth. Then, as pieces began to rot away and fall off, he cut off the tails and used them as patches. When buttons came off he substituted string, and small holes were darned with yarn of any colour which he could cadge off his parishioners. In the end there was very little left of the original material; it was more like Joseph's Technicolour Dream Coat, without the Technicolour.

Morgan Jones' hat was another masterpiece of miserly ingenuity. When the brim became too battered by years of constant wear he acquired a substitute brim from the hat of a convenient scarecrow. The fact that his own hat was russet brown and its new brim was black did not perturb him at all.

He was believed to have quite a stock of shirts but he preferred to wear only one of them. When he considered it needed washing, every three months or so, he went around shirtless until it was dry again. As with the coat, he patched and darned the shirt himself, removing pieces of the tail for use as patches until the shirt was too short to tuck into his trousers. 'This of course was a sad disaster', wrote one wry commentator, 'and there was some fear lest one of the new ones must be brought into use. But after a diligent search he fortunately found in one of his drawers the top part of a shirt with a frill on, which had probably lain by ever since his youthful and more gay days. With his usual sagacity this was tacked by him on the tail of the old one with the frill downwards, and was thus worn by him until the day before he left Blewbury'.

Morgan Jones dined as frugally as he dressed. He cooked only once a week, on Sundays, and all he cooked was bacon. He made this last throughout the week, supplemented with bread and cups of tea and whatever meals he could scrounge from his parishioners. Even the bacon, which he bought from a local farmer, afforded him the excuse of acquiring three free dinners – one when he went to order the bacon, another when he collected it, and a third when he went to pay for it. The farmer must have recorded a loss for every rasher he sold.

For lighting Jones relied on the stubs of candles he had used in church; for heating he gathered twigs in the churchyard. But he rarely had need of either, because on most days he stayed at a parishioner's fireside until it was dark, then went straight to his bed. He was a misogynist as well as a miser – it was reported that 'in early life he was deceived of a party whom he essentially served, and thereafter he distrusted all'. But in the end he had to rely on a woman, a distant relative, to look after him in his declining years, when he returned to Wales.

After the death of this woman-hating cleric in 1827 it was discovered that he had accumulated a very substantial sum of £18,000, and ironically it was a woman who benefited from his years of parsimonious living. The relative in Wales got the lot.

The REVD JOHN ALINGTON had no need to scrounge free meals or economise on shirts. He had a rich grandfather who presented him with a living and a manor house as a wedding present, and left him half his fortune when he died – a little matter of forty-three farms and a million pounds. He also got Letchworth Hall in Hertfordshire and took over from his grandfather as patron of the parish church. The rector, the Revd Samuel Hartopp Knapp, presumably in a spirit of friendly co-operation, invited his patron to assist him with the services – and soon wished he hadn't. It was the starting point for the eccentricities of the man who became known as 'Mad Alington of Letchworth Hall'.

Alington did not merely assist the rector, he took over the morning and evening services and even the baptisms and marriages, leaving Mr Knapp to cope with the funerals. And his sermons, when they were coherent enough to be understood, were based on the more romantic passages in the *Song of Solomon* and extolled the delights of free love.

Eventually the rector could take it no longer. He complained to the bishop, and the bishop suspended Alington from office. Mr Knapp no doubt thought that would be the end of it – but it was only the beginning. His infuriated patron installed a

Letchworth Hall, now a hotel, where the Revd John Alington installed a pair of pulpits and set up in opposition to the local rector.

couple of pulpits in Letchworth Hall and set up in opposition. Since most people in the village worked on his estate and lived in his cottages he had no difficulty in drawing away the congregation, and he augmented it by inviting tramps, gypsies, and anyone else who was passing, to come along too.

Not that they needed much persuading. Mad Alington pursued his theme of free love, and followed up his sermons by distributing beer and brandy and leading the congregation in dancing and drinking. If it got out of hand he produced a shotgun and drove the brawlers outside. And if any couple tried to put his free love theories into practice he warned them gently: 'No more of that. If you young colts want to roll about, there's plenty of grass outside'.

As a preliminary to the services he would perform on an old piano and two musical boxes, dashing from one to the other and playing voluntaries on each in turn. When the congregation had assembled he rode up and down amongst them on a hobby-horse, his servants propelling him at a great pace so that he frequently bounced against the walls, but this only delighted him the more. Having effectively got their attention he donned a splendid leopard skin as a vestment and began the service. He read love poems from one pulpit, then a love story from the other, but that was just a taster. He went behind a screen and re-appeared through a trapdoor in the minstrel's gallery to deliver his sermon. And finally, to signal the end of the service and the start of the festivities, he took off his wig and hurled it into the congregation.

JOHN ALINGTON IN THE 'VESTMENT' IN WHICH HE CONDUCTED HIS SERVICES AT LETCHWORTH HALL — A LEOPARD SKIN CLOAK.

Against this sort of opposition the hapless Knapp never stood a chance. But just to make certain, Alington would hold noisy prayer meetings in the churchyard during morning service, and during evensong he and his followers would bellow ribald ditties outside the church door. He even got at the rector financially, by reducing the agricultural activities on his estate to stacking flints into piles and digging holes which were filled up the next day; actual production was instantly reduced to nil, and so was the income from the estate. This did not bother Alington in the slightest, since he had ample money to spare, but it certainly bothered the rector, since he no longer received any tithes . . .

Working on the Alington estate must have been as odd an experience as attending his services, but he looked after his employees and indeed made efforts to educate them, albeit in unorthodox ways. He decided, for instance, to send them to London to see the Great Exhibition of 1851, and to make sure they didn't get lost in the big city he laid out tree trunks as a large-scale model of the streets they would have to traverse between King's Cross station and Hyde Park. For a week he marched them backwards and forwards along the route. Those on the way to Hyde Park wore hay bands round their right legs, and those on the way back to the station wore them on the left. At the end of the week they were still getting hopelessly lost, with hay bands wandering off in all directions. Alington gave up in disgust.

He was more successful at teaching them the elements of geography using another large-scale model, this time a pond with islands representing the continents. He took them on a world tour in a convoy of rowing boats, explaining the notable features of each continent as they splashed past them.

When he was not conducting services, baiting the rector, or trying to educate his workforce, Mad Alington liked to be carried

Alington rode a hobby-horse through his congregation at Letchworth Hall before conducting his services from both pulpits and gallery above.

round his garden in an open coffin. He explained that he was practising for the real thing. The real thing finally happened on a winter's night in 1863. He had been ill in bed, refusing medical aid, but eventually he agreed to sample some medicine. He found it tasted so unpleasant that he smashed the bottle in a fury and called for a tumblerful of brandy instead. He drank it down in a single draught, lay back on his pillow with a contented sigh – and died.

Another cleric who conducted a feud against the Church of England, though for very different reasons, was the REVD HAROLD DAVIDSON, the notorious Rector of Stiffkey in Norfolk. He was descended from a long line of Protestant clergymen, and he followed in their footsteps, but only erratically. He started his career as a stand-up comic, and when he did enter the church and became rector of this little fishing village on the North Norfolk coast, he outraged his parishioners by spending most of his time around his old haunts in London. His object, so he maintained, was to rescue prostitutes from a life of sin, but the Church took a rather different view of his nocturnal activities, and in 1932 Davidson was ritually unfrocked in the cloisters of Norwich Cathedral. Even on this portentous occasion he could not resist baiting the Establishment. Having arrived an hour late, instead of

WILLIAM POOLE'S MEDITERRANEAN-STYLE CHURCH IN THE HEART OF THE HEREFORDSHIRE COUNTRYSIDE. HE IMPORTED ITALIAN DESIGNS, ITALIAN MATERIALS AND ITALIAN WORKMEN; THE RESULT WAS NOT ONLY AN ITALIANATE CHURCH BUT SOME ITALIANATE CHILDREN.

In the days when country clergymen belonged to rich families and had money to spare, some of them used it to indulge their eccentric tastes in architecture. A couple of examples of their work can be found near the Welsh border.

The REVD WILLIAM POOLE was Rector of Hoarwithy, on the River Wye, for nearly fifty years, and seems to have spent most of that time building and embellishing his Italianate church, which would look more at home in sun-baked Sicily than among the green hills of Herefordshire. Its solid bulk is topped by a continental-style campanile, and inside there are marble columns, mosaics and lapis lazuli. Mr Poole imported Italian materials and Italian designs, and Italian workmen to put them all together. They got together with the locals too, and the result was not only an untypical Herefordshire church but some untypical Herefordshire families . . .

A little further north in Shropshire, the REVD JOHN PARKER designed his church at Llanyblodwel with surely the most eccentric-looking tower in England, a detached octagonal creation with little slit windows, tapering to a pointed tip one hundred feet high. It should be there still – unless someone has fired it into space.

The parish church at Stiffkey where the Revd Harold Davidson was rector. He outraged his parishioners by spending most of his time in London. He said he was rescuing prostitutes, but the bishop took a rather different view.

meekly following the bishop to the high altar he marched up the aisle ahead of him . . .

For the rest of his life he continued to protest his innocence, and found some unlikely platforms from which to do so. He preached from the mouth of a stuffed whale, and sat in a booth lined with his press cuttings haranguing passers-by. He also spent some time in a barrel, threatening to starve himself to death unless the Church reinstated him, and collected quite a lot of money for his campaign from sympathetic spectators. Their sympathy faded when they realised that, after several days of the hunger strike, he showed no signs of losing any weight. It transpired that he had managed to keep himself supplied with food by concealing it in the lavatory; each call of nature provided him with another quick snack.

Eventually Harold Davidson arrived in Skegness with a friendly lion called Freddie, and spent his days in Freddie's cage, still complaining about the Church's injustice and still extracting contributions from the spectators. But Freddie was not quite as friendly as he thought, and it all ended most unpleasantly. There are various versions of what went wrong – some say he was too fond of beating the lion and its patience ran out, others that he trod on its tail and the sudden pain made Freddie lash out. But

there is no dispute about the result. The lion reared up and mauled the ex-rector with his front paws, and although a sixteen-year-old girl lion-tamer entered the cage and tried to rescue him, she could not stop Freddie picking him up in its mouth 'like a cat with a mouse'. It was popularly rumoured at the time that the lion actually ate him, but in fact he died later in hospital.

At the funeral at Stiffkey in August 1937 his widow, a rather odd lady herself or she would hardly have married him, continued his tradition of eccentric irreverence. Instead of conventional black widow's weeds she dressed almost entirely in white – dress, hat, stockings, shoes. It would have been more appropriate at a tennis match than a funeral, but she did make one concession to the solemnity of the occasion – black shoelaces.

Harold Davidson and his 'friendly' lion Freddie. But Freddie proved less than friendly, and not even a youthful girl lion-tamer could rescue the rector.

There are not many clerics about these days who are quite as outrageously eccentric as Harold Davidson – if there are, they are a little more discreet about it. But happily the Church of England can still produce parsons whose interests extend far beyond the ecclesiastical, and who develop a passion for unlikely pursuits not normally associated with men of the cloth. They range from the Revd Ronald Lancaster, who is generally recognised to be Britain's foremost expert on fireworks, to the remarkable Boston brothers, Noel and Teddy, both now deceased but remembered with much affection by their flocks.

Mr Lancaster is happily still with us, alive and well and living at Kimbolton in Cambridgeshire, though he is not the incumbent. When he answers the phone it is not 'Kimbolton Rectory' but 'Kimbolton Fireworks'. After twenty-five years on the staff of Kimbolton School, where his subjects, predictably, were divinity and chemistry, he retired from teaching in 1988 to devote all his time to the unclerical world of catherine wheels, Roman candles, and whizz-bang rockets.

It all began when Ronald Lancaster was a lad in Huddersfield. Fireworks fascinated him – not just letting them off but actually making them. He was ordained and became a curate in the North of England, but the passion for pyrotechnics persisted. When he joined the staff at Kimbolton he continued to pursue his hobby, and built workshops where he carried out research for

The 800th anniversary of the City of London and the Revd Ronald Lancaster, the 'Pyrotechnic Parson', with some of his stock-in-trade. He has staged some of the biggest firework displays in the country.

the major fireworks companies. As his reputation spread, he started to stage firework displays at big national events. One of the first major ones was outside Buckingham Palace to mark the twenty-fifth anniversary of the Coronation, and other anniversary displays followed – the 800th anniversary of the City of London, the 550th anniversary of Eton College and, most recently, the fiftieth anniversary of the Battle of Britain. Whether it is the opening of the Humber Bridge, the completion of the Thames Barrier, or the annual Thames Day display for the GLC – if there is going to be a large-scale celebration anywhere in Britain they send for Ronald Lancaster, the 'Pyrotechnic Parson'.

In 1990 he opened a new factory on a three-acre site in Kimbolton, and Kimbolton Fireworks started a new chapter. While his fellow clerics may be pondering their next sermon, Ronald Lancaster's thoughts are also turning heavenwards – how to create bigger, better, more dazzling explosions in the sky. And business – I have to say it – is going with a bang . . .

Noel Boston was enthusiastic about explosions too, on a rather smaller scale, and it was appropriate that the Bishop of Norwich should designate him a canon, because he was devoted to antique firearms, particularly a miniature cannon which he would loose off at the slightest provocation. I attended many gatherings in Dereham in the 1950s when the vicar would intersperse a talk with a blast from his cannon; he is the only speaker I can recall who kept Dereham Rotary Club fully awake after lunch.

His passion for antique devices extended to musical instruments, and another memorable sight at such gatherings was Canon Boston playing the serpent, his ruddy cheeks growing ruddier beneath his large glasses as he puffed into this convoluted creation of an earlier, more fanciful age. I have to record that the sound which came out at the other end hardly seemed worth all the effort, but this in no way detracted from the fascination of his performance.

The Revd Teddy Boston was not into serpents, but steam. His rectory garden at Cadeby in Leicestershire is the headquarters of the Cadeby Light Railway, of which the rector was general manager, and he divided his spare time between driving his favourite engine *Pixie* round the garden, and running an elaborate miniature railway layout in a shed labelled 'Stationmaster's Office'. The clock in the shed was set to go at eight times the normal speed, so that a two-minute run around the track seemed to last for a quarter of an hour. Teddy shared his brother's unorthodox approach to music; he operated the control panel to the blast of Handel's organ concertos.

The Revd Teddy Boston could easily be mistaken for his brother Noel, but the railway equipment is the clue; while Noel went in for miniature cannon and ancient instruments, Teddy was such a train enthusiast he built his own railway in the rectory garden.

But it was the full-size track in the garden that occupied most of his time, with its signals, its sharp bend round the holly trees and past the churchyard, and its notices saying 'Passengers must not cross the line'. He was fortunate in finding a neighbouring vicar whose spare-time occupation was just as unusual for a cleric – he loved manual labour. So the two of them laid the track on stones from a nearby quarry; in one afternoon they moved four tons of ballast by wheelbarrow.

Teddy Boston's enthusiasm for steam soon spread to his parishioners. He liked to recall how an ex-Lord Mayor, his arms black to the elbows, turned to him while they were working on the valve gland of a 1903 steamroller and commented: 'Teddy, if anyone had told me thirty years ago, when I had to work on these things for a living, that I should one day be doing this for fun, I would have knocked his teeth in – but here we are!'

Teddy expected all his helpers, even ex-Lord Mayors, to lend a hand with the unglamorous jobs on his railway as well as operating signals and waving flags and actually driving the engines. He wrote in his book *Rails Round the Rectory*: 'There is more to be learnt about the permanent way by holding the business end of a sledgehammer for ten minutes than by sitting

Two examples of Revd Teddy Boston's collection of engines in the rectory garden at Cadeby.

Teddy Boston's church at Cadeby, which has a reminder of his other main interest.

in a comfortable chair reading track maintenance manuals for three hours'.

He drew up a list of railway regulations which included: 'Them as makes suggestions gets given the job'.

As well as the rectory garden, the rectory itself succumbed to his hobby. Beside the front door he put a huge board saying 'London, Midland and Scottish Railway', and inside he installed railway memorabilia in every available space – models, paintings, tickets, labels, magazines. The library is packed with reference books on railway history. It was a passion which Teddy Boston developed as a boy, which flourished when he ran the University Railway Club at Cambridge, and which occupied every spare moment away from his pastoral duties. It was a source of pleasure, not just to Teddy but to all those who became involved in it. I like to think of him happily sounding the whistle of some heavenly *Pixie* with perhaps brother Noel playing his serpent in the guard's van, as they head through the clouds in a trail of steam for the Last Great Terminus in the Sky . . .

Teddy Boston, at a garden fete in Cadeby Manor grounds.

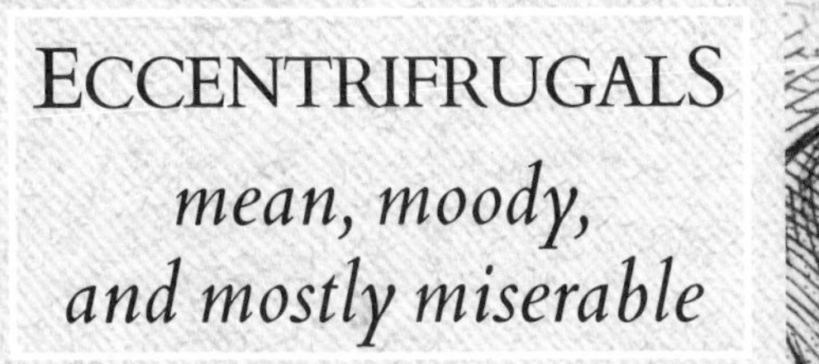

ECCENTRIFRUGALS

mean, moody, and mostly miserable

The first frugal recluses were not eccentric at all, they were early Christian hermits who fled into the desert to avoid persecution, and lived in solitude to preserve their faith. It was only in the fourth century that a degree of eccentricity began to creep in. Instead of retiring into desert caves, hermits spent their lives on top of pillars. Their inspiration was Simeon Stylites, who started off on a modest six-foot pillar and gradually gained elevation until he spent his last thirty years perched on a platform sixty-seven feet above ground level,

English hermits never seemed to take to this particular form of eccentricity; perhaps they had no head for heights. But by the Middle Ages there were hundreds of them tucked away in remote caves, or more conveniently, living in cells attached to churches or priories. Five hundred years ago there was one living almost on my doorstep. He was actually in our little village church just across the road, where a brass in the tower records that 'Hic jacet enim Thomas Leeke, Heremita'. Who Thomas Leeke was, and why he should choose to become a heremita in such a remote corner of Norfolk, nobody knows. Maybe, like me, he just wanted to get out of ye ratte race . . .

At that stage hermits were still motivated by their religious beliefs, but in the eighteenth century they took on a different significance – as prestige symbols. No fashionable country house was complete without a hermit at the bottom of the garden, and it reached the stage where one young aristocrat, CHARLES HAMILTON, actually advertised for a hermit to live on his estate at Cobham in Surrey.

'HERMIT COUNTRY': TWO FEATURES OF CHARLES HAMILTON'S ESTATE AT PAINSHILL PARK, COBHAM. THE RUINED ABBEY WAS A GOTHIC FOLLY, MADE OF BRICK AND PLASTERED TO LOOK LIKE STONE. BUT THE VINEYARD ALONGSIDE IT WAS ENTIRELY GENUINE. ELSEWHERE IN THE GROUNDS WERE A TEMPLE OF BACCHUS MADE OUT OF PAPIERMÂCHÉ, A CHINESE BRIDGE, A TURKISH TENT – AND THE HERMITAGE.

Another of Hamilton's eccentric creations, the grotto on an island in the middle of the lake. Ideally secluded surroundings for a hermit, but a little too damp. Hamilton's hermit had more comfortable quarters in the woods.

Hamilton, who was the youngest son of an earl, had already displayed a certain eccentricity in planning his gardens. They were dotted with follies – a Gothic temple made of stucco and wood, a Temple of Bacchus made of papiermâché, a Chinese bridge, a Turkish tent, a Roman arch. In the middle of this cosmopolitan confusion he built a hermitage in the side of a mound and started looking for someone to occupy it on a full-time basis.

The hermitage was quite luxurious by hermit standards. It had an upper compartment where the occupant could sleep or meditate, it was reasonably waterproof, and Hamilton undertook to provide a regular supply of food and water, plus a benefit on retirement of £700. In return the hermit was expected to live in

Hamilton's hermitage in the woods, nestling in the branches with a view across the river. Now all he needed was a hermit . . . And Charles Hamilton himself, recluse-by-proxy.

the grotto for seven years, wearing a camel-hair robe, studying the Bible, thinking great thoughts, and being civil to visitors. If during that period he strayed outside the garden or cut his hair or nails, he would not get a penny.

Not surprisingly, Hamilton was underwhelmed with applications. Only one prospective hermit turned up and agreed to have a go. He donned the camel-hair robe, installed himself in the hermitage and said goodbye to the outside world. But he was not true hermit material; after three weeks he told Hamilton what he could do with his camel-hair robe and went off for a glass of beer. Hamilton failed to find a replacement, and in due course the estate became too expensive for him to maintain, even hermitless, and he sold up. The buyer was presumably not bothered about ornamental hermits, and the grotto was never occupied again.

About the time that Charles Hamilton was hunting for a hired hermit, Daniel Dancer was setting up as one himself, not through any great religious conviction or an urge for solitary meditation, but like so many recluses of the eighteenth and nineteenth centuries, to save money. He inherited a profitable farm in what is now the Greater London suburb of Harrow Weald, but he preferred not to spend anything on cultivating it and the place was allowed to run wild. Instead of moving into the desert as the early hermits had done, Dancer stayed where he was and created a desert around him. He decided the farmhouse was too expensive to maintain and lived in a shack on the farm, sleeping on sacking. Soap and towels were also unnecessary luxuries; in summer he would wait for a sunny day to wash in a nearby pond and lie in the sun till he was dry, and in winter, one gathers, he gave up washing altogether. As a result, so one writer noted, 'notwithstanding his solitary tendencies he was never without a colony of insect friends attached to his person'.

Dancer was not entirely a recluse. His sister kept house for him – which, the way he lived, was not too arduous a task. She shared his views about economy and kept the weekly food bill down to one piece of beef and fourteen hard dumplings, which she cooked on Sundays. The highspot of her culinary career was when they found a dead sheep which had succumbed to some unknown disease, and nobody else would touch it. She made enough mutton pies to last for a month – and if the meat was a bit dodgy to start with, by the time they ate the last pie the flavour must have been quite memorable . . .

This bizarre pair only had one friend, their neighbour Lady Tempest, who unaccountably seemed to regard them with some affection. When Dancer's sister lay dying and he refused to pay for a doctor – 'if the old girl's time is come, the nostrums of all the quacks in Christendom cannot save her' – Lady Tempest took her away and tended her until she died. She continued to take an interest in Dancer himself, and on one notable occasion sent him a dish of trout stewed in claret. This faced him with the problem of how to heat it, since he never wasted money on a fire. His solution was to cover the dish and sit on it until he considered the trout was warm enough to eat.

DANIEL DANCER, THE MISER OF HARROW WEALD, WHO INHERITED A PROSPEROUS FARM BUT LIVED IN A SHACK, SLEPT ON SACKING, AND LIVED MAINLY ON BOILED DUMPLINGS. FROM HIS EXPRESSION, THEY WERE NOT TOO GOOD FOR THE DIGESTION.

Dancer lived like this for half a century, and when he died in 1794 the results of his parsimony were revealed. Money was tucked away all over the farm: £2,500 in a dunghill in the cow house, £600 in a teapot, £200 up a chimney, bowls full of guineas, bundles of banknotes stuffed down chairs. Lady Tempest, who was beside him at his deathbed, was rewarded for her years of devotion – he left it all to her. That was the good news; the bad news – she died herself three months later.

Daniel Dancer's incredible meanness was more than equalled some years earlier by JOHN OVERS, who made a fortune from operating the ferry across the Thames from Southwark to the City, at a time when there was no bridge. According to an early pamphlet: 'he hath gone in the night to scrape upon the Dunghill, and if he could have found any bones, but especially marrow bones, he would have borne them home in his Cap to have made Pottage with them'. He bought mouldy bread and cut it into thin slices, 'that it, taking the Air, might be harder to be eaten,' and he would happily eat meat which was so rotten that not even his dog would touch it.

'He needed to keep no Cats,' that tract continues, 'for all the Rats and Mice voluntarily left his House, for there were no Fragments or Crumbs left to feed them.' And it concludes: 'He was a most sordid Creature, who had no more of the Nobleness of Man in him than the mere Shape of Man, whose care was merely for himself and none else; who lived in an Hope that, being dead, he might have carried all his Wealth to the Grave with him'.

JOHN OVERS PRETENDED TO BE DEAD SO THAT HIS SERVANTS WOULD FAST IN SYMPATHY AND HE WOULD SAVE ON THEIR FOOD BILL. BUT THE SERVANTS CELEBRATED INSTEAD, AND FOR OVERS IT WAS ALL OVER . . .

The writer then takes considerable satisfaction in recording how John Overs' meanness led to his death. He had the idea of pretending to be dead for a day, believing that out of respect his servants would fast until after the funeral, thus reducing his food bill. He laid himself out under a sheet with a candle burning at his head and feet, and lay there pondering gleefully on all the money he was saving. But not for long. When the servants discovered he was apparently dead, they decided — not surprisingly — to skip the fasting and get on with the celebrating. They broke into his larder, tucked into all the food they could find, and held an uproarious wake around his 'body'.

The tract described what happened next: 'When he could endure it no longer, stirring and struggling in his sheet like a ghost with a candle in each hand, he purposed to rise up and rate them for their Sauciness and Boldness; when one of them, thinking that the Devil was about to rise in his likeness, being in great amaze, catched hold of the butt end of a broken Oar which was in the chamber, and being a sturdy knave . . . struck out his Brains'.

The after-effects of John Overs' meanness did not end there. Because of his 'usury, extortion

John Overs' daughter went into a nunnery after he died, and used his money to found the church of St Mary Overs in the City. The mean old ferryman is featured in one of the stained-glass windows — and his daughter is there too.

and the sordidness of his life', he was regarded as excommunicated and unworthy of a Christian burial. His daughter bribed the friars of Bermondsey Abbey to bury him in the Abbey grounds while the Abbot was away, but when he returned and saw the new grave he had the body exhumed and placed on an ass, which was taken outside the gates and left to wander where it wished. It ambled off along what is now the Old Kent Road, stopped at a place of execution known as St Thomas à Watering, and with a fine sense of the dramatic, shook off its burden immediately under the gibbet. The locals buried it there forthwith.

Overs' daughter Mary, somewhat depressed by all this, retired into a nunnery. But at least some good came out of the old man's miserliness. She used his fortune to found the church of St Mary in the City, later renamed St Mary Overs in her memory, and bequeathed to it all the income from the ferry.

The tract does not record John Overs' age when he died, except to call him old, and there is no telling how much older he might have become if that blow with the oar had not been fatal, but it does seem that miserly living conditions can lead to a long life, if not a very enjoyable one. Daniel Dancer lived until he was seventy-eight, and while he was ensconced in his wilderness at Harrow Weald, there lived in Clerkenwell a remarkable recluse who reached the age of 116. 'LADY' LEWSON, as she was known, was of very different stuff from Dancer and Overs; she was much liked and respected by the few people she kept in contact with, and she was not the sort to go hunting for marrowbones in dunghills. Nevertheless she lived a life of extreme frugality and seclusion after the death of her husband when she was only twenty-six. She occupied just one room of her large house, amid a gathering accumulation of dust and cobwebs, still wearing the style of clothes that had been fashionable at her wedding.

'LADY' JANE LEWSON IN HER WALKING-OUT DRESS, COMPLETE WITH GOLD-HEADED CANE. IT WAS THE STYLE SHE WORE AT THE TIME OF HER WEDDING, AND SHE STUCK WITH IT FOR EIGHTY YEARS.

It was the faded elegance of these garments which led to the locals dubbing her 'Lady Lewson', but she was actually plain Mrs Jane Lewson. One can understand the title, however, from a contemporary description of how she looked when she took an occasional stroll around the square. 'She always wore powder with a large *tache* (a kind of clasp) made of horsehair upon her head, over which the hair was turned up and a cap was placed which was tied under her chin, and three or four curls hung down her neck. She generally wore silk gowns, with the train long, a deep flounce all round and a very long waist . . . The sleeves came down below the elbows, and to each of them four or five large cuffs were attached; a large bonnet quite flat, high-heeled shoes, a large black silk cloak trimmed round with lace, and a gold-headed cane completed her everyday costume for the last eighty years.'

Like Dancer, Jane Lewson rarely washed, not out of meanness but for fear of catching cold. No doubt any small boys would say it was this shrewd decision which kept her alive so long. But they would hardly enjoy her alternative; she used to smear her face and neck with hog's lard, adding a dab of pink on each cheek to provide a little colour. Her antipathy to water extended to her room also – it was never washed and 'the windows were so crusted with dirt that they hardly admitted a ray of light'. But she had an ancient retainer who kept the beds made in all the bedrooms, ready for guests who never came.

If all this seems vaguely familiar, then you have probably read Charles Dickens' *Great Expectations*. It is believed he modelled his reclusive Miss Haversham on Jane Lewson, and if you saw the film you will need no further description of her – except to say that she is supposed to have cut two new teeth when she was eighty-seven years old, though I cannot imagine she allowed anybody to check.

After Jane Lewson's death in 1816, John Camden Neild took over as London's most famous recluse. He had inherited a quarter of a million pounds from his father, a public-spirited and generous gentleman renowned for his interest in prison reform. But Neild senior must have used up all the philanthropy in the family, because his son showed quite a different approach to life. 'It was soon apparent,' says one biographer, 'that avarice was his ruling passion. His parsimonious spirit increased till he became a confirmed miser, and for the last thirty years of his life he was entirely given over to the accumulation of wealth.'

Neild had a large house at Cheyne Walk in Chelsea, but like Mrs Lewson he occupied only one room. For many years he slept on a bare board, though he later permitted himself an old bedstead. The house was scantily furnished and his housekeeper had to exist on a pittance. Again like Mrs Lewson, when he did emerge he always wore old-fashioned dress, in his case a blue swallow-tailed coat with gilt buttons, brown trousers, short gaiters and patched shoes. But he took his miserly habits far beyond those of

Cheyne Walk in Chelsea, where John Camden Neild lived as London's most famous recluse in Victorian days. He lived in one room in his large house, and for many years slept on a bare board, though he later permitted himself an old bedstead.

the genteel and generally kindly recluse of Clerkenwell. He refused to have his clothes brushed in case it wore them out, and he never went to the extravagance of a greatcoat, even in the bitterest weather, though he did carry a gingham umbrella. His stockings and linen were full of holes, and his nightshirt was so tattered and rotten that, when he left it behind after staying with one of his tenants, his hostess threw it in the fire.

It was on his excursions to the family properties in Buckinghamshire, Middlesex and Kent that his meanness was displayed to the full. He did not pay an agent but collected the rents himself, cadging overnight board and lodging from his tenants, and happy to take a lift on a coal cart or a farm waggon rather than pay for a carriage. He did travel in and out of London by coach, always booking the cheapest seat on top, and the story goes that at one village halt, when he stayed in his seat in the bitter cold rather than spend money in the inn, his sympathetic fellow travellers sent out a brandy-and-water to the 'poor gentleman' who apparently could not afford it himself. He accepted it without a murmur, even though he could have bought the brandy, the inn, and probably the entire village . . .

Some of his property was at North Marston in Buckinghamshire, where he was responsible for keeping the church in repair. The present Rector of North Marston, the Revd Peter Lawrence, described in an article how Neild had cracks in the lead roof covered up with strips of canvas and calico painted with tar, saying it was sufficient to last out his time. 'That was before there were advisory committees and Archdeacon's certificates to control standards,' the rector commented wryly. 'Heady days!'

He added however that Neild did have odd moments of generosity. He gave a sovereign to the village Sunday School and a fiver to another at nearby Aston Clinton; and when he discovered that the young son of one of his tenants was unusually bright, he paid for his school and college education. But in the main it was his miserliness that people remembered, and it achieved national notoriety when the terms of his will were published. Thanks to his years of parsimony he had doubled the sum his father left him; in present-day terms it was probably worth twenty million pounds. He left almost his entire fortune 'to her most Gracious Majesty, Queen Victoria, begging her Majesty's most gracious acceptance of the same, for her sole use and benefit, and her heirs'.

His tenants must have heard the news with mixed feelings; they would probably have appreciated a few bob

The memorial to John Camden Neild. Thanks to his meanness he left a fortune — and bequeathed it all to Queen Victoria. He has gone down in history as 'The Queen's Miser'.

themselves. On the other hand, the Queen was hardly likely to treat them quite as meanly as their previous squire – and indeed she did the right thing by Neild's old housekeeper, who was left nothing in his will. She increased the few bequests he had made, and at North Marston she had a stained glass window put up in the church in his memory. I hope she also did something about the roof.

However, she kept the bulk of his money, and it is popularly believed that she spent the lot on buying Balmoral Castle, her Scottish holiday home. There is no proof, of course, but certainly

The chancel of North Marston Church in Buckinghamshire, where John Camden Neild is buried. The east window and reredos were given by Queen Victoria out of the fortune he left her – worth about twenty million pounds in today's terms. It is thought she spent most of it on buying Balmoral Castle.

she did acquire the castle soon after Neild had left her his fortune. As for Neild himself, he has gone down in history as 'The Queen's Miser'. He died in 1852 in his house at Chelsea, and the body was taken to North Marston for burial. It was probably the most comfortable journey – and the most expensive – he ever made. As one villager commented as he watched the hearse go by: 'Poor wretch! Had he known how much would be spent on his funeral, he would have come down here to die'.

But at least John Camden Neild maintained some sort of respectability and did not shut himself away completely from the world. He was not in the same league of recluse as JAMES LUCAS, 'The Mad Hermit of Hertfordshire', who turned his family mansion into a fortress and lived for most of his life

EDWIN JEHOSOPHAT ODELL was a recluse in reverse. He did not retire into his own house to escape from the world, because he had no house to retire into. At the age of ninety he decided to take up residence in his London club, the Savage – not in a bedroom, but on one of the sofas. This quite amused most of the members but profoundly displeased the committee. It took them a little time to displace him; he was a formidable figure, a former actor whose appearance was described as 'a fearsome compound of Rasputin, Wallace Beery and The Old Man of the Sea'. However the committee did summon up the courage to withdraw his membership, and for some days he hung about outside the building until his friends launched a campaign to reinstate him.

They parked a carriage outside the front door for him to sleep in, and smuggled meals out to him from the dining-room. The committee members had to endure his icy stare each time they entered or left the Club, and eventually they admitted defeat and allowed him back, no doubt in the hope that, as he was already ninety, he would not trouble them too much longer.

They underestimated Edwin Jehosophat Odell. He lived to be over one hundred, and became so cantankerous that his friends may have wished they hadn't bothered. He refused to allow anyone to use his favourite chair – even the Duke of York, later George VI, was peremptorily ordered to vacate it. He was also inclined to borrow money from unsuspecting new members and never pay them back. When one young man reminded him after six months that he still owed him ten shillings, Odell snapped back: 'I haven't finished with it yet'.

However, there must still have been some goodwill towards him when he eventually gave up his membership for good. The members placed a brass plate on his chair: 'Here Odell Sat'. They omitted to put one on the sofa saying: 'Here Odell Slept' – there is a limit to eccentricity, even at the Savage.

in the kitchen, in the most appalling squalor.

The story of 'Mad Lucas' was first told in numerous penny pamphlets soon after his death in 1874, and more comprehensively a century later by a former BBC colleague of mine, the reporter and television news reader Richard Whitmore, who lives not far from the site of Lucas' home near Hitchin. Richard has delved deeply into Lucas' eccentricities, and a picture emerges of a sad, mentally ill but intelligent man with a paranoid fear of being attacked.

JAMES LUCAS, 'THE MAD HERMIT OF HERTFORDSHIRE', WHO LIVED MOST OF HIS LIFE IN SACKCLOTH AND ASHES BEHIND THE BARRED WINDOW OF HIS KITCHEN.

The fear arose as a result of the macabre events that followed his mother's death. Lucas was devoted to her, to such an extent that he personally embalmed her body, put it in a glass coffin in the drawing-room, and refused to allow the undertaker to enter the house, let alone take her away. For thirteen weeks he sat by his mother's coffin, barricaded inside the house, until his exasperated brother got the police to break in and take away the corpse. When they had gone James Lucas replaced and strengthened his barricades, loaded every weapon in the house, and settled down to being a full-time hermit.

He cleared most of the furniture out of the kitchen and slept on a pile of cinders

A TEA-SET FEATURING HIS HOME, ONE OF SEVERAL SOUVENIRS MADE FOR TOURISTS AFTER HIS DEATH.

from the fire. His only clothing was a horse-rug, and he never washed, or combed his hair, or cut his nails. 'Gradually,' says Richard Whitmore, 'his entire body, covered by an ever-thickening film of grease and grime, turned grey and then almost black. Only his bright eyes could be clearly discerned beneath the long matted hair and the wild straggling beard that hid much of his face . . . A hermit of old, a wild biblical figure sitting amid the trappings and fast-decaying elegance of an upper class Victorian household.'

In spite of his unsavoury appearance Lucas had no shortage of visitors. He kept a supply of sweets and pennies for small girls, and tots of gin and water for the gentry, whose idea of an entertaining afternoon out was to visit 'Squire James' in his cell. But mostly he entertained tramps, with whom he had a much greater affinity. The more privileged were allowed inside the kitchen, the others had to converse through the thick bars on the window.

His most notable visitor was Charles Dickens; it was not a happy encounter, and it finished up with Lucas threatening the distinguished author with a shotgun. It also led to Dickens

Elmwood House, where 'Mad Lucas' lived in appalling squalor in the kitchen. He boarded up the windows to keep out intruders, and employed two bodyguards (in the foreground) to patrol the grounds.

writing *Tom Tiddler's Ground*, a semi-fictional story in which Lucas, although not actually named, was unmistakably portrayed as a 'slothful, unsavoury, nasty reversal of the laws of human nature'.

Dickens did escape without actually being fired at, though if Lucas had known what he was going to write about him he might well have let fly. Certainly he took a potshot at some local

THE CHURCH OF ST JOHN-AT-HACKNEY IN EAST LONDON, WHERE JAMES LUCAS WAS BURIED. THE INSCRIPTION ON THE TOMB IS STILL JUST READABLE. 'MAD LUCAS' IS RECORDED, MORE CORRECTLY, AS 'JAMES LUCAS ESQ' AT THE BOTTOM OF THE STONE.

hooligans who attempted to get into the house on the pretext that he was a wicked Papist; and he used his gun again years later when a group of drunken soldiers tried to do the same thing. But in the main he tolerated the attentions of the inquisitive strangers who came to peer into the darkened kitchen and talk to the weird figure crouched in a far corner. Sometimes he would come to the window and sit on the sill to chat – a disconcerting sight at close quarters.

'There is no disguising the fact,' wrote one visitor, who was treated to this experience, 'the man is dirty. Not partially or temporarily dirty, but dirty comprehensively and permanently. His hair is dirty, his scalp is dirty, his face is dirty, his hands and arms are dirty, his body and legs are dirty, his feet are dirty. In a word, he is dirty all over.' No room for argument there.

But Lucas could be equally scathing about his visitors. When a dark-skinned lady from Martinique declined to answer his civil 'Good afternoon', he raised a broken monocle to his eye and commented coldly, 'A little of the coolie caste, I should say'. And when a supercilious society matron enquired loudly, 'Does he do tricks?' he gave her the monocle treatment also while

'The Hermit of Redcoats' at Great Wymondley, which was re-named in memory of James Lucas at the end of the last century.

observing, equally loudly, 'Now there's an old ewe dressed lamb-fashion if ever I saw one'.

In his final years he retreated further inside the house, and spent much of the time in his mother's bedroom. Two bodyguards were employed to keep trouble-makers away, and he rarely saw anyone not known to him. On Good Friday 1874, the day when traditionally he gave presents to the local children, an unusually large number of people flocked to the house, and Lucas, apparently in good form, talked to each little girl through a landing window and gave each a small gift. Then he disappeared inside. A few days later the police broke into the house again for the second time in twenty-five years, and found he had suffered a stroke. He died two days later.

In death James Lucas provided his final surprise. This is how Richard Whitmore describes it: 'As the women engaged to perform the last offices began to wash the crust of his hermit years away, it was as if the covering of soot and grease had preserved him from old age. His cleansed skin had the pure white smooth alabaster quality of a boy. His hands, the nails trimmed, were small and delicate like those of a woman . . . In death his face was serene, even handsome, that of a distinguished and intellectual man of high birth . . . Esther Palmer, who helped to lay him out, commented afterwards: "A more beautiful-looking corpse I never saw"'.

Happily not every recluse has to be miserly, or over-fearful, or slightly dotty. Sometimes their only eccentricity is their inordinate shyness. HENRY CAVENDISH was such a man. Although he was a brilliant scientist and a member of the Royal Society he found it difficult to get along with people and detested talking to them. One of his contemporaries suggested that he spoke fewer words in his seventy-eight years than anyone of a similar age in history – including Trappist monks.

In order to avoid talking to his servants he left notes in letter-boxes around his splendid house in Clapham. He once met a maid on the staircase and was so put off by the experience that he built another staircase for his own exclusive use. Even his closest relative and eventual heir, Lord George Cavendish, was only granted an annual audience of half an hour.

Cavendish did not need to leave his house to conduct his scientific activities; the drawing-room was converted into a laboratory, one of the bedrooms was an observatory, and he took his meteorological readings up a tree in the garden. Whenever he did venture out to attend a scientific meeting he avoided conversations by talking incessantly to himself in his high-pitched squeaky voice. And even on his deathbed he elected to die alone – he told the servants he had 'something particular to think about and did not wish to be disturbed'.

Perhaps it was through his shyness, and the fear of having to speak in public, that he failed to publish two of his most notable discoveries, the fundamental principles of electricity which became known as Coulomb's Law and Ohm's Law. Coulomb and Ohm made the same discoveries much later, but were not so reticent about it.

He also never talked about money. His father left him a fortune, in which he was supremely uninterested. When his banker asked what he should do with it, Cavendish reprimanded him for interrupting with such trivial matters. Fortunately the banker took his responsibilities more seriously, and invested wisely. When Henry Cavendish died in 1819 he left his cousin George £1,175,000.

CHARLES SEYMOUR, sixth Duke of Somerset, also went to great lengths to avoid talking to his servants, but this was not due to shyness, just downright snobbery. He only communicated with

HENRY CAVENDISH, A BRILLIANT SCIENTIST, BUT SO SHY THAT HE LEFT NOTES AROUND THE HOUSE FOR HIS SERVANTS, RATHER THAN SPEAK TO THEM. HE ONCE MET A MAID ON THE STAIRS AND WAS SO SHAKEN BY THE EXPERIENCE HE HAD ANOTHER STAIRCASE BUILT FOR HIS EXCLUSIVE USE . . .

Charles Seymour, sixth Duke of Somerset, who built houses along the route from his country estate to London so that he did not have to mingle with the lower orders at public hostelries.

them by sign language, and when he travelled from his country estate to London he built houses along the route, where he could stay without having to mingle with the lower orders at public hostelries.

This attitude was not uncommon among the aristocracy, though few took it to such lengths. But Lord Crewe, for example, was so determined not to encounter his servants that any maid seen in the corridors or rooms of Crewe Hall after ten in the morning was subject to instant dismissal. Perhaps that was why nobody spotted the fire which broke out in the Hall and burnt it to the ground. His lordship seems to have taken as lofty an attitude to his family as to his servants. When the fire was at its height he is said to have observed to his distraught sister: 'On this occasion at least, you cannot complain of your bedroom being cold'.

George Edward Dering, the squire of Lockleys, near Welwyn, had little difficulty in avoiding the servants in his mansion, because in later years he was rarely there to see them. For a long period he only visited the house just before Christmas, when he paid the wages and read the mail. Then he went away again on Christmas morning, nobody knew where. But a staff of seven was maintained at Lockleys, and their instructions were to have a mutton chop always ready by the stove, just in case he arrived unexpectedly.

In his younger days when de did live in the house he demanded absolute quiet, so he could study his books and develop his inventions; altogether he took out seventeen patents between 1850 and 1881, mostly electrical devices. If flocks of sheep were grazing in the park near the house, all new-born lambs had to be removed in case they disturbed him with their bleating. The shutters were kept closed all day, which was when he slept, and he was inclined to take dinner at two in the morning. When a road near the house became too noisy for his liking he spent £20,000 diverting it to a more distant route.

The most unlikely feature of Dering's activities was his friendship with Jean Francois Gravelet, better known as Blondin the tightrope walker. The eccentric Hertfordshire squire was a high wire enthusiast himself, and he and Blondin used to practise

on a rope stretched across the river at Lockleys. When Blondin went off to perform a rather more spectacular feat across Niagara Falls, he left his host with a set of Venetian glass and the popular title of 'the tightrope-walking inventor'.

Then came Dering's years of absence from Lockleys, and when he eventually came back permanently in 1907 he occupied just one room of the fine old mansion, and never allowed anyone in to clean it. It was only after his death four years later that the mystery of his missing years was explained; he had been living in a house he owned in Brighton with a wife and daughter who knew nothing about his other life at Lockleys. His wife had died, his daughter had married, and so he returned to spend his final years in the house where he was born.

Lockleys was found to be full of archaeological treasures he had collected in his earlier years, and the cellar was full of wines which had been laid down by his father and never touched. His daughter presented the archaeological collection to the British Museum and, I trust, drank a few glasses of the wine to his memory. Lockleys was sold and became a boarding school. I can't think George Dering would have enjoyed all that noise . . .

LOCKLEYS, THE HOME OF GEORGE EDWARD DERING, LATER TO BECOME A BOARDING SCHOOL, AND DERING HIMSELF, APPARENTLY TAKING A REST DURING TIGHTROPE PRACTISE OVER THE RIVER MIMRAM.

These days intellectual recluses are thin on the ground. One of the more recent ones was Solomon Pottesman, who lived with his aged mother in a squalid flat in Bloomsbury, near the British Museum. Its only furniture was one old bed. There was much speculation that he shared it with his mother, but in fact he dossed down in the kitchen. The rest of the place was piled high with musty volumes, because Pottesman was an antiquarian bookseller who hated to sell his books. He stored the most valuable of them in bank vaults and safe deposit boxes, and in a private strong-room underneath Harrods; the rest he kept in the flat.

Solomon Pottesman, recluse and antiquarian bookseller, in typical pose at a book fair, in grubby cloth-cap, always the same shirt (supplemented by layers of *The Times* in cold weather), and his latest purchases in a brown paper parcel — or is it his lunch?

Like Daniel Dancer and Jane Lewson he had a great dislike of water, but in his case it was because he feared it might damage his books. For this reason he disconnected the lavatory cistern, in case it leaked and flooded the flat. He discouraged any visitors, but one Bloomsbury bookseller who got past the door reported that when he accepted a cup of tea there was only one cup in the place, and Pottesman drank his out of a half-pint milk bottle.

Pottesman frequented only two sorts of places — book auctions and libraries. It was said he knew nearly all the books in the British Museum Library, and which shelves they occupied. During his final illness he announced with some satisfaction that he had acquired the medical book which first mentioned the disease from which he suffered.

He was not a prepossessing figure, and not always welcome in the sale-rooms. He constantly wore the same shirt, supplemented by two or three layers of *The Times* in cold weather, and his grubby cloth-cap remained on his head, indoors and out. He carried sheets of brown paper to wrap up any purchases, and finished up with armfuls of untidy brown paper parcels. At auctions he would infuriate everyone by talking through the bidding and obstructing the view of the other bidders. He was also inclined to eat his lunch in the sale-room, generally a sordid-looking sandwich wrapped in the ubiquitous brown paper. But in spite of all this he was highly regarded for his expert knowledge and held in grudging affection by auctioneers and fellow dealers. It is perhaps unfortunate that his nickname amongst them was, inevitably, 'Potty' . . .

NATTICENTRICS

Dressed to kill, or just to confuse?

It is not easy to define eccentricity in dress. In the Garden of Eden it was considered eccentric for some time to wear anything at all; then the height of fashion became a fig-leaf. The early Britons must have thought the Vikings looked very odd in those fancy horned helmets, and the Vikings must have blinked to see chaps dressed solely in woad. As early as the first century, people like Ovid were shaking their heads sadly as they wrote: 'I cannot keep track of all the vagaries of fashion. Every day, so it seems, brings in a different style' – and we've been saying much the same thing ever since. One man's fashionable turnout can be the height of eccentricity to another; and in the space of a single generation we can look back and mock the football heroes of yesteryear, in their very long shorts and very short haircuts. I suspect that every man at some time or other has added a touch of eccentricity to his dress, be it only a pair of yellow socks or a particularly nauseating tie. As for the ladies, I dare not quote any examples; their fashions are a constant source of wonderment. It was a brave fellow who wrote: 'A man has his clothes made to fit him; a woman makes herself fit her clothes'.

GEORGE 'BEAU' BRUMMELL, GRANDSON OF A VALET, WHO BECAME SO OBSESSED WITH CLOTHES THAT HE MADE HIS OWN VALET POLISH HIS SHOES WITH THE FROTH OF CHAMPAGNE – INCLUDING THE SOLES.

So back to the question: how do you define eccentricity in dress? In my book – literally – it can be either wearing something extremely odd which nobody else had thought of before, or carrying popular fashion to ridiculous extremes. Even this second classification is a matter of opinion; how extreme does it have to be before it becomes ridiculous? I take as my guideline the man who is generally recognised, I think, as the epitome of the fashionable eccentric – the man who took three hours to tie his cravat, changed his shirt three times a day, and sent them off to be laundered in the country 'so they smelt of new-mown hay'; and who insisted that his valet polished his shoes – the soles as well as the uppers – with the froth of champagne.

Appropriately, though perhaps surprisingly, GEORGE 'BEAU' BRUMMELL was the grandson of a valet himself. His father shrewdly married a wealthy heiress and sent young George to Eton and Oxford. George, equally shrewdly, edged his way into London society and endeared himself to the Prince of Wales. The Prince gave him a commission in the highly exclusive 10th Light Dragoons, and Brummell's dazzling Hussar uniform started him off on his career as the king of the dandies.

He managed to keep his uniform exquisite by avoiding any kind of actual soldiering. He had a nasty moment when his regiment was posted to Manchester, but he appealed to his friend the Prince in terms which, at the risk of offending my Mancunian friends, I cannot resist quoting. 'Think!' he cried. 'Think, your Royal Highness. **Manchester**!' He never went.

Brummell's real fame began to build up after he bought himself out of the army in order to concentrate on clothes. He introduced an idea which, at the time, was the height of eccentricity – he washed. It was the practice for men of fashion not to bother with such preliminaries before donning their finery, but Beau Brummell spent two hours washing, and scrubbed his whole body with a stiff brush before even donning a sock. This may have been one reason for his popularity; certainly it gave him novelty value, since he had no need to douse himself with perfume to conceal the smell.

Beau Brummell socialising with the Duchess of Rutland at a ball in 1815. He was a popular figure at such gatherings, perhaps because he was eccentric enough to have a wash before dressing.

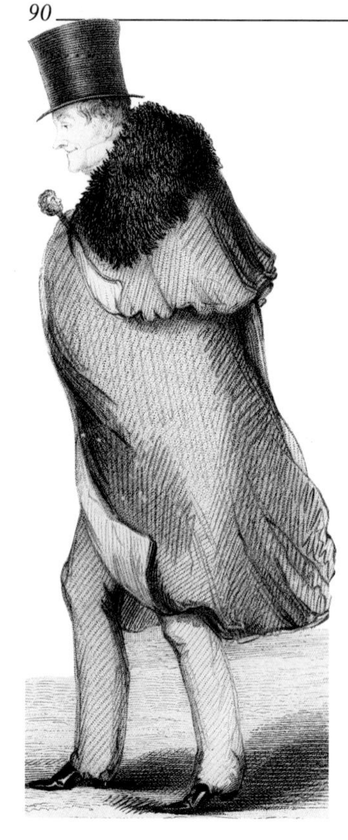

Beau Brummell in his later years. He would never raise his hat to a lady in case he could not replace it at precisely the right angle.

Having spent so much effort on preparing himself for the public gaze, he would not risk dirtying his shoes on the pavement, or having a hair blown out of place by the breeze. His sedan chair was brought indoors to the foot of the stairs, and he boarded it there. His insistence on not having his clothing disturbed by too much movement could lead to certain discourtesies – he would never raise his hat to a lady in case he could not replace it at precisely the right angle, and at dinner he would not turn his head to talk to his neighbours in case he creased his cravat.

However, for eighteen years his foibles were tolerated by the Prince and his court. He even dared to criticise the cut of the Prince's clothes, whereupon it is said the Prince burst into tears. But at last he went too far. He met the Prince, who by now was extremely overweight, walking in Bond Street with his friend Lord Alvanley. 'Ah, Alvanley,' said Brummell, 'who's your fat friend?' The Prince was touchier about his figure than his clothes; instead of bursting into tears, he never spoke to Brummell again.

It would be nice to record that the king of the dandies departed this life as elegantly as he lived. Alas, he gambled away his money and ran up enormous bills. No longer able to indulge in his expensive eccentricities, and shunned by the court, his mind finally went. He died in Caen Lunatic Asylum in 1840 at the age of sixty-two.

A contemporary of Brummell's, and a rival for the Prince's favours, was another eccentric dandy with a much more distinguished pedigree. Charles Stanhope, Viscount Petersham, later the fourth Earl of Harrington, had no need to edge his way into society, he was born into it, and when, like Brummell, the Prince gave him a commission in one of his fashionable regiments he showed his more soldierly qualities and rose to be a major-general. But he still found time to pursue his passion for clothes, which dated back to his days at Eton. A friend of the family, Lady Bessborough, noted at the time: 'He seems a good-natured boy, but I am sure he wears stays, like Misses used to wear some years ago. Anne will never resist feeling him to find out'.

As a young man he cut out all his own clothes, not trusting a tailor to achieve a perfect fit. He had a special liking for brown; his carriage and horses were brown, his servants wore long brown coats down to their brown boots, and glazed hats with brown cockades. This fixation extended to other objects besides clothes; he was a great connoisseur of teas and of snuff. He collected enough snuff boxes to use a different one on each day of the year, and on one occasion, when someone admired the fine Sèvres snuff box he was using, he agreed that 'it was a nice summer box, but it would not do for winter wear'.

As a young dandy at the Prince's court, Viscount Petersham invented a coat which became known as a Petersham. It was greatly admired by the Prince, who ordered one for each day of the week but, in spite of this royal patronage, the Petersham failed to catch on, unlike other garments named after the gentlemen who devised them — we are still familiar with 'cardigans' and 'raglan' coats and 'wellington'

VISCOUNT PETERSHAM, LATER EARL OF HARRINGTON, WHO INVENTED THE PETERSHAM COAT. THE PRINCE OF WALES ORDERED SEVERAL, BUT IT NEVER CAUGHT ON.

boots, but petersham only lives on as a kind of corded ribbon for strengthening belts, and its connection with the original Petersham coat is somewhat obscure.

He also had a hat named after him, but to save confusion with the coat it was named after his earldom instead of his viscountcy, and was called the Harrington. It had a tapering crown and a square brim turned up at the sides. The effect was a little too eccentric even for his friend the Prince, and it has long since disappeared from the nation's hat-stands.

When Stanhope was fifty and inherited the earldom, along with Elvaston Castle in Derbyshire, he married an actress young enough to be his daughter and switched his curious designing talents to reorganising the gardens and creating what has been called the biggest wedding present in the world. He tried to engage Capability Brown to give him a hand, but Mr Brown decided that Elvaston's flat acres did not have sufficient capability, and William Barron of Edinburgh Botanical Gardens got the job instead. He was still at it thirty-five years later, along with some eighty gardeners. The centre-piece was a Moorish temple designed in what has been called Sino-Mooresque-quasi-

Elvaston Castle in Derbyshire, Lord Harrington's stately home, where he switched his eccentric designing talents from clothes to landscape gardening.

One of Lord Harrington's curious garden decorations, a Moorish temple in Sino-Mooresque-quasi-Gothic — to name but a few. Like the Petersham coat, it never caught on.

Gothic, and the rest of the vista was just as jumbled — Italian and Spanish gardens intermingled with yew hedges and tunnels, avenues and arbours, grottos and follies, rock gardens and caves. As one of Stanhope's biographers put it: 'An outrageous phantasmagoria of artificial rock and growing wood threatened to engulf the house itself. . . The grounds became nowhere to lose a child after dark!'

There was little danger of that. The gardens were entirely for the benefit of Stanhope's young wife, and he gave instructions to his head gardener to keep the *hoi polloi* out. He made one exception. 'When the Queen comes, Barron, show her round, but admit no one else.' The Queen never did come, and when the Earl died his wife hastily escaped from this horticultural hotchpotch and made tracks for London. These days the *hoi polloi* are more than welcome; the castle and grounds have become a country park owned by Derbyshire County Council.

The world of Beau Brummell, Charles Stanhope and their fellow dandies was not confined entirely to London. Thanks to the various interests the Prince Regent had in Brighton, the

Steyne became a popular venue for the fashionable set to promenade and preen in front of the peasantry, and one or two ambitious locals joined in. Undoubtedly the most eccentric Brighton beau was one HENRY COPE, known to everyone as 'The Green Man of Brighton'. Just as Lord Petersham had a bent towards brown, Henry Cope was gripped by green. A contemporary writer records every detail: 'Green pantaloons, green waistcoat, green frock coat, green cravat; and though his ears, whiskers, eyebrows and chin were powdered, his countenance, no doubt from the reflection of his clothes, was also green. He ate nothing but green fruits and vegetables, had his rooms painted green, and furnished with green sofa, green chairs, green table, green bed and green curtains. His gig, his livery, his portmanteau, his gloves and his whip were all green. With a green silk handkerchief in his hand, and a large watch-chain with green seals fastened to the green buttons of his green waistcoat, he paraded every day on the Steyne'. How politically fashionable he would have been today . . .

HENRY COPE, 'THE GREEN MAN OF BRIGHTON', WHO ADOPTED THE COLOUR A CENTURY OR TWO BEFORE IT BECAME ENVIRONMENTALLY FASHIONABLE. HIS CLOTHES WERE ALL GREEN, SO WAS HIS FURNITURE, HIS CARRIAGE, HIS LUGGAGE — AND HE ONLY ATE GREEN FRUIT AND VEGETABLES.

The public loved 'The Green Man of Brighton'. The *Lewes and Brighthelmstone Journal* noted that 'the Green Man continues daily to amuse the Steyne promenaders with his eccentricities', and an old local history records proudly that 'Brighton, in its merry days, could turn all other eccentrics green with envy. The specialised greenness of the Green Man still keeps green his memory'. But not everybody was so enthusiastic. In 1806 a contributor to the Journal signing himself merely 'Quiz', wrote a poem about Henry Cope which started favourably, then fell away:

A spruce little man in a doublet of green
Perambulates daily the streets and the Steyne.
Green striped is his waistcoat, his small-clothes are green,
And oft round his neck a green 'kerchief is seen.
Green watch-string, green seals, and, for certain, I've heard,
(Tho' they're powdered) green whiskers, and eke a green beard.
Green garters, green hose, and, deny it who can,
The brains, too, are green, of this green little man!

I hope it was not that final dig which upset Mr Cope, but manifestly something did, because a fortnight later he featured again in the Journal. 'On Saturday morning, a little after six o'clock, the gentleman who, from his singular garb of green, and other eccentricities (exhibited on the Steyne for several weeks past) had obtained the appellation of the Green Man' – at last they come to the point – 'leaped from the window of his lodging on the South Parade, into the street, ran from thence to the verge of the cliff nearly opposite, and threw himself over the precipice to the beach below.'

It seemed like a dramatic end to the story of 'The Green Man of Brighton', and indeed many historians have treated it that way and called it suicide, but in fact Henry Cope survived the twenty-foot drop. Perhaps it would have been better if he hadn't. Five days later the Journal noted sadly: 'Mr Cope, the Green Man, is pronounced out of danger from his bruises; but his intellects have continued so impaired as to render a straight waistcoat necessary'.

The paper never refers to him again, and one can only assume that Henry Cope, like his hero Beau Brummell, ended his days in an asylum, clad in a 'straight waistcoat'. I hope that at least it was green . . .

Perhaps as a reaction to the extravagancies of Brummell and his fellow dandies, the DUCHESS OF QUEENSBERRY insisted on wearing such down-to-earth attire at court that it led to a Royal Order being issued on correct court dress. Until then she insisted on wearing a red flannel dress and a maid's apron. She was equally down-to-earth in her attitude to her guests; anyone who arrived late was turned away at the door, and when she got bored with the others, she produced a broom and swept the floor until they took the hint and departed. She was also inclined to get irritated if the male guests formed their own groups and ignored the ladies – a social phenomenon not unknown today. At one of her parties she came upon Horace Walpole and two other distinguished gentlemen gossiping on their own in an adjoining room. They realised their error when a servant appeared and took the door off its hinges.

THE DUCHESS OF QUEENSBERRY, WHO WORE A RED FLANNEL DRESS AND A MAID'S APRON TO COURT UNTIL A ROYAL ORDER WAS ISSUED ON CORRECT DRESS IN THE PRESENCE OF ROYALTY.

But it was the Duchess' disregard for fashionable clothes that made the greatest impact at functions. No matter how important the occasion she never worried about dressing up or powdering her hair. She preferred to put her time to better purpose by setting out early on foot, often startling her hosts by arriving on the doorstep 'cheerful, sweaty and red faced with exertion'. Beau Brummell would have thought her not just eccentric, but quite mad.

The acting profession, not surprisingly, has produced some notable dress eccentrics. In most cases it has been as much to attract attention as to satisfy any eccentric urge; there were just a few who took it to such extremes that it got beyond simply showing off.

William Cussans, for example, was an eighteenth-century performer at Covent Garden and Sadler's Wells who favoured an enormous cocked hat on his shaven head, paper ruffles round his neck and wrists, a heavy chain hanging from his neck and a sword at his belt. He not only wore odd clothes, he did unexpected things with them; he visited a coffee shop in Bath wearing a bright yellow suit, called for a jug of water, and promptly poured it over himself. Then with his meal he ordered a bootjack, a Bible, a pint of vinegar, a paper of pins and some barley sugar. The proprietor was all right for barley sugar, but short on Bibles and clean out of bootjacks. On learning this, Mr Cussans forthwith produced six shirts from his case, put them all on, one on top of the other, and swept off — but not before giving instructions that for his evening meal he would require a dish of cold fried milestones, without sugar.

His instructions to his tailor were often just as bewildering. He told him on one occasion: 'Cut the skirts of my coat into strips and sew them on my waistcoast, breeches and stockings'. Fortunately he was not wearing this cumbersome garb when he took it into his head to jump fully clothed into the Thames, after learning from some ladies he met that they had never seen a man in the river before. The ladies, it seems, were not too surprised; it is reported that the reputation of 'the eccentric Mr Cussans' had already reached them.

He never achieved much fame on the stage — which perhaps is why he tried so hard to attract attention off it — but I can offer one example of his repertoire which received 'universal applause', so it is said, when he rendered it at Sadler's Wells and the Royal Circus. It was a song he dedicated to Robinson Crusoe, and its only merit, so far as I can judge, was that in one verse he actually found a new rhyme for Crusoe:

He got all the wood that ever he could,
And he stuck it together with glue, so.
He made him a hut and in it he put
The carcase of Robinson Crusoe . . .

After that, perhaps it was not surprising he jumped in the river.

But for sheer awfulness on the stage, combined with eccentricity in dress, you could hardly beat ROBERT COATES, who made an enormous impact on the theatre-going public in the early 1800s with his incredibly bad portrayal of Shakespeare's Romeo. This was the only role he was really interested in, though he did sometimes have a crack at Lothario, which was possibly even worse.

For his Romeo role he invariably wore a blue silk cloak covered with spangles, a Charles II wig and a top hat; for Lothario he switched into a silver suit with a pink silk stole, and a large hat decorated with ostrich feathers. As for his acting, critics had difficulty in deciding just how appalling it was, but audiences came to love him, particularly when he greeted friends across the footlights in the middle of a speech, or interrupted the action to threaten a heckler with his sword. The highspot of his performance was the death scene; before actually dying he dusted the stage with his handkerchief to preserve his spangled costume, then placed his hat carefully on the floor before settling himself

One of the more endearing forms of eccentric dressing is the re-creation of historical or fictional characters. The energetic gentlemen who dress up as Roundheads and Royalists, in order to thump each other with staves and broadswords, are an example of 'groupie' dress eccentrics; individual examples include the Nottinghamshire man who became so entranced by the story of Robin Hood that he adopted his name by deed poll. ROBIN HOOD donned a green costume complete with longbow and arrows and feathered hat, and went to live in a well-camouflaged tent in Sherwood Forest. He emerged from this during working hours – still I trust in his Robin Hood gear – to pursue his more mundane career of installing automatic cash dispensers. Maybe he hoped to find one which only dispensed to the poor . . .

But surely the most distinguished of these dress eccentrics in recent years was BARON GORE-BOOTH of Maltby, at one time High Commissioner in India and later a director of Grindlays Bank. His clubs listed in *Who's Who* predictably included the Athenaeum and, less predictably, the Baker Street Irregulars. Lord Booth was in fact President of the Sherlock Holmes Society of London, and it was his wont to don an Inverness cape and deerstalker hat, and take himself off to the Reichenbach Falls in Switzerland to re-enact the final struggle with a reincarnated Professor Moriarty.

I gather that he read the Conan Doyle stories as a boy and became devoted to the 'sacred writings'. He was a great expert on all the characters, particularly Dr Watson, who had apparently married two or three times – it varies from story to story – but it was never made clear when, or where, or to whom. It was a mystery which this Holmes, alas, will never solve: Lord Gore-Booth died in 1984.

comfortably alongside and delivering the final lines. Audiences, we are told, were so overcome by emotion at this routine that they often demanded an encore, and were seldom denied.

Coates' carriages were as eccentric as his costumes. One was in the shape of a large cockleshell, drawn by two white horses, and the other looked like an enormous kettledrum, decorated with serpents. The silver buttons on his servants' livery bore the emblem of a cock, as a reminder of his family motto – or so he claimed – 'While I live, I'll crow'. It earned him the sobriquet 'Cock-a-doodle Coates', but he preferred to describe himself as 'The Celebrated Philanthropic Amateur' – and so he was, since he paid the expenses of all his performances, and if he happened to make a profit he gave most of it to charity.

Such flamboyance is rare among Shakespearean actors these days; there seems a tendency to perform in more modern dress remarkable only for its dullness. Eccentricity in the entertainment world seems limited to pop groups who are quite as appalling in their own way as Robert Coates was in his, without his endearing features. Just occasionally one comes across a distinguished character connected with the legitimate theatre who has no need to attract publicity by dressing peculiarly, but chooses to do so merely because he feels like it. I am thinking of JOHN CHRISTIE,

JOHN CHRISTIE, FOUNDER OF THE GLYNDEBOURNE FESTIVAL, AT A FORMAL MEETING OF HIS PRODUCTION DIRECTORS IN 1960 – THAT'S HIM ON THE EXTREME RIGHT IN THE TENNIS SHOES.

founder of Glyndebourne Festival Opera, who wore a pair of old tennis shoes with his formal evening dress because he felt more comfortable that way. He went through a lederhosen period in 1933, when all his visitors at Glyndebourne were expected to follow his example and don Tyrolean costumes for dinner. There was also a time when all the lady guests were provided with knitting needles and wool, so they could be gainfully employed while they chatted; and as he never felt the cold himself he limited his heating arrangements at house parties to a small electric fire with a long lead, which he carried with him from room to room.

GLYNDEBOURNE, WHERE JOHN CHRISTIE WENT THROUGH A LEDERHOSEN PERIOD IN 1933, AND LIKED HIS GUESTS TO WEAR TYROLEAN COSTUME AT DINNER.

Wilfred Blunt, who recorded many of Christie's funny little ways, confirmed that he was not calculatedly eccentric: 'Often the perfectly logical solution of a problem resulted in apparently abnormal behaviour'. That accounts for the occasion when a friend was driving him along the Bayswater Road in London and he opened his attaché case, took out several old collars and socks, and threw them out into the gutter, explaining: 'It's the easiest way of getting rid of them'. It also accounts for him leaving some

John Christie in his later years with his favourite pug.

valuable jewels in a railway carriage, wrapped in brown paper, while he went to buy a magazine; he argued that if something was wrapped in brown paper, nobody would think it worth stealing. Sure enough, the jewels were still there when he returned.

This was not his only eccentricity on train journeys. If the light bulbs were too bright for his liking, he either put up an umbrella to protect his eyes or, more drastically, removed the bulbs altogether – a practice which caused considerable alarm among any ladies in the compartment . . .

Christie used the same kind of logic when he was ordering clothes; he liked to save money by buying in bulk. This is how he came by 2,000 pairs of cheap plastic dancing pumps – not that he wore this kind of footwear, but he thought they might come in handy. He finished up trying to sell them to fellow members of his London club, with predictably little success. He would come home from a shopping expedition with three umbrellas or seven suits of silk pyjamas, and his wardrobe contained 230 shirts, 132 pairs of socks, and 180 handkerchiefs. He always had seven copies of *The Times* delivered to Glyndebourne so his guests had something to read at breakfast, and when his office manager asked for a typewriter he told him to buy half a dozen – 'I'm sure we shall need them'.

His most spectacular bulk buy was just after the Second World War. He acquired a ton of sugar and rice in America and brought it home on the *Queen Mary*. Rationing was still in force at the time, and it was quite against the rules for one person to bring such large quantities into the country, so he persuaded his fellow passengers to take small portions of sugar and rice through Customs in their hand luggage. Once ashore he retrieved it all from them, loaded it in a lorry and took it off to Glyndebourne, where he stored it under one of the cellar floors. Perhaps the extra helpings of sweet rice pudding at subsequent house parties were some consolation to his guests for the enforced knitting before dinner, and having to read *The Times* over breakfast . . .

Apart from show business and the Beau Brummell Brigade there used to be a fair sprinkling of eccentric dressers among hermits. I can offer a pair of them, a couple of centuries apart, whom I saved up from the last chapter: John Bigg the 'Dinton Hermit,' and William Lole, the self-styled Old Hermit of Newton Burgoland.

DINTON HALL IN BUCKINGHAMSHIRE, WHERE JOHN BIGG SPENT THIRTY YEARS AS A CLERK BEFORE DEVELOPING HIS ECCENTRIC TASTE IN CLOTHING AND MOVING INTO A CAVE IN THE GROUNDS.

JOHN BIGG spent his first thirty years in considerable comfort at Dinton Hall in Buckinghamshire, as clerk to Simon Mayne, one of the judges who signed Charles I's death warrant. It was rumoured locally that Bigg was actually the king's executioner; certainly he had no sympathy for the Royals. The restoration of the monarchy put Simon Mayne into the Tower and John Bigg into a deep melancholy; neither of them ever emerged. Mayne died in the Tower a year later; Bigg lived on for another thirty-six years in his own equivalent of the Tower, a cave in the grounds of Dinton Hall.

It was here that he developed his eccentric taste in clothes. There is a graphic description of them in an article in the *Bucks Free Press* published in 1882: 'Although he lived by begging, it is related that he never asked for anything else but leather, and upon receiving a piece he would at once nail it to his garments, so that they became at length a wonderful example of patchwork in which it was difficult to find a piece of the original material. His garments were fastened together, so that he put them all on or off at once. He mended his shoes in the same way by fastening fresh pieces of leather or cloth over the decayed parts, until they became of more than tenfold thickness, composed of above a thousand different pieces. Round his waist he wore a girdle and suspended from it he usually had three bottles, one of which he kept for ale, one for small beer and the other for milk'.

Three hundred years later John Bigg's remarkable shoes still exist. One is at Dinton Hall, the other in the Ashmolean Museum. The cave has long since disappeared, but John Bigg can be found today at another location, a pub at nearby Ford called The Dinton Hermit, which features on its sign perhaps the first eccentric dresser to develop a leather fetish.

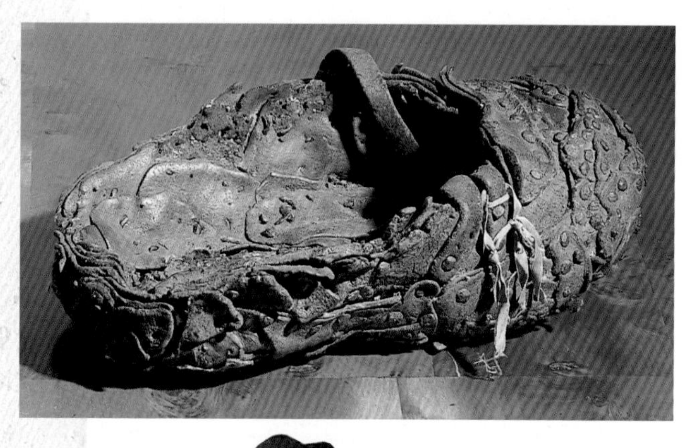

John Bigg in his patched-up clothes and boots (above). One of the boots (above, right) is still preserved at Dinton Hall, and Bigg himself appears on the inn sign of The Dinton Hermit (right).

William Lole was a very different class of hermit. Indeed, on the face of it he was not a hermit at all. He lived in a comfortable cottage at Newton Burgoland, near Ashby-de-la-Zouch in Leicestershire, and in the words of a contemporary writer in the 1860s, 'he can enjoy a good dinner, can drink his glass of beer, and smoke his pipe with as much relish as any man, yet according to his own definition he is entitled to the appellation of a hermit. "True hermits," says he, "throughout every age, have been the first abettors of freedom" '.

One way he abetted freedom was through his choice of clothes. He had a selection of hats and costumes which he designed himself 'to symbolise the Eternal Truths contained in the Emblems or Mottos'. Unfortunately the emblems and mottos he devised were so obscure that it was none too clear what Eternal Truths they contained. His Oddfellow's suit, for instance, was a loose-fitting white tunic tied round the waist with a white girdle; on the left breast was a heart-shaped badge bearing the words 'Liberty of Conscience'. The hat that went with it was bound with black ribbon and inscribed with the staccato message: 'Bless, feed — good allowance — well clothed — all working men'. However the motto that went with the suit was: 'Without money, without friends, without credit'. Without much meaning either, I imagine, to the good folk of Newton Burgoland, but no doubt it all made sense to Mr Lole.

William Lole, who designed his own clothes and hat 'to symbolise the Eternal Truths'. This was his Oddfellow suit. How true . . .

The names and mottos attached to his other suits were just as baffling. 'Patent Teapot', for instance, had the motto: 'To draw out the flavour of the tea best — Union and Goodwill'; 'Washbasin of Reform' was explained as: 'Whitewashed face and collyed heart'. 'The Beehive' was a bit clearer: 'The toils of industry are sweet; a wise people live at peace', and his 'Military' did indeed look like an old-fashioned uniform, except that the cocked hat was adorned with two horse's ears sticking out of the crown. This came to an unfortunate end when Mr Lole encountered some youths in the village. A rather unsympathetic chronicler recorded what happened: 'His fantastical hat, his antiquated military costume, the whimsical mixture of his reverent and defiant air, might have conquered the gravity of a Stoic. No wonder the merry youths were convulsed with laughter. They rushed round the old hermit, knocked off his hat, tossed it into the air, kicked it about for a football, and finally tore it in tatters . . . The old hermit still mourns over his lost hat, and descants its glories with melancholy pleasure'.

Wisely, perhaps, William Lole spent much of his time inside his garden, which was as symbolic as his clothes. At the entrance were the 'Three Seats of Self-Inquiry', inscribed with the searching questions: 'Am I vile?' 'Am I a Hypocrite?' and 'Am I a Christian?' If you felt you had satisfactory answers, you could then proceed into the garden itself, where all the flowers symbolised something, and Mr Lole helpfully spelt out with pebbles what it was. Some were patriotic: 'Britain Never Shall be Slaves'; some were cautionary: 'The Henpecked Husband Put On Water Gruel'; and some were a little more mystical: 'The Bank of Faith', 'Conjugal Bliss', or simply: 'The Saloon'. Having absorbed the significance of all this, you found yourself at a large tub and desk which served as Lole's pulpit and lectern, and you were liable to be harangued about the Papacy, which was illustrated by another of William Lole's garden ornaments, a gallows from which dangled a mock Pope. Eventually, with any luck, you may spot the only floral inscription that really made sense; it said simply: 'The Exit'.

WILLIAM LOLE IN WHAT HE CALLED HIS 'MILITARY'. AND SO IT APPEARED — EXCEPT THAT THE COCKED HAT HAD TWO HORSE'S EARS STICKING OUT OF THE CROWN.

William Lole's eccentric pursuit of Freedom came expensive. He spent half his income on his clothes and the other half on his garden, and finished up relying on the generosity of the villagers, but he refused an invitation to go and live with his brother. 'What would then become of my garden?' he pointed out. 'My heart is in my garden. I cannot leave it.' And I hope he donned his 'Helmet' suit, the one with the motto: 'Will fight for the birthright of conscience, love, life, property and national independence'. Good for him . . .

TOURICENTRICS

better to travel oddly than to arrive

Before the era of package tours and Southern Region commuting, when travelling was still an adventure, there was great scope for the English to demonstrate to foreigners that they were superior to them in eccentricity as in everything else. Thus the reputation of the mad English was established all over the globe, wearing weird and unsuitable garb, travelling in unlikely conveyances, and of course going out in the mid-day sun. In the eighteenth century one of the first travellers to export genuine English eccentricity to America and Europe was CAPTAIN PHILIP THICKNESSE, described succinctly by one biographer as 'gentleman, scoundrel and professional tourist'. He was also a highly successful travel writer; the account of his economy version of the Grand Tour, undertaken in a two-wheeled cabriolet in the company of his wife, two daughters, a spaniel, a pet parakeet and a monkey, was reprinted into three editions, translated into French and German, and sold briskly for years.

Yet the author himself seems to have been universally detested. He was described by various writers as irascible, aggressive, quarrelsome, vindictive, 'and with an inordinate capacity for making enemies'. The politest word they could find for him was 'eccentric' – but that'll do me. Judge for yourself . . .

He was born in 1719, the son of a Northampton rector. His school-days ended in expulsion – 'a joyful sentence', he called it – and his apprenticeship to an apothecary ended just as abruptly when he told the customers that all patent medicines were quite useless. At sixteen he undertook the first of his eventful journeys; he emigrated to America.

In Savannah he launched his long career of slander, libel and litigation by spreading a story that John and Charles Wesley, who were visiting the town on an American tour, were concentrating too much on converting the ladies. One of these converts, according to Thicknesse, had a lively bedroom romp with Charles – 'she laid violent hands upon him, threw him upon the bed, and threatened him with immediate loss of life – or what some men might deem as dear life . . . Nor did she dismiss him until she had deprived him of all the Adonis locks which at that time adorned one side of his meek and godly countenance'.

It is difficult to find a portrait of Charles Wesley with half his whiskers missing, so the story is unconfirmed, but nobody seemed too upset on this occasion and the Wesleys departed in search of more respectful congregations, and possibly a barber.

Perhaps disappointed that he had not caused a greater stir, Thicknesse struck up a friendship with the local Indians and decided to go native. He set up home on an island in the Savannah River, lived mainly on home-killed duck and squirrel, and acquired the services of an attractive Indian lady for the price of a pair of boots, some paint, a looking-glass and comb, and a pair of scissors. According to his own account he intended to consummate the union – 'one buffalo-skin would certainly have held us,' as he delicately put it – but then he had a vision which apparently put him off his stroke. He was strolling on the beach playing his flute – quite a normal activity for someone like Thicknesse – when his mother appeared before him. She urged him to leave the Indian lady, and the island, and indeed Savannah. Thicknesse made an excuse, and left.

Back home he applied for a commission, became an instant captain (commissions worked like that in those days, even for eccentrics) and was posted to Jamaica, where he was sent slave-hunting. The going rate was £70 'for every pair of wild Negro's ears'. To his credit, he took a poor view of this; he decided to make another excuse . . .

He spent the next thirty-odd years in England, forsaking travelling in favour of marrying – three times altogether. He also pursued his subsidiary career as a scandalmonger, and managed to offend, among others, the Archbishop of Canterbury, the Earl of

Captain Philip Thicknesse, 'gentleman, scoundrel and professional tourist', making his Grand Tour in the company of his wife and three children, their pet spaniel, Callee the horse and Jocko the monkey (riding postilion). There is also a parakeet, nestling out of sight, in Mrs Thicknesse's bosom. The French peasantry, as can be seen, were a little stunned by this curious ménage.

Coventry, the Lord Chancellor, his own two sons and the entire House of Lords. In 1775, with court cases piling up against him and the threat of imminent imprisonment, Captain Thicknesse set off again, this time on his Grand Tour.

Besides being an eccentric traveller, Captain Thicknesse was also said to have 'an inordinate capacity for making enemies'. It was presumably one of them who composed this caption.

This was a popular occupation among the eighteenth-century gentry, but Thicknesse decided to boldly go where no English tourist had gone before; the fact that he was also on the run probably influenced his decision. He crossed the Channel with his party in a four-wheeled post-chaise, then to raise a little capital – and perhaps confuse any pursuers – he replaced it in Calais with a two-wheeled cabriolet and a horse, 'a little touched in the wind', which he christened Callee.

The modest carriage must have been a tight squeeze for the four members of the Thicknesse family, let alone the pets. Generally the spaniel ran alongside, the parakeet nestled in Mrs Thicknesse's bosom, and Jocko the monkey, dressed in red jacket, jackboots, a hard hat and a detachable pigtail, rode postilion on Callee's back. This remarkable ménage wandered off into the French countryside, to the utter bewilderment of the local peasantry – which increased further when Mrs Thicknesse brought out her bass viol to provide background music.

Captain Thicknesse took notes of all the unlikely incidents which made his subsequent book such a success. In Lyons, for instance, he found that all the little ferryboats were rowed by attractive young ladies. 'I asked one of these female scullers how she got her bread in the winter. "Oh sir," said she, giving me a very significant look – such a one as you can better conceive than I convey, "dans l'hiver j'ai un autre talent".' The gallant captain adds very frankly: 'I can assure you I was glad she did not exercise both her talents at the same time of the year. Yet I could not refrain from giving her a double fee, as I thought there was something due to her winter as well as her summer abilities'.

He had a less pleasing encounter in the same town on his return journey several months later. When he arrived at his hotel he saw a flat basket on the ground containing boiled spinach. 'As my dog and several others in the yard had often put their noses into it, I concluded it was put down for their food, not mine, till I saw a dirty girl patting it into round balls and two children playing with it. I asked the maid what she was about and what it was she was so preparing. She told me it was spinage. "Not for me, I hope," said I. "Oui, pour vous et le monde". I then forbade her bringing any to table'.

But the story did not end there. 'Nevertheless with my entrée came up a dish of this delicate spinage, with which I made the girl a very pretty *chapeau anglais*, for I turned it, dish and all, upon her head'.

Captain Thicknesse, in fact, would have made an excellent inspector for the *Good Hotel Guide*. If he was not satisfied with an establishment he did not pull his punches — or his spinach. But if he found a meal to his satisfaction he described it in great detail, like the dinner at Pont St Esprit which featured 'a larded hare roasted, a roasted poularde, stewed pigeons, becca fica roasted — evidently warblers of some sort that had been fattened on figs — cream custard, roasted truffles and coffee'. But no cheese?

His motley caravan headed southwards down the Rhône on the deck of a barge, with the family still inside the cabriolet, Callee still in the shafts, and Jocko still on Callee's back, making quite an impressive water-borne montage. They crossed the Spanish border, where Thicknesse confused the Customs men by assuring them he was a Hottentot, pointing out the obviously African origins of Jocko and the parakeet. Once in Spain he became enchanted with the mountains of Montserrat, and the family abandoned Callee and the cabriolet for several weeks while they explored the mountainsides and chatted up the monks and hermits who lived there.

He was so enchanted, in fact, that he tried to buy his own plot and join them, but failing in that he created his own hermitage when he got back to England, a ramshackle cottage on the hills above Bath, with a huge oak tree growing through the kitchen and the faithful cabriolet propping up one of the walls. That is where he wrote the story of his year-long tour, and that is where he might have died, but more appropriately the end came when he was on the road. In 1792, when he was 73, he decided to make another visit to Paris. He was on the Paris-bound stage-coach just south of Boulogne when he was taken suddenly ill, and died in his seat. Mrs Thicknesse was at his side — and I am sure that, in spirit, so were Callee, the spaniel, Jocko the monkey and the pet parakeet . . .

If Captain Thicknesse had included Venice in his Grand Tour he would doubtless have found a kindred spirit in another eccentric English traveller, EDWARD WORTLEY MONTAGU. He could hardly have missed him in his Turkish costume and flowing beard, and he would have been entertained sitting cross-legged on cushions, drinking Turkish coffee served by a young negro slave. This was the life-style that Montagu assumed after spending most of his life roaming the Middle East, mostly in local costume speaking the local tongue, and making love to the local ladies.

Montagu had an even less auspicious school career than Thicknesse. By coincidence they attended the same school, Westminster, though Montagu was the senior by six years. He was the son of an English diplomat, and when he was three years old his father was made ambassador to Constantinople. Young Edward got through a succession of tutors, who had to suffer being sworn at in Greek, Turkish and French, before being sent home to Westminster where he was just as miserable as Thicknesse – it really does sound a pretty grim school. He ran away several times, and on one occasion changed places with a young sweep. As one biographer put it: 'He followed for some time that sooty occupation'. Next time he apprenticed himself to a fisherman and sold flounders in Rotherhithe, and on the third escape he went off to Oxford, enrolled himself as a student of Oriental languages, found some lodgings and seduced his landlady. Or perhaps it was the other way round – he was only thirteen.

Each time he was brought back and soundly beaten. Finally he dressed up as a cabin-boy and sailed off on a merchant ship to Portugal, where he became a mule-driver. Even in Portugal there was no escape; the British consul in Oporto, no doubt a member of the Diplomatic Corps Old Boy Network, spotted him and shipped him home. But Edward Montagu's bizarre travels had begun.

Westminster at last decided it had had enough of him, and one imagines that by now his parents felt much the same way. They sent him off to the West Indies with a tutor, but the tutor was no match for this experienced absconder, and this time he ran away in reverse, and returned to London. His early adventure with his Oxford landlady had obviously given him a taste for female company, and on a night out in London he encountered a young lady 'who aspired to a character no higher than that of an industrial washerwoman,' as his biographer put it. Montagu did not take such a condescending view of washerwomen, and married her forthwith. He was now all of seventeen years old.

'As the marriage was solemnised in a frolic,' our supercilious biographer continues, 'he never deemed her sufficiently the wife

It might be Nebuchadnezzar, or even Ali Baba, but it was actually the notable English eccentric, Edward Wortley Montagu, who roamed the Middle East with various female companions, ranging from an Egyptian serving-girl to the wife of a Danish consul. He finished up in Venice with a couple of eunuchs and an African servant — but still in his Turkish gear.

of his bosom to cohabit with her, but she was allowed a maintenance. She lived contented and was too submissive to be troublesome. Mr Montagu on the other hand . . . had wives of almost every nation'.

He goes on to catalogue them: 'When he was in Egypt he had his household of Egyptian females. At Constantinople the Grecian women had charms to captivate this unsettled wanderer. In Spain, a Spanish brunette; in Italy, the olive-complexioned females were solicited to partake of the honours of his bridal bed'.

This aspect of his travels, while fascinating, was not strictly eccentric, just greedy; but in other aspects they were odd in the extreme. Before he embarked on them seriously, however, there were one or two preliminaries. He fitted in a spell as an army officer, became an acknowledged scholar in Oriental languages, and got elected to Parliament as MP for Huntingdon – the same seat which was to produce Mrs Thatcher's successor, but in Montagu's day, like so many parliamentary seats at that time, it produced just another absentee eccentric.

In his thirties Montagu startled fashionable London by bringing home from Paris an iron wig, which he wore with a different set of diamonds each day. Also, according to Horace Walpole, 'he had more snuff boxes than would suffice a Chinese idol with a hundred noses'. He piled up enormous debts, expecting to inherit his father's fortune, but all he got was a small annuity, and Montagu decided it was time to take up travelling full-time.

He left behind another minor complication, a bigamous marriage with a young lady whom he met while visiting a highwayman in prison – he seemed very prone to these bizarre liaisons. However, this did not stop him eloping with the wife of the Danish consul at his first port of call, Alexandria. The consul was away on business at the time, so Montagu assured the lady he had been drowned at sea, and they sailed off down the Nile for yet another marriage ceremony. The consul duly returned and set off after them; Montagu decided to follow the example of Moses

Most travellers on foot prefer to carry as little luggage as possible; SIMEON ELLERTON took quite a different view. In the eighteenth century he walked regularly from his home in Durham as far afield as London, carrying messages for the local gentry. On his journeys he collected stones for a cottage he was building, and always carried one or two of them on his head. By the time the cottage was built, he had got so used to this ballast on his head that he found it uncomfortable to walk without it, and for the rest of his life he did his walking thus laden.

It could have done him no harm. When he died in 1799 he was reputed to be 104 years old. And the constant pressure of his cranium does not seem to have blunted his wit; when passers-by asked why he had a rock on his head he explained simply: ''Tis to keep my hat on'.

– though for rather different reasons – and disappear into the wilderness, taking his 'wife' with him.

As one biographer put it, this was an odd sort of honeymoon. 'Edward wandered through Sinai with an Old Testament in one hand and the Danish consul's wife in the other. But the travel papers he sent home were read admiringly at meetings of the Royal Society.' Even though he must have left out the juicier bits . . .

Eventually his companion got a little fretful about this nomadic life, so he put her in a convent and went off to Venice, ostensibly to try and get her marriage to the consul annulled. Why Venice, you may ask. I have no idea, I have to reply. Nor is it explained how he managed to remain away from her for some years while he continued his wanderings, and then still found her waiting when he got back. Such were his charms, however, that he persuaded her to go through another wedding ceremony, this time in a Roman Catholic church, and for a while they set up home in Egypt.

But Edward Montagu was not cut out for the domestic life, and in due course he became involved with his black Egyptian serving-girl, Ayesha. He switched his religion again, this time from Catholic to Moslem, and Ayesha joined the ranks of Mrs Montagus.

Alas, this marriage ended like all the rest, and Montagu next turns up in Venice again, but attended this time by a couple of half-naked eunuchs and a young black servant called Massoud. Here he lived the life of a Turkish prince, holding court in his Venetian palazzo and flying the Turkish royal pennant on his gondola. This is where Captain Thicknesse might have paid his respects.

Then came the final eccentric twist to Edward Montagu's travels. He heard that his first and only legal wife, the London washerwoman, had died, and under his father's will any woman he now married legally would get a settlement, and any son would get the family estate. Montagu forthwith had an advertisement placed in the London papers:

> *MATRIMONY: A gentleman who hath filled two succeeding seats in Parliament, is near sixty years of age, lives in great splendour and hospitality, and from whom a considerable estate must pass if he dies without issue, hath no objection to marry any widow or single lady, provided the party be of genteel birth, polished manners, and five, six, seven or eight months gone in her pregnancy.*

Several applied to his London agent and he prepared to travel from Venice to pick the winner. It was one journey he failed to make. While he was eating supper before he left, a bone stuck in his throat and could not be dislodged. It went septic, the infection spread, and on 29 April 1776, Edward Montagu set off on quite a different kind of journey – alone this time, but not single. Ironically the news of his wife's death had been incorrect; he died, as he had so spectacularly lived, a very married man.

Montagu was not the only English traveller who succumbed so completely to the call of the mysterious Middle East. One year after he died, LADY HESTER STANHOPE was born at Chevenings, niece to William Pitt, member of a famous aristocratic family, but destined to spend twenty-five years of her life in a Lebanese monastery, waiting to be crowned Queen of the Jews.

Hester may have inherited her eccentric nature from her father, who in spite of being Lord Stanhope was a confirmed Republican. He sold all his coaches because they were symbols of privilege, and after the French Revolution insisted on calling himself Citizen Stanhope. Hester didn't mind what he called himself, but she was very fed up about the coaches, and for some time walked about on a pair of stilts, assuring her father that without any transport it was the only way she could keep her petticoats out of the mud.

Although she never went to Westminster she shared the scholastic attitude of Montagu and Thicknesse, and followed their example by running away. On a visit to Hastings with her governess she helped herself to a rowing-boat and set off for France, but her rowing was not quite up to it and she had to return. She was thirty-three when she did manage to leave these shores successfully, on board the frigate *Jason*, inspired by a prophecy that she would be crowned Queen of the East. The fact that the prophecy originated from an inmate of Bedlam lunatic asylum did not at all deter her. And she never came back.

All went well as far as Constantinople, and Lady Hester was following in Montagu's wake to Egypt when her ship sank in a storm. She was rescued and landed at Rhodes, but all her luggage was lost, and she had to find fresh clothes locally. She refused to follow local custom and wear a veil; instead she borrowed a man's Turkish robe and turban, and like Montagu before her, she never donned European clothes again.

In this guise she rode around the Middle East, travelling in some style on a saddle of crimson velvet embroidered with gold, and wearing a white hooded cloak over her splendid Turkish costumes. She kept her face uncovered and never wore women's clothes even in the most fanatical Moslem cities. The Moslems, instead of being offended, were enormously impressed, and she was received with great honour and respect wherever she went.

This no doubt strengthened her belief that she was destined for regal status, and when her friends jokingly addressed her as Queen Hester, she took it quite seriously.

Her final journey was to the ruined city of Palmyra in the Arabian desert, a remote area full of rampaging Bedouin tribesmen. Hester dressed as a Bedouin herself, led her caravan across the desert like some female Lawrence of Arabia, and was received with much the same acclaim. In Palmyra itself she actually went through a crowning ceremony, which must have finally convinced her that her moment had come. On her return she declared her wandering days over and set up court in the disused monastery of Mar Elias in Lebanon.

She did a full-scale conversion job on the monastery, equipping it with such queenly essentials as a stable and a gazelle house, and creating a flower garden where the cloisters used to

LADY HESTER STANHOPE IN HER ROYAL ROBES, RECEIVING A VISITOR IN HER ROOM AT DJOUN MONASTERY. SHE NO DOUBT HOPED IT WAS AN EMISSARY TO TELL HER SHE HAD BEEN ACCLAIMED AS QUEEN OF THE EAST; BUT THE MESSAGE NEVER CAME, AND THIS IS WHERE SHE DIED.

be. Her redecorating ran into a problem with a persistent discolouration on one wall, which was accompanied by an unattractive smell. Eventually the wall was knocked down, and the body of a former Patriarch was found inside; it had been embalmed, but had long passed its 'sell by' date . . .

At Mar Elias, and later at another monastery at Djoun, Lady Hester spent the rest of her life awaiting the call which never came. She had a steady flow of visitors, whom she received sitting majestically and expectantly in her royal robes, but none of them brought the message she wanted. However, she had her compensations. She had had her affairs in earlier days, and at Mar Elias a young French officer called Captain Loustenau joined her entourage and made the waiting less tedious. He died before her and was buried at the monastery. When Lady Hester died some years later, at the age of sixty-three, he featured in her final eccentric gesture – her midnight funeral procession was lit by candles stuck in the eye-sockets of his skull.

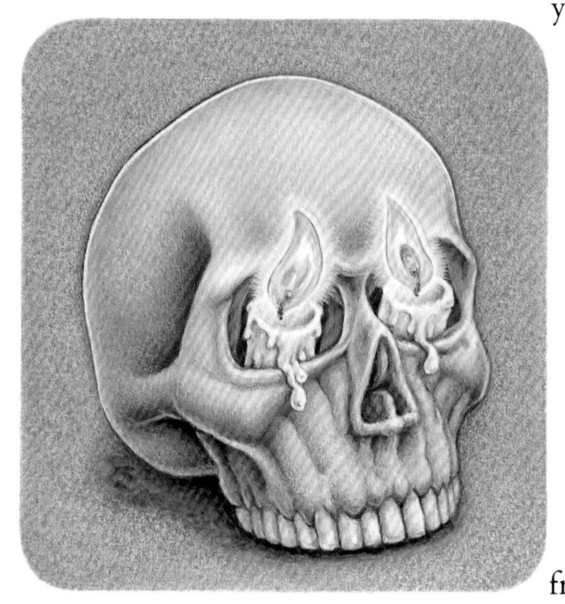

Lady Hester's last wish was that her midnight funeral procession should be lit by candles stuck in the eye-sockets of her dead companion's skull.

She died, not as a queen, but in abject poverty. Because of the debts she had run up during her travels the British government stopped her pension, and in spite of distinguished connections, nobody back home would help her. Her servants robbed her, her followers deserted her, her authority disappeared. She ended her days a sad old lady, mocked or forgotten by her former friends in England. But a century later *The Times* put the record straight:

> *An immense amount has been written about the morbid state and squalor of her court . . . of her queer food, clothes and habits, of her towering pride of birth, her belief in magic, in astrology and in transmigration . . . What Kinglake (a writer who visited her at Mar Elias) saw in her was a great English lady with all the pride and audacity of her class, exaggerated by seclusion from her proper fellows and distorted by the mystic influence of the East.*

Margaret Fountaine was another strong-willed English lady who insisted on travelling in her own style and wearing her own choice of costume. In her case it was not a Turkish robe and turban, but a man's check shirt with several canvas pockets sewn on, a striped skirt with more pockets, a large cork helmet, and plimsolls. Miss Fountaine was in fact a collector of butterflies, and in pursuit of her specimens she journeyed unescorted to the most obscure and unwelcoming corners of the uncivilised world.

The Fountaines are still a well-known family in West Norfolk. Margaret was born at South Acre Rectory in 1862, one of seven brothers and sisters, and led a conventional enough rural life until she became involved with a member of the Norwich Cathedral choir, an Irishman called Septimus Hewson. They were almost engaged when Septimus decided to take his affections elsewhere, and Miss Fountaine decided to take her broken heart elsewhere too. The butterflies took over.

She pursued them through Italy by bicycle, she was virtually kidnapped by a Corsican bandit but managed to run away – the plimsolls must have helped – and she trekked through Hungary travelling twelve hours a day and living on bread and sheep's milk. Various men, including the Corsican bandit, entered her life and moved on, but in Damascus a Syrian courier called Khalil Neimy entered it and stayed for

MARGARET FOUNTAINE AT THE AGE OF TWENTY-EIGHT, DRESSED CONVENTIONALLY AS A VICTORIAN COUNTRY LADY. THAT WAS BEFORE SHE EMBARKED ON HER TRAVELS AND MET THE ROMANTIC SYRIAN COURIER, KHALIL NEIMY (LEFT). SHE KEPT THIS PHOTOGRAPH OF HIM IN HER DIARY.

Miss Fountaine in her later years in full butterfly-hunting gear, and some of her 22,000 butterflies.

twenty-eight years. Together they roamed the world, and when he died she kept on roaming. Her travels took her from North Africa, where she bathed in diluted creosote to keep off the leeches (her complexion was never quite the same again), to the mountains of Tibet, riding a pony along precipitous tracks 'through a world of wild winds and bitter cold and strange, curious faces'.

She was still travelling when she was seventy, covering forty-five miles a day, mostly at a gallop. And she was still encountering amorous locals. She wrote rather charmingly of a meeting with an enthusiastic Brazilian in her later years. Somehow – she does not explain how – she found herself closeted with him in his pyjamas. 'It forced itself upon my unsuspecting brain that very soon he would be *out* of his pyjamas . . . It reminded me of the days of long ago!'

Margaret Fountaine died as she had lived, on the road. She was butterfly-hunting in Trinidad in 1940 when she collapsed with a heart attack, and was found dying on the dusty roadside. Her butterfly net lay beside her.

Unlike Lady Hester, her death was universally mourned at home. She left her unique collection of 22,000 butterflies to the Norwich Castle Museum, and it is a reminder, not only of this

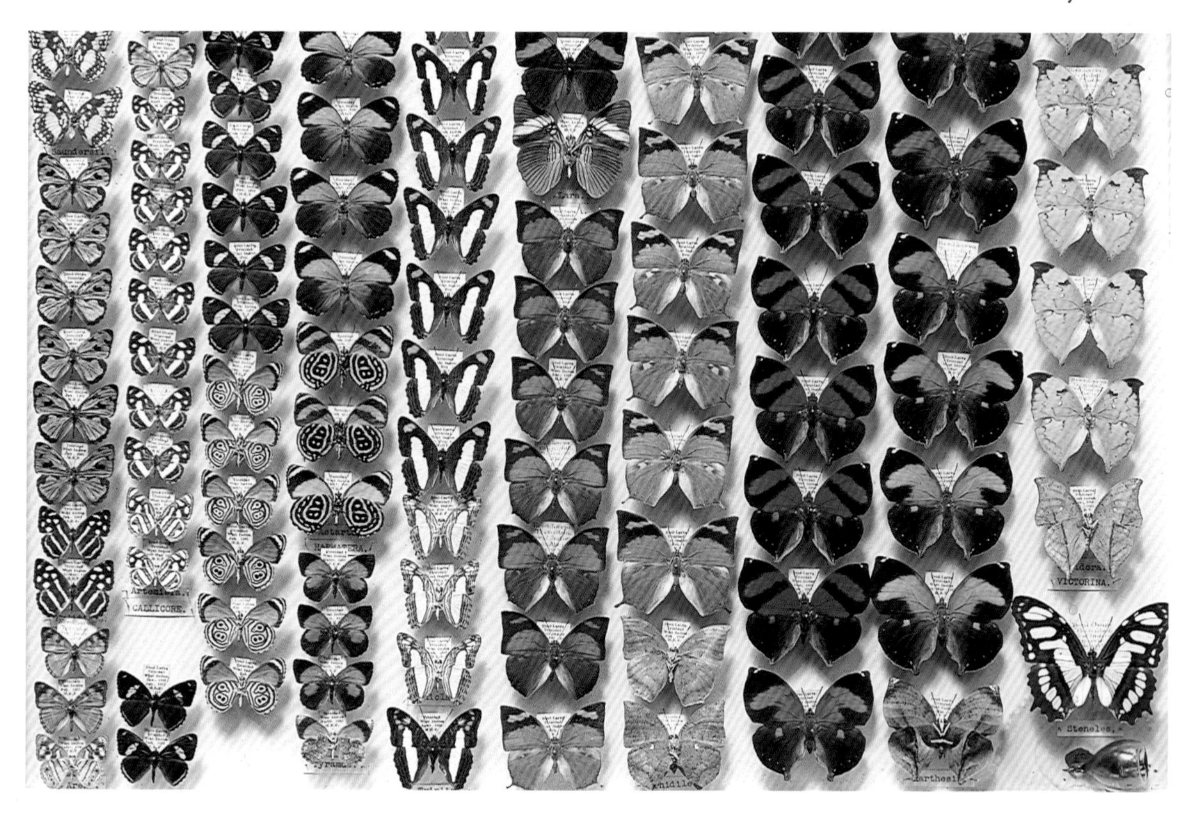

remarkable Norfolk lady but of the Syrian courier who shared her travels for so long. She insisted that it be called the 'Fountaine-Neimy Collection'.

Of all the eccentric travellers and travel writers of the last two centuries, I would nominate as the most astonishing an ex-naval officer called James Holman. 'He traversed the great globe more thoroughly than any other traveller who ever existed,' wrote the editor of *The Times*, which may be pushing it a bit but it wasn't far wrong. Holman did go all over the world and toured every continent, almost entirely on his own. He wrote five volumes about the journeys, which were eccentric as travel books go because he never described the scenery and never identified the people he met. The reason was simple, but quite staggering: James Holman was completely blind.

During his first twenty-five years, twelve of them spent in the Navy, his sight was normal; a bout of scurvy was blamed for causing the blindness, and he left the Navy in 1810 with apparently a bleak future ahead. He spent eight years coming to terms with his affliction, then packed his bags, headed for the Dover ferry, and was off across France and Italy. His friends expected he would be back within the month; he was actually away for three years.

In that time he went swimming from a boat off Marseilles, confident that the shouts of the other passengers would guide him back. In Rome he climbed into the dome of St Peter's and wanted to scale the lightning conductor, arguing that as he couldn't see the drop below, it would be no different from climbing a tree. He was prevented on that occasion, but nobody stopped him walking round the edge of the crater on Vesuvius, where again he could not see the unpleasant fate that awaited a false step.

He was home for only a few months before setting off again. This time he only got as far as Gravesend when his journey was interrupted. As his ship was sailing down the Thames it was rammed by a collier and they locked together. Holman, the ex-Navy officer, volunteered to take the wheel, and the captain, unaware of his blindness, shouted commands which he fulfilled with great efficiency until the ships parted and they tied up safely at Gravesend. When the captain took a closer look at his helmsman and discovered he was blind, he must have felt the need for a stiff drink, but in fact he was so impressed that when they set out again two days later, he invited Holman to take the helm again until they were safely out of the estuary.

The commemorative plaque, by the track in Trinidad, where Margaret Fountaine collapsed and died on her last expedition at the age of seventy-eight. Her butterfly net lay beside her.

JAMES HOLMAN, WHO TRAVELLED TO THE MOST INACCESSIBLE CORNERS OF THE WORLD — EVEN THOUGH HE WAS COMPLETELY BLIND.

Holman left the ship at St Petersburg, and this was the start of an epic journey across Russia and Siberia, which even a traveller who could see would have thought twice about. The fact that he had no official permission, he spoke no Russian, and nobody in their right mind wanted to visit Siberia anyway, did not deter him. He acquired a pavoshka, a singularly uncomfortable Russian cart, from another extraordinary traveller, Captain Cochrane, whom he met in Moscow. Cochrane had planned to travel across Siberia into Alaska and Canada, but at Kamchatka he fell in love with a fifteen-year-old Indian girl and changed his mind. He returned to Moscow, sold his pavoshka to Holman, and headed for home with his young companion, making no secret of his view that Holman was even crazier than he was himself.

'There is so little to be seen in Siberia by those who have the use of their eyes that I cannot divine what interest he can have to attempt it,' he wrote. To which Holman replied that if there was nothing to see, then he wouldn't be missing much. And off he went on the 3,500-mile journey to Irkutsk, the capital of Eastern Siberia and in effect the end of the semi-civilised world.

In his book he explains how he acquired lodgings and fresh horses with a wad of introductory letters, which he had organised, to local officials and chiefs. The roads were appalling, and to have a break from the discomfort of his springless pavoshka, he often ran alongside, tied to it with a rope to keep him on course.

A month after leaving Moscow he crossed the Urals, and a month after that he was in Tobolsk, capital of Western Siberia, where he was entertained by the Governor. He records an embarrassing moment when the Governor left him with his other guests and he heard a heavy breathing at about knee-level. He asked his companions if it was 'some nondescript Siberian animal' that had joined them. 'Unfortunately it was one of the principal counsellors of Tobolsk,' he confessed, 'a gentleman of very diminutive stature, who had a peculiar obstruction in his nasal organs which produced the singular wheezing noise.'

Holman survived the *faux pas* and set off again, this time through foggy marshes alive with Siberian mosquitoes, a particularly vicious variety which not only caused malaria and other diseases, but attacked in such multitudes that they could kill by suffocation. Holman thwarted them by wearing a beekeeper's gauze netting, and emerged safely from the marshes to arrive at Irkutsk in triumph, just three months after leaving Moscow.

He had every intention of pressing on into China, but like Cochrane his plans were changed, not by a fifteen-year-old Indian girl, but by an official sent from the Emperor with orders to escort him back to Moscow. His extraordinary journey had not gone unnoticed, and the Russians, not yet familiar with the eccentricities of the English, assumed that in spite of his obvious blindness he must be some sort of spy. His protests were ignored and he had to retrace his steps.

Winter had arrived, and although this meant travelling was a little smoother in a sledge than in his bone-shaking pavoshka, it also meant that the temperature was down to fifty degrees of frost, which was no weather to be out on the steppes. Holman avoided frost-bite by wearing two pairs of stockings under two pairs of fur boots, but the driver was not so lucky and lost a big toe. Holman wrapped himself in a greatcoat over his normal clothes, and over that a cloak made of wolves' skins, but it was

James Holman's gruelling journey back to Moscow by sledge, after his epic journey across Siberia. A Russian officer was with him, but judging by this episode he seems, in spite of his blindness, to have managed rather better on his own . . .

still too cold to sleep and when he reached Moscow, for the first time on his travels, he was completely exhausted. He got little sympathy from the Russians, and in due course he was extradited to Poland.

It was an ignominious end to an historic journey – but it made a good story. The book was published in 1825, dedicated by special permission to King George IV, and immediately ran to four editions. Holman was famous, financially comfortable, but still restless. Two years later he was off again, to the west coast of Africa, to South America, to Australia, India and China. In Brazil he rode to the Mato Grosso, in South Africa he trekked for 500 miles round the coast, in Ceylon, astonishingly, he went hunting for elephant and alligator. In some places like Zanzibar, Ceylon and Tasmania he explored entirely on foot, and nearly everywhere he travelled alone. At the end of four years he had achieved his ultimate ambition; he had encircled the world.

Herbert Spencer, the social philosopher, who invented the phrase 'survival of the fittest'. He ensured his own comfort surviving on train journeys by taking a hammock.

Unlike so many travellers James Holman died in his own bed, a venerable seventy-two-year-old. The books he left give little indication that throughout all these adventures he was totally blind. Certainly there is no note of self-pity – but there is just one expression of regret:

> *On the summit of the precipice and in the deep green woods, emotions as palpable and as true have agitated me as if I were surveying them with the blessing of sight . . . It entered into my heart and I could have wept, not that I did not see, but that I could not portray all I felt.*

But really, he didn't do so bad . . .

For some eccentric travellers it is neither the destination nor the route which is odd, it is the accoutrements needed for the journey. Herbert Spencer, noted nineteenth-century social philosopher and the man who first devised the phrase 'survival of the fittest', ensured his own survival on train journeys by taking with him his own carrying chair, a good supply of rugs and cushions, and most essential of all, a hammock which had to be slung in his private compartment. He reclined in this throughout the journey, thus avoiding any unpleasant jarring and jolting. He had his own security system for any manuscript he took with him; it was wrapped in brown paper and tied to his waist with a thick piece of string.

Spencer's journeys by horse and carriage did not require all this paraphernalia, but he had a disconcerting habit of halting the coach suddenly in order to take his own pulse. 'The carriage was at once brought to a standstill,' wrote his biographer, 'no matter where he might be, whether in a quiet place or in the middle of the busiest traffic in Regent Street. Silence reigned therein for some few seconds in order that he might feel his pulse. If it was regular the driver continued. If not, and he feared injurious consequences, the order was given to return home'. The effect on the pulse-rate of his fellow passengers, or indeed on the drivers immediately behind, is not recorded.

At home he had his little idiosyncrasies too. If he became bored with the dinner conversation he put on his ear-plugs, which looked like headphones but had velvet-coloured knobs on each side. 'Very practical and sensible, no doubt,' says his biographer, 'but irresistibly funny to see, and a ready butt for parody'. However, Spencer liked to have jokes at other people's expense too; in his younger days he unnerved a colleague by placing each day an extra strip of paper inside his hatband, to make him believe his head was expanding – at the same time telling him about the unpleasant symptoms of water on the brain . . .

Sir Tatton Sykes of Sledmere in Yorkshire was another nineteenth-century traveller who took unusual precautions to protect his health on the road. Because of a delicate stomach, on

Sledmere in Yorkshire (below), the home of Sir Tatton Sykes (above). When he left it to go globe-trotting he always took his cook with him, to keep him supplied with his favourite milk pudding.

Sir Tatton's devotion to milk pudding was such that, when Sledmere caught fire while he was eating dinner, he refused to leave the table: 'First I must finish my pudding'. And he did.

his long-distance travels to America, Russia and China he always took his cook with him, just to supply him with his favourite milk pudding. On his daily walk he ensured that his body maintained a constant temperature by starting out in several overcoats, then shedding them one by one as he got warmer. Instead of carrying the discarded coats – the extra exertion might have overheated him – the local children were paid a shilling for each coat they retrieved in his wake and took back to the house.

Sir Tatton often wore two pairs of trousers for the same reason, and must have caused quite a stir among passers-by when he started removing the outer one. He carried a stick to knock down any flowers he found growing in his village, part of a long-standing campaign against the 'nasty untidy things'. When he inherited his estate in 1863 he had all the gardens ploughed up and his tenants were told: 'If you wish to grow flowers, grow cauliflowers'.

His final journey might have been the most eccentric of all. He died in a London hotel in 1913, and the manager was so anxious not to let the other guests know there had been a death amongst them that he planned to smuggle out the corpse inside a hollow sofa. Not unnaturally Sir Tatton's son objected. 'However my father leaves this hotel,' he said firmly, 'he shall leave it like a gentleman.' Sir Tatton himself might not have been too bothered; at his own request he was taken to his grave, not in a formal hearse but in the back of a farm cart.

RELICCENTRICS

if it's old, collect it

Collecting things, in itself, is not particularly eccentric. At various times I have collected American stamps, threepenny bits, coloured pebbles, engine numbers, and the coupons off cornflake packets, and if anybody thought that was odd they were civil enough not to say so. These days the range of collectable items has expanded astonishingly, and perfectly sane collectors pay ridiculous sums for what they would once have regarded as junk. How many of us are now regretting that we threw away mother's old fire-irons, or those hideous art-deco ornaments from Auntie Flo, or the spoons they gave us at school to mark the Coronation?

No, if a collection is to be considered eccentric these days, it has to be very odd indeed. And the truly eccentric collector has to be obsessed with whatever it is he is collecting. It is not necessarily something tangible; there are those who 'collect' experiences – how many railway stations can they collect on a day's train journey, how many peaks can they collect on a week's holiday in the Lakes, how many pubs can they collect on an evening pub-crawl? And having done it, how many people can they bore by telling them all about their collections . . .

Let's start with the collectors whose hobby became a fixation, so that even the pursuit of mundane items like books rendered them eccentric. In short, the bibliomaniacs, people like THOMAS RAWLINSON, an eighteenth-century collector who filled his rooms at Gray's Inn so full of books that he had to sleep in the passage. So he bought a mansion, which he shared with his brother, and filled that up too. He died early, aged forty-four, which at least gave his brother more room in the passage . . .

The most scholarly bibliomaniac of that period was RICHARD HEBER, whose wealth allowed him almost unlimited scope, not only to acquire books but to acquire the space to store them. He was born in Cheshire in 1774, and already had a sizeable library when he was eight, all properly catalogued. Until his father died he had to limit himself somewhat, but once he inherited the family fortune there was no holding him. He accumulated a vast library, frequently buying extra copies of books which he possessed already. He explained why: 'No man can comfortably do without three copies of a book. One he must have for his show copy, and he will probably keep it at his country house. Another he will require for his own use and reference; and unless he is inclined to part with this, which is very inconvenient, or risk the injury of his best copy, he must needs have a third at the service of his friends'.

Cynics suggested that his real reason for buying all these copies was to keep them out of the hands of rival collectors, but Heber was in fact very generous about lending out his library, and many contemporary authors were grateful for the chance to refer to them – most notably Sir Walter Scott, who paid tribute to him in his own books and wrote a rather rambling poem in his honour. Here is a typical excerpt:

How just that at this time of glee,
My thoughts should, Heber, turn to thee!
For many a merry hour we've known,
And heard the chime of Midnight's tone.
Cease then, my friend! A moment, cease,
And leave these classic tomes in peace . . .

But he did not leave them in peace. He kept on collecting, until two houses in London were full of them. So was the family home in Cheshire, and so were other houses in Paris, Brussels, Antwerp and Ghent. He virtually built up an international network of branch libraries – and again came under attack from his critics. One described him as 'a bibliomaniac in the most unpleasant sense of the word – no confirmed drunkard, no incurable opium-eater has less self-control. To see a book is to desire it, to desire it is to possess it'. But it was his own money, so why not?

At one stage Heber contemplated marriage to a Miss Richardson Curren of Yorkshire, who just happened to be an enthusiastic book-collector too. It is not clear whether he had mainly in mind a union of souls or a union of libraries, but perhaps Miss Curren suspected the latter, because the marriage never took place.

There was also a period when Richard Heber found himself in Parliament, as so many eccentrics did in those days (only in those days?); but he rarely attended, and his speeches were even rarer. Instead, he continued to pursue his obsession elsewhere. 'On hearing of a curious book,' wrote one biographer, 'he has been known to put himself into the mail coach and travel three, four or five hundred miles to obtain it, fearful to entrust his commission to a letter'. He purchased an entire library of 30,000 volumes in Paris, 'and was in constant communication with most of the old booksellers in every town and city in the United Kingdom'.

RICHARD HEBER, AN EIGHTEENTH-CENTURY BIBLIOMANIAC, HAD A SIZEABLE LIBRARY, FULLY CATALOGUED, BY THE TIME HE WAS EIGHT. HE FINISHED UP WITH SEVEN HOUSES FULL OF BOOKS LOCATED AROUND ENGLAND, BELGIUM AND FRANCE.

THE HON. MAURICE BARING WAS NOT ONLY A BIBLIOMANIAC BUT ALSO — IF THERE IS SUCH A THING — A LEAFOMANIAC. IF HE CAME UPON AN INTERESTING PASSAGE HE WOULD TEAR OUT THE PAGE AND STICK IT IN A NOTEBOOK. TO BE FAIR, HE ONLY DID IT WITH HIS OWN BOOKS.

Heber was still in constant touch with them in his final weeks. Indeed he had just sent a substantial order to a bookseller when he died in 1833. A visitor to his Pimlico house after his death described the scene: 'I looked around me in amazement. I had never seen rooms, cupboards, passages and corridors so choked, so suffocated with books. Treble rows were here, double rows were there. Hundreds of slim quartos, several upon each other, were longitudinally placed over thin and stunted duodecimos, reaching from one extremity of a shelf to another. Up to the very ceiling the piles of volumes extended, while the floor was strewn with them, in loose and numerous heaps'. The house, in fact, spoke volumes . . .

The absolute antithesis of Richard Heber and his fellow bibliomaniacs must be the HON. MAURICE BARING, member of the famous banking family, diplomat, poet, essayist, linguist, war correspondent, and if there is such a thing, leafomaniac. Mr Baring did not collect books, he collected pages from books. If he came upon an interesting passage he would tear out the page and paste it in a notebook. It should be said that it was his own books he despoiled in this way, not copies from the local library. However, once he had extracted what he wanted, the books did not stay with him long. Each time he moved house he gave away his entire library and started afresh. No doubt the recipients were a little disconcerted when they got the books home and found several of the pages missing . . .

The exception was Sir Ronald Stows, who lost his books in a fire in Cyprus. He received a message from his friend Baring saying simply: 'Sending library. Maurice'. The library consisted of his entire stock of miniature editions of the classics in seven languages – with every page intact.

Maurice Baring took this carefree attitude to all his possessions, not just his books. On a train journey in Germany he was chatting with a friend while trying to put his new overcoat into a case. When he found it would not fit inside, he threw it out of the window – then continued his conversation.

When he died in 1945 *The Times* wrote a glowing obituary, referring to his literary talents, his linguistic skills, his generosity and his urbane good humour. It did not mention his propensity for page-ripping, but it did reveal one other curious failing. His efforts to enter the Diplomatic Service were apparently thwarted for years because of his 'extraordinary incapacity to deal with figures'. *The Times* notes drily: 'In 1899, after his father's death, the end was achieved, half-marks for arithmetic being awarded him on the strength of his performance in other papers'. I wonder if examiners still take such a generous view . . .

LORD BERNERS, a contemporary of Baring's was another distinguished diplomat and writer who went in for unorthodox collecting. In his case it was not pages out of books but other people's calling cards. The reason for the collection was just as unusual as the collection itself. When he lent out his house in Rome to friends, he selected from his collection the cards of the most notorious bores in London, and sent them to the butler in Rome with instructions to deliver one or two of the cards each day. Thus the guests spent much of their holiday diving for cover every time they heard someone at the door.

This was only one of Lord Berners' little eccentricities. At his home, Faringdon House in Oxfordshire, he kept whippets which were decorated with diamond collars, and doves dyed in various pastel shades. Notices round the estate said:

Dogs will be shot; cats will be whipped –

though of course they weren't. In 1935 he built the Faringdon Folly, a 140-foot tower of his own design. When asked what it

FARINGDON HOUSE IN OXFORDSHIRE, WHERE LORD BERNERS PUT UP NOTICES WARNING THAT CATS WOULD BE WHIPPED AND DOGS WOULD BE SHOT — BUT OF COURSE THEY WEREN'T. IN FACT HE KEPT WHIPPETS HIMSELF, WHICH HE PROVIDED WITH DIAMOND COLLARS.

Lord Berners' practice of dyeing his doves is still repeated each Easter — and Faringdon Tower, built with the object of being 'entirely useless'.

was for, he explained: 'The great point of the tower is that it will be entirely useless'. And to discourage anyone who thought of one obvious use for it he put up a notice saying:

> *Members of the public committing suicide from this tower do so at their own risk.*

Lord Berners was in fact an inveterate practical joker. During his years as a diplomat he worked with an important official who made great play with his spectacles to emphasise a point, picking them up from his desk with a grand flourish. Berners arrived ahead of him one day, found the glasses on the desk, and tied them with a thin piece of thread to the ink-bottle, the letter-opener, and all the contents of the pen-tray. When the

WHEN LORD BERNERS WANTED TO PAINT A PICTURE OF HIS HORSE HE DIDN'T GO TO THE STABLE — THE HORSE CAME TO THE HOUSE . . .

official next flourished his glasses, everything else on the desk came too . . .

Even when he was a well-known public figure, and perhaps old enough to know better, Lord Berners adopted the most schoolboyish methods of keeping other passengers out of his railway carriage. At each stop he would don a black skull-cap and spectacles, lean out of the window and beckon invitingly. This was normally most effective, but if some hardy spirit remained undeterred and insisted on joining him, he had another trick up his sleeve. He produced a large clinical thermometer every few minutes and took his own temperature, studying each reading with increasing gloom. The intruder generally left at the next station.

Obviously Lord Berners did not take his collecting too seriously, any more than he took life very seriously. HENRY CONSTANTINE JENNINGS, however, regarded collecting as a very serious business indeed, to the extent that it frequently landed him in jail for bankruptcy. In the early 1800s he collected almost anything, from stuffed birds and sea shells to a statue of Venus which joined him at the dinner-table each evening, attended by two liveried footmen. Unfortunately there were periods when not only his collection, but even the dinner-table, had to be sold to meet his debts. Eventually he devised a way of retaining his treasures, if not his liberty. In 1816, when he went bankrupt again, instead of paying his debts he went to jail and took his favourite

. . . AND WHEN HENRY JENNINGS WENT TO JAIL FOR BANKRUPTCY, SOME OF HIS FAVOURITE ITEMS WENT WITH HIM.

pieces with him. He was allowed to keep them with him in prison until he died.

Contemporary with Henry Jennings was another eccentric collector whose treasures did not land him in jail, they actually killed him. THOMAS PITT, the last Lord Camelford, was a bellicose gentleman whose great pride was his collection of duelling pistols. His house was full of them, 'a veritable armoury strongly expressive of the pugnacity of the peer,' as one writer put it. He accumulated other offensive weapons too; the pride of his collection was a large bludgeon which he hung on the wall, adding smaller cudgels and canes above, 'until a pyramid of weapons gradually arose, tapering to a horse-whip'.

LORD CAMELFORD, WHO BUILT UP A COLLECTION OF DUELLING PISTOLS. HE LIKED TO USE THEM TOO — AND ONE OF THEM EVENTUALLY KILLED HIM.

Lord Camelford, in short, enjoyed a fight — or at any rate, thumping people. As an officer in the Navy he shot dead a lieutenant who refused to accept an order from him, and was acquitted at the court-martial on the grounds that he was quelling a mutiny. At Drury Lane Theatre, when an elderly man courteously asked him to move away from a window he was obstructing, he knocked him down a flight of stairs and beat him so violently he nearly lost the sight of an eye; Camelford had to pay £500 in damages. When peace was declared in 1801 he complained publicly because the fighting was over, and his house was attacked by an angry mob. He laid about them with his favourite bludgeon, but there were too many of them and this time he got a nasty beating himself.

He got involved in numerous brawls and duels until in 1814, at the age of twenty-nine, he fell out with a friend called Captain Best. Somebody suggested that, as far as duelling was concerned, Best was indeed the best. Camelford promptly challenged his friend to a duel to make him prove it. Out came a pair of duelling pistols from his collection, and they met at dawn. Camelford had the first shot — and missed. Captain Best had the second — and didn't. The pugnacious peer died three days later, saying he had never really felt any ill will towards any man. Alas, he had an eccentric way of showing it.

A third eccentric collector of that period, with a very different kind of collection, was SIR JOHN DINELY-GOODERE, who had a grace-and-favour home at Windsor Castle and very little else. Because of this Sir John collected wealthy prospective wives. He calculated that any woman should be proud to pay £10,000 for the honour of sharing the Dinely name; if she was young and pretty he was prepared to knock off £500. So he advertised regularly in the papers, not actually quoting any figures but emphasising the bargain he was offering. The advertisement was addressed 'To the angelic fair of the true English breed,' and the wording was chosen carefully, if not over-modestly:

'Sir John Dinely, of Windsor Castle' – technically accurate, if a little misleading – 'recommends himself and his ample fortune' – ample, compared with the average beggar – 'to any angelic beauty of good breed, fit to become, and willing to be, a mother of a noble heir, and keep up the name of an ancient family, ennobled by deeds of arms and ancestral renown . . . The lady who shall thus become my wife will be a Baronetess, and rank accordingly as Lady Dinely of Windsor . . . Paeans of pleasure await your steps!'

Three times a year Sir John visited London to interview the applicants. In due course his search for a wife became so widely known that the advertisements were hardly necessary. As soon as word got round that he was in town, eligible ladies besieged him with offers of matrimony wherever he went. He was an easy target to spot; at the end of the eighteenth century he still wore clothes more suited to the seventeenth – faded velvet breeches, coat and waistcoat, and a powdered wig held on by a strap under his chin.

Perhaps none of the ladies would produce the requisite £10,000, perhaps Sir John enjoyed his collecting so much that he forgot his financial problems, but the right woman never seemed to come along. He died at the age of sixty-nine, still single and still broke, but with his collection intact and his reputation established as an eccentric English gentleman.

They don't come like that any more, but there are still English gentlemen around with an eccentric taste in collections. THE MARQUESS OF BATH is such a one, though perhaps there is an element of commercialism in his eccentricity. At Longleat House, safe from all those lions, he has a remarkable collection of Churchilliana, displayed around two life-size effigies of Winston himself, one relaxing on a sofa in a red siren suit smoking a cigar, the other in a blue siren suit hard at work on a painting. He has Churchill's books, Churchill's letters, Churchill's passport, Churchill's luggage labels, even a half-smoked Churchill cigar. The stub was purloined for Lord Bath by his cousin, who was playing cards with the great man when he had to leave the room for a call of nature . . .

The Marquess has a special section for what he calls Churchillian rubbish – toby jugs, biscuit tins, tea caddies and the like. At the other extreme there is his collection of

LORD BATH'S COLLECTION OF CHURCHILLIANA AT LONGLEAT INCLUDES WHAT HE CALLS CHURCHILL RUBBISH, AND THIS MUST BE AN EXAMPLE – NOT A TOBY JUG OR A TEA CADDY OR A CANDLE HOLDER, JUST A RATHER AWFUL ORNAMENT.

Churchill stamps, considered the finest in the world. The unlikeliest item is the road sign in the corridor which leads to the collection: 'Churchill 1½ miles'. Lord Bath is on record as admitting that he and a friend acquired it many years ago, 'somewhere off the Axminster Road'.

Churchill is not the only subject of Lord Bath's enthusiasm for memorabilia. Adolf Hitler has a corner at Longleat, surrounded by unpleasant reminders of his days as Führer – rubber truncheons, the master keys of Belsen concentration camp, a painting of the Nuremberg trial – and, a little incongrously, an empty bottle of 1933-vintage German wine, and a matchbox made in the village where the Nazi movement began.

Another room features Edward VIII souvenirs, ranging from tea strainers to jigsaw puzzles, with a model of Edward himself in Coronation robes, which he never actually wore. There is also a letter-box carrying his royal coat of arms, which Lord Bath managed to retrieve before the EVIIIR cipher was replaced by GVIR. Finally a corner of the library is devoted to Margaret

HITLER BROODING AMONG THE SWASTIKAS AT LONGLEAT, WHILE THE MARQUESS VISITS ADOLF'S OLD ENEMY TO SEE HOW THE PAINTING IS PROGRESSING; NOT VERY WELL, FROM THEIR EXPRESSIONS . . .

Thatcher, including a couple of Spitting Image masks which Lord Bath considers 'unfair but unmistakable'. Somehow I doubt that he will devote any space to her successor; apart from any other consideration, Longleat is just about full up.

Christopher Proudfoot also has a space problem for his collection. He has no mansion to use as a store-room, just a very large garden shed. If he collected gnomes or flowerpots it would be perfectly adequate, but Mr Proudfoot's gardening treasures are rather bulkier. He is actually a mower buff, and the shed is stuffed full of well over one hundred lawn-mowers, dating from the 1880s to the 1950s, and nearly all in working order. When he cuts the grass at his home in Kent the neighbours never know whether he will be pushing a little six-inch American 'New Excelsior', about one hundred years old, or a 1930 cast iron Shanks's 'Ivanhoe' with eight blades on the cutting cylinder. It all adds a little variety to what most of us find a very tedious chore.

Christopher Proudfoot presiding over his collection of antique lawn-mowers. He probably finds it difficult to pick the best one, but Ransomes (above) were in no doubt at all.

JACK HAMPSHIRE FEARED THAT THE TRADITIONAL PERAMBULATOR WAS BEING OUSTED BY THE CARRY-COT AND THE BABY BUGGY, SO HE DECIDED TO PRESERVE A FEW FOR POSTERITY. NOW THEY HAVE TAKEN OVER HIS HOUSE.

JACK HAMPSHIRE is another Kent collector who is devoted to objects you can push. In his case it's prams. This is not because Mr Hampshire and his late wife produced a vast family which involved large-scale pram pushing; they only produced two sons and one daughter, and he left most of the pramwork to his wife. But in the sixties they feared that the traditional coach-built perambulator was disappearing in favour of the carry-cot and the baby buggy, and he has been collecting them ever since. Inside his moated manor house there are ten prams parked in his bedroom, prams on the landing, prams in the sitting-room and dining-room, and even prams in the lavatory, amounting to some 450 in all. Some are made of metal, some are chip carved wood and reedwork; some are built for twins, some fold, some are not technically prams at all but bassinets and mail-carts. One day the old style prams might come back into fashion; until then Mr Hampshire is their self-appointed guardian.

There is no such lofty purpose behind JAMES REEVE's collection down on Exmoor. What could be lofty about a skull picking its teeth with a lobster claw, or a stuffed ferret swallowing a mouse? In the bathroom there is a dried snake's skin for guests to rub themselves down with, and in the library is a hairless baby monkey and a pickled hand under a glass dome. There are two negro heads on the dining-room table, next to a papier maché toadstool and a china ornament portraying a buxom lady cradling a sailor on her lap. And so it goes on throughout the rest of the house. James Reeve, in short, collects anything which nobody else would particularly want to have, under the general heading of 'curios'.

The collection started in just as bizarre a fashion as it developed. Reeve was a monk at the time, languishing on his monastery sick-bed, when he saw an advertisement in *Country Life* (approved reading in monasteries, I assume) asking for a good home for an old staircase. He decided, for reasons best known to himself, to answer the advertisement, and his parents were startled to find a removal van on their doorstep laden with newel posts, banisters and some very large stairs.

Exhilarated by this unlikely acquisition, he cast aside his monk's habit and acquired a much odder one, roaming the world in search of peculiar mementoes. His family contributed too. It was his sister who gave him the pickled hand, which she obtained from some Portuguese nuns during a trip down the Amazon. Like Reeve, the nuns had given up their vocation to concentrate on the macabre, and built up a useful business selling pickled hands to the tourists. Who or what the hands were originally attached to, they did not explain, but James Reeve is convinced that his specimen has grown hairs since he has had it, and the nails are distinctly longer. He would not be surprised if it

James Reeve with some of his bizarre curios, including a mummified hand which he is sure has grown hairs since he acquired it, and he says the nails are distinctly longer. Will it one day escape from its glass prison and chase him upstairs?

eventually broke out of its glass dome and chased him upstairs. He is not the only person, of course, who has read *The Monkey's Paw*. . .

This is not the only occasion on which a severed limb has entered Mr Reeve's bizarre world. When he was a student at the Academy in Madrid, where they used real bodies in their anatomy classes, he was given a foot to study at home. On the metro the foot fell out of its brown paper wrapping, and he found himself under arrest on suspicion of murder. He spent three days in jail before they accepted his explanation . . .

That is just one of James Reeve's traveller's tales. He will tell you how he was attacked by fifty holy men in the Yemen when he closed the main door of the Great Mosque, to give a better effect for a picture, and blocked the path of an incoming funeral party; how he came upon a small boy assaulting a little girl in a graveyard in Haiti, hauled him away by his ears, and was assaulted

JAMES CURTIS was a nineteenth-century collector who had nothing to show for his efforts over twenty-five years except for a large wad of notebooks. He spent those years at the Old Bailey, taking down a verbatim report of all the proceedings — not because he was an official court reporter, but because he just liked collecting court cases. It was said that only a public execution could draw him away from the courtroom. He liked to follow the fate of the prisoners all the way from the trial to the gallows, and often introduced himself to them and helped them through their final days.

The star 'exhibit' in his collection was the trial of Corder, the man who murdered Maria Marten in the Red Barn. Curtis was actually allowed to stand alongside him in the dock, on this occasion at the Suffolk Assizes in Bury St Edmunds, and in due course wrote his biography. His privileged place in the courtroom led to a bizarre mistake on the part of a provincial newspaperman who was sent to the trial to draw a sketch of Corder. He confused the two men in the dock and sketched Curtis instead. It could have been a case for substantial damages from the newspaper when his picture appeared above Corder's name, but in fact James Curtis seemed quite gratified by the error.

To make up for his long hours in the courtroom Curtis did a great deal of early-morning walking; he liked to cover eight miles or so before breakfast. This stood him in good stead when he wanted to attend more distant executions, such as one at Chelmsford which took his fancy. He walked the twenty-nine miles from London to a Chelmsford lodging house, only to be refused admission at first because the landlady thought he had come to carry out the execution. Thus Curtis found himself mistaken for a hangman as well as a murderer. His collection must have been complete.

by the boy's parents; how he was imprisoned in a fortress in Jerash for rebuking some unruly children – he has encountered as many unpleasant children on his travels as severed limbs – and only survived there with the help of a crate of white wine provided by the American ambassadress; how he was nearly poisoned by his landlady in Madagasgar, and how he lived off kangaroo croquettes in Australia, and explored the jungle armed only with a volume of *Balzac* and a bottle of Dr Collis Brown. The stories are endless and if, perchance, you wonder at times if such weird and wonderful events could really have happened, then you only have to catch the eye of James Reeve's stuffed peacock – the one that wears the pince-nez – or any of the other extraordinary creatures in his collection, and it all becomes perfectly believable.

He showed his first interest in collecting the unusual when he was a small boy; he used to pull tufts of fur out of visitors' coats while they were taking tea with his mother. CHARLES BROOKING started early too, but on a more practical theme. When he was still only three he became fascinated by the different styles of house numbers near his suburban home in Cheam, and began to build up a collection. At four he turned his attention to

CHARLES BROOKING WAS THREE YEARS OLD WHEN HE STARTED COLLECTING DISCARDED HOUSE NUMBERS; NOW HE HAS 20,000 ARCHITECTURAL BITS AND PIECES. WHAT STARTED AS AN ECCENTRIC HOBBY HAS DEVELOPED INTO THE FAMOUS BROOKING COLLECTION.

door-handles and latches; by the time he was six he was into windows. And so it went on.

'At the age of thirteen,' he later wrote, 'I reappraised my whole collecting philosophy, and decided to specialise in the building components that not only interested me most but were not covered by any other collection – doors and their furniture, windows of all types, fire grates, staircases and rainwater heads . . . Although I knew that I was leading a rather unconventional life, and possibly in danger of being labelled an eccentric, I saw no reason to let that worry me.'

Today the Brooking Collection contains some 20,000 items, and coping with it is a full-time job. It has been exhibited at the London Building Centre, architects have waxed lyrical over it, there is even a Brooking Collection Trust devoted to finding it a permanent home. Collecting the bits and pieces which builders would once have thrown away is now a respectable and respected occupation, and Mr Brooking writes on elegant notepaper with 'Architectural Historian and Consultant' printed at the top. But I wonder if he used to enjoy himself rather more in those early days, when he cadged house numbers off the neighbours, followed building workers around to pick up discarded door knockers, and was 'in danger of being labelled an eccentric?'

I rather think he did.

Part of Brooking's collection of door furniture, including some helpful advice on how to get into an early public convenience.

INHERICENTRICS

oddness can run in the family

Some people are born eccentric, some achieve eccentricity, and some, it seems, have eccentricity inculcated in them through their families. Sometimes the eccentricity develops in a different form, occasionally it is exactly the same from one generation to the next. In the case of the eighteenth-century Elwes family, it was an eccentric uncle who inspired his nephew to follow his strange example, and indeed surpass it. The two of them were known jointly as the 'Misers of Ashen'.

SIR HARVEY ELWES lived at Stoke-by-Clare in Suffolk, and owned most of the land and property in the village of Ashen, just across the Essex border. Although he was one of the richest men in England he kept his annual expenditure down to £100 a year – and that included the wages, such as they were, of his three servants. He never bought new clothes; instead he kept a chest of old suits which belonged to his grandfather, and wore each suit until it fell to pieces. He rode round his estate in a moth-eaten greatcoat and a ragged black cap, on a broken-winded old horse which looked nearly as disreputable as he did, and he lived entirely on partridges which he shot himself, or occasionally a fish, plus one boiled potato per meal. If he was alone, instead of a fire he paced up and down to keep warm; if he had a guest he would stretch a point and light a fire, but only burned one stick at a time. Guest or no, the household went to bed at nightfall to save on candles.

STOKE COLLEGE ON THE SUFFOLK BORDER, IN RATHER BETTER SHAPE NOW THAN IT WAS IN THE DAYS OF THE EIGHTEENTH CENTURY 'MISERS OF ASHEN', SIR HARVEY ELWES AND HIS NEPHEW JOHN. SIR HARVEY KEPT HIS ANNUAL SPENDING DOWN TO £100 A YEAR — AND THAT INCLUDED THE WAGES OF HIS THREE SERVANTS.

A regular visitor to Sir Harvey's home, Stoke College, was his nephew JOHN MEGGOTT. As a young man John showed no sign of Sir Harvey's miserly nature, but he did respect it, to the extent of changing out of his smart London suit into shabby old clothes at an inn in Chelmsford before presenting himself at Stoke. In London he enjoyed a hectic social life in high society, devoting himself to the standard pursuits of an English city gentleman – gambling and riding, with a little dancing thrown in.

It seems however that his regular visits to Stoke began to influence him. He no longer thought it odd that Stoke College was never repaired, that dinner always consisted of a partridge, a potato, and one glass of wine shared with his uncle, and that as soon as dusk fell, everyone went to bed. On the contrary, he developed his own little economies. On the ride from London, instead of stopping at inns for refreshment, he carried two boiled eggs to last him the journey; if he was thirsty he drank from a stream, alongside his horse.

One biographer suggests that John's mother also set him an example in meanness, and starved herself to death. It would fit the story nicely, but it seems more likely she was killed by her physician, the curiously-named Dr China, who put her on a strict diet to cure her various ailments, when she really needed to build up her strength with a few extra calories. Whatever the cause, she died in 1753 a very rich woman. She left her son a fortune, and when Sir Harvey died ten years later, John changed his name to Elwes and inherited another.

Thus provided for, he moved into Stoke College and embarked on a way of life which displayed the most extraordinary contradictions. He invested much of his money in bricks and mortar, building magnificent town houses in expensive areas of London like St James's and Marylebone, but allowed no work at all to be done on his own home at Stoke, which had already been neglected for years by his uncle. When he visited friends in London he ate and drank voraciously, but on his own he only had a bun or a slice of bread. He never hired a cab, but always accepted a lift. Going out for a dinner or to a ball he wore the height of fashion, but during the day he dressed like a pauper.

While his house fell into disrepair, Elwes restored the stable block for his hunters and built new kennels for his hounds. He did not however take on any more staff. His solitary manservant, according to one writer, 'successively milked the cows, prepared breakfast, saddled the horses, unkennelled the hounds, conducted them to the chase, rubbed down the horses on their return, laid

JOHN ELWES WAS A GREAT HUNTING MAN, AND HIS OWN MISERLY LIVING CONDITIONS DID NOT EXTEND TO HIS HORSES AND HOUNDS. WHILE HIS OWN HOME AT STOKE FELL INTO DISREPAIR HE RESTORED THIS STABLE BLOCK AND BUILT NEW KENNELS.

the cloth, waited at dinner, again milked the cows, and fed and littered the horses for the night; and yet his master called him an idle dog, who wanted to be paid for doing nothing'.

Astonishingly, John Elwes was elected to Parliament and spent twelve years as an MP, but he had no interest in politics, never made a speech, and sat on whichever side of the House seemed convenient at the time. In spite of mixing with politicians, who are not usually noted for their frugality, he did not alter his own parsimonious habits. His shoes were never cleaned in case the friction wore them out. He rode on the grass verge to save wear and tear on the horseshoes, and made wide detours to avoid paying at the toll-gates. For clothing he delved into Sir Harvey's old chest in the attic; his one luxury was a wig he found in a hedge, topped by a hat he removed from a scarecrow.

His meals became steadily more gruesome. The meat was so mouldy it moved on the plate; he is said to have supped off a moorhen that had been gnawed by a rat, and he was thrilled to bits when he caught a pike which had an undigested fish in its stomach. 'This is really killing two birds with one stone,' he exulted.

One biographer records that he broke both legs in an accident and would only allow the doctor to put a splint on one, saying he could copy it on the other leg and thus halve the bill. Another version has it that his legs were not broken but badly cut; again he would only allow the doctor to treat one of them, wagering the amount of the bill that the untreated leg would get better first. He won the bet by a fortnight. Whichever version is the correct one, it was entirely in character with the rest of his economies.

But there was another side to his character too. He was a rider of great skill and courage, as a magistrate he was renowned for his fairness and integrity, and surprisingly in someone who was so ludicrous in his meanness, he retained a remarkable sense of humour. When he was out shooting and one of the other guns, a hopeless shot, put two pellets in his cheek, causing considerable pain, Elwes merely commented wryly: 'My dear sir, I give you joy on your improvement – I knew you would hit something by-an-by'. But no doubt he made sure who paid the doctor . . .

WHEN JOHN ELWES WAS BURIED IN 1789 HE LEFT BEHIND A SEMI-DERELICT HOUSE, A WILDERNESS OF A GARDEN – AND A FORTUNE WORTH, IN TODAY'S FIGURES, ABOUT TWENTY MILLION POUNDS.

John Elwes' eccentric life-style and revolting diet seemed to do him no harm at all. He lived until the age of seventy-six, and remained remarkably fit until his peaceful death in 1789. He left a house at Stoke full of rotten floor-boards, cracked windows, peeling paint and sagging doors on broken hinges, and a garden which was a desolate wilderness. He also left the equivalent in today's figures of about twenty million pounds.

During the period that Elwes was at Stoke College consolidating his reputation as an eccentric miser, the first MARCHIONESS OF SALISBURY was establishing a dynasty of eccentrics in quite a different field, as the flamboyant hostess of Hatfield House. As one bewildered observer wrote: 'I never heard anything like the manner of living at Hatfield – five hundred fed every Tuesday and Friday for six weeks at Christmas, the house full of company eating and drinking all day long . . . Lady Salisbury goes a-fox-hunting in the morning and to all the balls in the county at night. In short she does anything and everything all day long'.

She hunted in a costume she designed herself, featuring a blue and silver riding coat and a black velvet jockey cap. When her husband got bored with being Master of the hunt she took it on herself, and she was still hunting when she was eighty years old and almost blind. She was strapped to her horse, which was on a leading rein controlled by her groom. When they came to a hedge the groom cried: 'Damn you, my lady, jump!' – and she did.

In the summer she staged concerts in the park, either on the terrace or on the banks of the River Lea, where she listened to the music from a state barge rowed up and down by twelve oarsmen in full livery. She also liked to drive around the estate tossing guineas to any passing peasantry.

Lady Salisbury had little time for religion. Indeed she held card parties on Sundays, which was quite shocking by eighteenth-century standards. On one rare visit to a service she listened, apparently for the first time, to the story of how Adam excused himself for taking the apple by putting the blame on Eve. She announced loudly and with great disgust: 'Shabby fellow indeed!' She was just as unselfconscious when she took a dislike to the box which was allocated to her at the Handel Festival in Westminster Abbey, a very ceremonial occasion attended by George III and his

The first Marchioness of Salisbury leading the hunt at Hatfield House in the blue and silver riding habit she designed herself. She still rode when she was eighty and almost blind – she was strapped to her horse, and her groom told her when to jump.

family. She insisted that carpenters should be sent for to remove a partition in the box, and for part of the concert there was a great hammering as her instructions were carried out. The King, it is reported, enquired about the noise, but when told that Lady Salisbury was involved, enquired no further . . .

In her later years she was known disrespectfully as 'Old Sarum', but while she accepted the Sarum she never admitted she was old. She dressed in girlish clothes and tried to mingle with young people, even though her youthful looks had long since gone. One fellow guest at a house party, a shabby fellow indeed, wrote this ungallant description: 'It is impossible to do justice to the antiquity of her face. If, as alleged, she is only seventy-four years old, it is the most cracked, or rather furrowed piece of mosaic you have ever saw. But her dress, in the colours of it at least, is absolutely infantine . . . white muslin, properly loaded with garniture, and she has just put off a very large bonnet, profusely gifted with bright lilac ribbons, leaving on her head a very nice lace cap, not less adorned with brightest yellow ribbon'.

It was her inappropriate choice of dress which led to her death. It is thought that, while writing a letter at Hatfield House, the feathers in her high-piled hair – the style of her youth – caught in the candle on the desk and started a fire which burned down the entire west wing. In the morning all that was found of Lady Salisbury was a heap of charred bones.

The eccentricity of the first Marchioness seems to have skipped a generation. The second Marquess led an orthodox political life at Westminster and an orthodox feudal life at Hatfield. He restored the house and modernised the estate, and was shrewd enough to allow the railway to cross his land so long as a station was built for his benefit. It was the third MARQUESS OF SALISBURY, later to become Queen Victoria's Prime Minister, who brought a touch of his grandmother's eccentric style back to Hatfield House – along with a pet boarhound he named Pharaoh 'because it won't let people go'.

HATFIELD HOUSE, WHERE THE FIRST LADY SALISBURY DIED IN A FIRE WHICH DESTROYED THE WEST WING. IT IS THOUGHT THE FEATHERS IN HER HAIR – PART OF HER ECCENTRIC ENSEMBLE – WERE SET ALIGHT BY THE CANDLE ON HER DESK WHILE SHE WAS WRITING.

His idiosyncrasies, however, were the opposite of Lady Salisbury's. Instead of her extravagant entertaining he shrank from humanity in the mass. As his grandson put it: 'This was an inconvenient reaction for a Prime Minister. It was said that going for a walk with him in a public place was like accompanying somebody wanted by the police and trying to avoid arrest!' And instead of flamboyant clothes he dressed so scruffily when he was pursuing his hobby of botany that he was once arrested by a farmer who thought he was a poacher.

'Throughout his life my grandfather was eccentrically indifferent to his own appearance,' wrote David Cecil. 'In later years, and when Prime Minister of England, he was refused admission to the Casino at Monte Carlo because his clothes were so disreputable that he was taken for a tramp.' Why the Prime Minister wished to get into the casino is not explained . . .

AN IMPRESSION OF LORD SALISBURY, ONE OF ENGLAND'S MORE IDIOSYNCRATIC PRIME MINISTERS, BY THE FAMOUS CARTOONIST 'SPY'.

One similarity between the eccentric little ways of Lord Salisbury and the first Marchioness was their propensity for making unexpected remarks in public places. The Prime Minister, who was a little vague about recognising faces, was standing behind the throne at a court ceremony when he saw a young man smiling at him. 'Who is my young friend?' he asked his neighbour. 'He's your eldest son,' was the reply.

David Cecil records that he had little respect for the treasured furnishings at Hatfield House. 'He thought nothing of cutting through a piece of ancient tapestry to make a door, or of nailing a tray for his letters on to the veneer of a beautiful table.' This disregard was further demonstrated when he installed the newfangled electric lighting in the Long Gallery, with uninsulated wires running along the ceiling. The wires had an unfortunate habit of catching fire, but Lord Salisbury was able to cope. 'My grandfather, conversing below, would look up, and he, or his sons, would nonchalantly toss up a cushion to put the flames out, and then resume their conversation. The fact that he was risking the destruction of a masterpiece of Jacobean interior decoration did not bother him.'

Another innovation he brought to Hatfield was less of a threat to the decorations, but just as disconcerting for his guests. He installed an inter-communicating telephone, one of the first in the country, and liked to test it by reciting nursery rhymes into it. 'Unsuspecting visitors, sitting as they thought alone, would be alarmed to hear, emerging from a mysterious instrument on a neighbouring table, the spectral voice of the Prime Minister intoning: "Hey diddle diddle, the cat and the fiddle"'.

But his most public demonstration of eccentricity came in his later years. At the age of seventy, in a brave attempt to reduce his considerable weight, Lord Salisbury took a daily ride on a tricycle. Londoners were treated to the sight of their portly, bearded Prime Minister, wearing a shabby cloak and a wide-brimmed felt hat, trundling around St James's Park on his trike. 'Since he was too infirm to start the machine rolling, he was usually accompanied by a groom or a grandchild whom, when he found himself forced to slow up, he would politely request to push him from behind till he had achieved the required impetus. In spite of his and their efforts, my grandfather's weight did not noticeably diminish.'

I cannot leave the third Marquess on such an undignified note. We should remember how remarkably self-possessed he was — these days it would be called 'laid back' — when he made his maiden speech in the House. He paused in the middle of it — and yawned! Disraeli turned to a colleague and murmured, 'He'll do'. And he did.

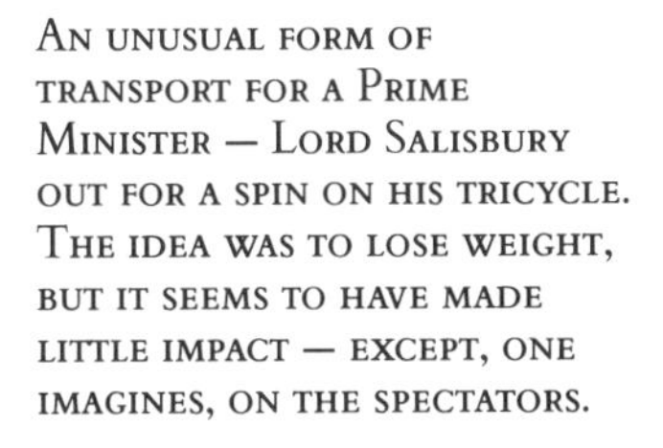

An unusual form of transport for a Prime Minister — Lord Salisbury out for a spin on his tricycle. The idea was to lose weight, but it seems to have made little impact — except, one imagines, on the spectators.

The Harpur-Crewe family of Calke Abbey in Derbyshire had a distinctive idiosyncrasy which spanned not just one or two generations but two centuries. It was a trait which first appeared in the eighteenth century with SIR HENRY HARPUR, who was known as 'The Isolated Baronet', and ended in 1985 when the National Trust acquired Calke Abbey, 'The House Where Time Stood Still'. It was not reclusiveness on the scale of the hermits recorded elsewhere; it was just an extreme version of traditional English reserve – the ultimate in unsociability. The Harpur-Crewes, with one or two exceptions, liked to keep themselves to themselves; in one case it even meant that father and daughters

In the 1950s the best-known eccentric in England was probably 'MAD JACK' WINTLE, epitome of the English officer and gentleman, whose monocle remained in place no matter how dire the situation, and whose immaculate umbrella he unfurled only once, to insert a note reading: 'This umbrella has been stolen from Colonel A D Wintle'. This was the man who wrote in his diary: 'There are essentially only two classes of Englishmen; those who believe themselves superior to foreigners – and those who know they are!'

To the general public there was only one eccentric in the Wintle family, but the most publicised incident of his astonishing career came about through the eccentricity of one of his relations, a second cousin called Kitty Wells. It was the very odd will she left that resulted in Colonel Wintle luring her solicitor into a hired flat, where he forced him at gunpoint to remove his trousers, photographed him wearing a dunce's cap made out of newspapers, and released him, still trouserless, into the street. It was an exploit which earned him a six-month prison sentence, but also the applause of the nation – even more so when he became the first layman to conduct his own appeal in the House of Lords, and won. Even *The Times* became a little light-headed; its headline read: 'Calvalry Officer Jumps Last Fence to Win'.

The case of the debagged solicitor was the high spot of a career which combined gallantry with idiosyncrasy. In the First World War, when the man next to him in the trenches was blown to pieces, Wintle forced himself to stand at attention with the shells bursting round him 'until I was able to become again an Englishman of action'. At Ypres he was blown up by a mine, lost one eye and much of the sight of the other, plus a kneecap, five and a half fingers and one and a half thumbs. But he discharged himself from hospital, returned to the front, captured thirty-five prisoners single-handed and won the Military Cross. He was still only twenty.

Between the wars he met Cedric Mays, who was to be involved in his famous court case and in his final touch of eccentricity. Wintle was in military hospital after a riding accident when he found Mays, a boy trumpeter, in part of the ward known as the 'Stiffs Retreat', suffering from mastoiditis and diphtheria, usually a fatal combination. 'What's all this nonsense about dying, Mays?' he roared. 'You know it is an offence for a Royal Dragoon to die in bed. You will stop dying at once, and when you get up – get your bloody hair cut.' As Mays said later: 'After that, I was too terrified to die'.

Wintle began the Second World War as dramatically at he ended the first. He tried to commandeer an RAF plane to fly to France and lead the French air force to freedom. When he was stopped and told by the Director of Intelligence he would be court-martialled he drew his revolver and shouted: 'You and would only communicate by letter – and they all lived in the same house.

The Harpur family were at Calke from the days of James I. They were conventional enough during the first 150 years or so, until Sir Henry inherited the estate. It marked the beginning of what the National Trust describes and 'that congenital unsociability that was to be a characteristic of the family for 200 years, and which gives them a special place in the gallery of English eccentrics'.

When Sir Henry moved into Calke Abbey he moved out of society, both literally and figuratively, because he took with him a

your kind ought to be shot'. Now suspected of being a spy, he was taken to the Tower of London, but his young officer escort lost the committal paper en route. Wintle snapped: 'For God's sake wait here while I get another'. He duly got it – and as no senior official was available, he signed it himself.

After a few weeks in the Tower the War Office had second thoughts, reduced the charges against him to a minor one and gave him a severe reprimand. And in 1941 he did get to France at last, as an undercover agent, was captured, escaped, and then captured again. At this stage he decided his Vichy French guards looked too scruffy, and threatened to go on hunger-strike if they did not smarten up. Such was the glare of that one monocled eye that, amazingly, they cleaned their buttons, polished their boots and promised to shave every day. The next time he escaped, most of the prison garrison went off too and joined the Resistance . . .

Meanwhile Wintle's sister Marjorie was looking after his eccentric cousin Kitty, a reclusive lady who sent herself letters, bulky envelopes stuffed with old bus tickets, to impress the postman. Marjorie tended her for twenty-five years, but when Kitty died after the war it was found she had left only forty pounds; the bulk of her estate, about £100,000, went to her solicitor, Frederick Nye, who had drawn up the will.

Wintle was outraged, especially when he found the will was phrased so obscurely that even his solicitors could not understand it. He appealed to Nye to give his sister a better deal, but Nye returned his letters unopened. Then he wrote insulting letters about him in the Press; still no reaction. Finally, to get Nye into court one way or another, he undertook 'Operation De-Bag'.

At Lewes Assizes in 1955 his grievances over the will were ignored, and he was sentenced to six months for assault. With the help of Cedric Mays, the former boy trumpeter, he compiled a dossier on Nye, appealed to the High Court – and lost. So he fired his solicitors, mortgaged his last possessions, and with Mays' continued help took the case to the House of Lords. It lasted six days, and at the end of it Nye was ordered to forfeit all his benefits under Kitty's will and pay all the costs. It was a famous victory.

Lieutenant Colonel Wintle often said that he had fought clots all his life, and expected to die of one. In 1966 he did. He had told Cedric Mays that he would dearly like the band of his old regiment, the Royal Dragoons, to play Schubert's *Serenade* at his funeral, but it was serving overseas, so ex-trumpeter Mays displayed the kind of eccentric gallantry which Mad Jack would have much appreciated. He fortified himself with a bottle of whisky, then stood to attention in the Chapel of the Cavalrymen of Great Britain in Canterbury Cathedral – and sang the entire *Serenade* himself.

Calke Abbey in Derbyshire, home of the reclusive Harpur-Crewe family. When the National Trust took it over they found it was 'The House Where Time Stood Still'.

lady's maid as a mistress, and later – worse still in the 1790s – he married her. He spent the rest of his life in seclusion, emerging occasionally to landscape the park, to raise a troop of yeomanry during the Napoleonic Wars, and to take his wife on holiday to unfashionable resorts like Aberystwyth 'where the scenery was more interesting than the society'. He also changed his surname to Crewe in the hope of reviving a dormant barony, but it failed to materialise, and his descendants compromised by using both names and a hyphen.

Sir Henry died in a carriage accident in 1819 – he would probably have thought it a judgment on him for going out in public – and his son George brought life back to normal at Calke, but the next generation, George's son Sir John Harpur-Crewe, retreated into the family shell again. He lived at Calke for forty-two years and his epitaph records that he was 'averse to a public life and spent the great part of his days at Calke among his own people, in the exercise of unostentatious charity and doing good to all around him'.

He set the tone for his son Vauncey, who was descended from the reclusive Sir Henry on both sides of the family, and thus got a double dose of the family reserve. He was more interested in butterflies and stuffed birds than people, and rarely left the house, where he was something of a martinet to his family. It was

he who wrote letters to his daughters instead of speaking to them, even though they all lived under the same roof. 'The Misses Crewe do not marry,' he used to say, and was very put out when two of them did. The third must have regretted not following their example; she made a more ignominious departure, turned out of the house by her father for smoking.

When he died in 1924 one of his married daughters inherited Calke Abbey and moved in with her husband, but little alteration was made to the house or its contents, and Hilda herself wore old-fashioned clothes and refused to allow electricity to be installed. Even when the Army commandeered the Abbey during the last war, only a small part of it was used, and when Hilda died in 1949 and Calke Abbey went to her nephew Charles Harpur-Crewe, the old family trait reappeared. As the National Trust puts it: 'Unmarried, and more shy, retiring and socially isolated than any of his predecessors since Sir Henry, he made Calke for thirty-two years one of the two or three most impenetrable country houses in England'.

Charles did play a limited part in local life, reluctantly agreeing to be High Sheriff of Derbyshire, and serving as a district councillor and a governor of Repton School, but at their meetings he was notorious for his silence. In 1981 he died suddenly while setting traps for the equally reclusive moles in his park. Because of death duties Calke Abbey went to the National Trust, and many of the rooms were found to be almost unchanged since Sir Vauncey inherited the estate one hundred years before. 'Here was

The Saloon at Calke Abbey (left), undisturbed since it was remodelled for Sir John Harpur-Crewe in 1841. The Calke State Bed (above), a wedding present to Sir Henry Harpur and his wife, from George II's daughter in 1734, but never used because it was too high for their bedroom. The National Trust have erected it in what used to be the housemaids' room.

a family,' the Trust sums up, 'who threw nothing away, but simply stored their treasures in a room – and shut the door.'

In contrast to the retiring and unsociable Harpur-Crewes, the three most famous eccentric families in England during the early twentieth century seemed unable to avoid the glare of publicity; sometimes they went out of their way to attract it. There were the Mitfords, the six remarkable sisters and the young brother they nicknamed 'Tuddemy' because they thought it rhymed with 'adultery'; the talented Sitwell trio, Osbert, Sacheverell and Edith (who wrote her own book on eccentrics, obviously with inside knowledge); and the Sackville-Wests, notably the unconventional Victoria, whose complicated love life featured in a quite daring television serial.

The activities and sometimes chequered careers of the Mitford girls, the Sitwell trio and the televisual Vita have already been extensively chronicled. I think it is the heads of these families who are worth looking at more closely, because they never hit the headlines so spectacularly as their offspring, but they created a home life for their families which was just as unusual as their public ones.

DAVID BERTRAM OGILVY FREEMAN-MITFORD, second Baron Redesdale, addressed by his children as 'Farve', but referred to

THE MITFORD FAMILY HOME AT SWINBROOK, BUILT BY LORD REDESDALE. JESSICA MITFORD SAID HER FATHER MADE IT SOMETHING OF A FORTRESS, DIFFICULT FOR THE FAMILY TO ESCAPE FROM OR FOR OUTSIDERS TO ENTER.

privately as 'The Old Sub-Human', was born in 1878 and served with distinction in the Boer War. Then his career took an odd turn; he became editor of *The Lady*, which for a man who had no interest in female pursuits, no talent for journalism and rarely read a book, might reasonably be considered a trifle eccentric. His next move was even odder; he built a family home at Swinbrook in Oxfordshire which, according to his daughter Jessica, had many aspects of a fortress, difficult for the family to escape from or for outsiders to enter.

These oak pews in Swinbrook Church were donated by Lord Redesdale in memory of his father, the first Baron, from the proceeds of a winning bet on the Grand National.

'According to my father,' wrote Jessica, '"outsiders" included not only Huns, Frogs, Americans, blacks and all other foreigners, but also other people's children, the majority of my older sisters' acquaintances, and almost all young men . . . He was in general unaware of distinctions between different kinds of foreigners. When one of our cousins married an Argentinian of pure Spanish descent he commented: "I hear that Robin's married a black!"'

Visitors who did penetrate the house, even on business, never knew quite what to expect from his lordship. When a doctor came on a medical call to any member of the family, Lord Redesdale always remained in attendance. He supervised the births of all the children, and when the infant Nancy appeared to stop breathing he became so impatient with the doctor's ministrations that, in his own words, 'I seized him by the neck and shook him like a rat'. Nancy survived – and so, fortunately, did the doctor.

Lord Redesdale was patron of the living at Swinbrook; he interviewed prospective incumbents in quite terrifying fashion, according to Jessica, who used to eavesdrop with her sisters. He made it clear that he chose all the hymns – 'None of those damn complicated foreign tunes. I'll give you a list of what's wanted: "Holy, holy, holy", "Rock of Ages", "All Things Bright and Beautiful" and the like'. He warned that sermons must never exceed ten minutes, and he timed them with a stopwatch and signalled when to stop – 'If you disregard this I shall precipitate you out of the pulpit by the scruff of the neck'. And his final question was always: 'Do you go in for smells and lace, and all that Popish nonsense?' Any cleric who accepted the living must have needed a job pretty desperately . . .

The memorial to Lord and Lady Redesdale in Swinbrook Church, with the Mitford coat of arms and motto: 'God Careth for Us'.

He ruled his own family just as firmly. When Nancy had her hair shingled at the age of twenty there was a monumental row, and meals were eaten in tearful silence for a week. The same thing happened when she bought a ukulele, which he considered 'fast', and yet again when, far worse, she started smoking. But she did get her own back by portraying him as the irascible General Murgatroyd in her novel *Highland Fling* – though one gathers he rather enjoyed being immortalised thus.

In spite of, or perhaps because of, his iron rule, the children liked to bait 'The Old Sub-Human'. Unity and Jessica devised a secret language called Boudle-didge, into which they translated dirty songs and performed them in his presence. Debo spent much of her time in the chicken house, learning to imitate the pained expression of a hen at the moment of laying an egg, while Jessica's favourite trick was to give her father 'palsy practice', which consisted of gently shaking his hand while he was drinking his tea. 'In a few years, when you're really old, you'll probably have palsy,' she explained to him. 'I must give you a little practice before you get it, so you won't be dropping things all the time.' Astonishingly, she got away with it.

Pets played a major part in the Mitford household. The children were encouraged to keep pigs, calves and chickens, but their father charged them a small rent for the plot they occupied, which they had to recoup by selling eggs and litters. When the family went to church the pets went too, and were parked in the churchyard on whichever graves had railings. When Lord Redesdale decided to acquire a Shetland pony to add to the collection, he brought it from London in the same railway compartment as his family.

When he died in 1958, just after his eightieth birthday, *The Times* described him as a man 'who adhered to somewhat old-fashioned views with tenacity and boisterousness' — which was putting it rather mildly. It also said that, compared with the ladies of his family, 'he was a rather shadowy personality'. As one biographer commented, this was further proof that you can believe nothing in a newspaper except the date.

If Lord Redesdale's attitude was a survival from Victorian times, SIR GEORGE SITWELL's was positively medieval. A sign in his manor house at Eckington in Derbyshire made his position quite clear:

> *I must ask anyone entering the house never to contradict me in any way, as it interferes with the functioning of my gastric juices and prevents my sleeping at night.*

Sir George's attitude to his three talented children was just as unequivocal; he disapproved of almost everything they did. Their reaction was predictably rebellious, with Edith well to the fore. As a teenager, when her father insisted on taking her to the races, she sat with her back to the course. When he took her to the Albert Hall for a brass band concert, which she apparently disliked even more than horse-racing, she managed to make herself violently sick. And although she was expected to wear white tulle like other society girls of her age, she wore long black velvet dresses, forerunners of the Plantagenet style she adopted later, explaining frankly: 'If one is a greyhound, why try to look like a Pekinese?'

Sir George's disapproval of his children seemed to increase as they grew older. When Osbert said he planned to write a novel he was advised strongly against it: 'My cousin had a friend who utterly ruined his health writing a novel'. He had no time for Edith's literary talents either; in later years he observed: 'Edith made a great mistake by not going in for lawn tennis'. And he tried to keep them under surveillance as long as possible; as he told Osbert: 'It is dangerous for you to lose touch with me for a single day. You never know when you may need the benefit of my experience'.

As a result Osbert and Sacheverell invented a non-existent yacht, from which they wrote to their father on notepaper inscribed: 'On board the *Rover*', saying they could not be contacted. They baited him in other ways too. Osbert used the word 'blotto' in front of him, and explained it meant 'very tired'. There was much delight in the family when Sir George later suggested to a guest that he took a rest before lunch because he appeared to be blotto . . .

The remarkable Sitwell trio, Osbert, Edith and Sacheverell, drawn by Alan Stern in 'The Graphic'.

He never did catch up with the twentieth century. When Sacheverell went to Eton Sir George offered to pay the fees in pigs and potatoes. He worked out Osbert's allowance on the basis of how much a Lord of the Manor gave his eldest son in the days of the Tudors. And his idea of modern warfare was just as antiquated; when Osbert was serving in the trenches in 1914 he wrote to him: 'Though you will not of course encounter anywhere abroad the same weight of gunfire we had to face here' – he was writing from Scarborough – 'yet my experience may be useful to you. Directly you hear the first shell, retire as I did to the Undercroft, and remain there quietly until all firing has ceased . . . Keep warm and have plenty of plain nourishing food at frequent but regular intervals, and of course plenty of rest. I find a nap in the afternoon most helpful; I advise you to try it whenever possible'.

Although Sir George had little regard for his children's writing talents, he had no doubts about his own. Seven sitting-rooms in the house were earmarked as his studies, and he embarked on various literary works with titles ranging from *The Origins of the Word Gentleman* and *The History of the Fork*, to *Acorns as an Article of Medieval Diet* and, closer to home, *Osbert's Debts*. None was ever completed.

His main passion, however, was for landscape gardening. At one stage 4,000 men were reputed to be employed on digging an artificial lake in the grounds, with wooden towers sticking out of the water from which he could survey his other projects. These included stencilling Chinese willow patterns on his white cows, which he had to abandon when the inartistic cows objected. So did Sacheverell, I imagine, when his father visited his Northamptonshire home in 1924 and remarked casually, as he surveyed the garden, 'I don't propose to do much here; just a sheet of water and a line of statues'.

THE SITWELL FAMILY MANSION AT ECKINGTON. SIR GEORGE USED SEVEN SITTING-ROOMS AS STUDIES, WHERE HE WROTE LITERARY GEMS LIKE 'THE HISTORY OF THE FORK' – ALL UNPUBLISHED. TO IMPROVE THE VIEW FROM THE WINDOWS HE PAINTED CHINESE WILLOW PATTERNS ON HIS WHITE COWS.

Sir George's eccentric landscaping schemes were hardly in the same class as the horticultural skills of Vita Sackville-West, who produced the magnificent gardens at Sissinghurst, but her eccentric mother, LADY SACKVILLE, had no time for gardening at all. She much preferred artificial flowers, notably tin delphiniums, mainly because they were impervious to slugs. However she did respect her daughter's feelings sufficiently to add colour to her own garden before a visit from Vita, by filling the bare beds with flowers made of velvet, sequins, paper and beads.

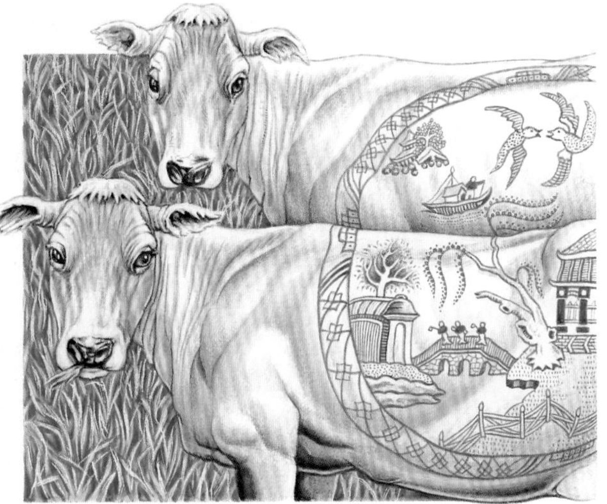

Lady Sackville alternated between wild extravagance and positive meanness. At one time she used to cut off the unused

LADY SACKVILLE, WHO PREFERRED ARTIFICIAL FLOWERS TO THE REAL THING — UNLIKE HER DAUGHTER VITA, WHO CREATED THE GARDENS AT SISSINGHURST (BELOW).

parts of postage stamps and piece them together to use again. She utilised any available paper for writing letters, ranging from the backs of advertising leaflets to the toilet paper from the ladies' room at Harrods. She devised unlikely charities like the Million Penny Fund, which was intended to eliminate the National Debt, and urged famous people on their birthdays to contribute a penny for each year of their life. The impact this had on the nation's finances was, I fear, undetectable.

Quite undeterred, in 1928 she launched the Roof of Friendship Fund, asking her friends for the price of a tile as a symbol of their regard; she was much put out when one of them actually sent her a tile. She had better luck, however, when she decided to hold a white elephant sale at her home and wrote to the King of Siam, a land with a good supply of elephants, asking for a white one. Astonishingly, he sent her a small, but valuable, solid-silver elephant, a gesture which could not have been widely publicised at the time, or the poor chap would have been bombarded by every Women's Institute in the country . . .

VITA SACKVILLE-WEST's idiosyncrasies were rather different from her mother's and considerably more sensational. Their relationship was often stormy, and perhaps gardening provided a haven from her turbulent personal affairs. Certainly at Sissinghurst, where she turned a wilderness into what is now the most-visited National Trust garden in England, she had a special relationship with her fellow gardening enthusiasts, whatever their social status. 'These homely souls,' she wrote, 'will travel fifty miles by bus with a fox-terrier on a lead and pore over every label, taking notes in a penny notebook . . . Between them and myself a particular form of courtesy survives, a gardener's courtesy in a world where courtesy is giving way to rougher things.'

I doubt if old Lady Sackville would have understood that, but then to her — and indeed to me — any enthusiasm for gardening is eccentric in itself . . .

Colossucentrics

build it extravagantly,
and build it big

Follies can come in all shapes and sizes, and these days they don't have to be buildings. My farming neighbour in Norfolk has planted a round wood of oak and chestnut and cherry, surrounded by a hedge of hawthorn and holly, slap in the middle of a sugar-beet field, to recreate what the landscape looked like a few centuries ago, but we'll all be dead before it comes to full fruition. His wife has christened it 'Robin's Folly' – though I prefer to think of it as 'Robin's Legacy'. But traditionally a folly was some sort of eccentric building, erected by somebody with more money than sense, for reasons which nobody else can fathom. And surely the biggest folly of all was the eighteenth-century Fonthill Abbey in Wiltshire, the creation of a man who decided he wanted the tallest private house in England.

WILLIAM BECKFORD, ENTHUSIASTIC TOWER-BUILDER. THEY WERE VERY EXPENSIVE AND VERY IMPRESSIVE — BUT THEY MOSTLY FELL DOWN.

When WILLIAM BECKFORD's father died in 1770, leaving an estate worth a million pounds with an income of a hundred thousand pounds a year, his son became probably the richest ten-year-old in the country. It was enough to unsettle the most level-headed of lads, and young William grew up to be an eccentric in the grand manner. Whenever he travelled, which for fifteen years was most of the time, he took with him his own doctor, baker, valet and cook, plus three footmen, twenty-four musicians and a Spanish dwarf. There were also a couple of dogs called Mrs Fry and Viscount Fartleberry . . .

Wherever he stayed he supplied his own bed, cutlery, plates – and wallpaper; his bedroom had to be repapered with his own designs before he would occupy it. And it is said that on one occasion in Portugal he also took with him a flock of sheep, not to provide fresh English lamb for the dinner-table but to improve the view from his window.

In his late thirties he developed a passion for building, and he settled down on the family estate at Fonthill with plans to build himself a new abbey with an octagonal tower 300 feet high. But first he built a wall around the estate, seven miles long and twelve feet high, to discourage intruders. Only one person is recorded to have climbed it, for a bet. He was discovered in the grounds by Beckford who, to his surprise, entertained him most courteously. But Beckford left him at the dinner-table, and the butler who escorted him to the door gave him the encouraging message from his master that, as he had found his way into the grounds without assistance, he could no doubt find his way out again – 'and he hopes you will take care to avoid the bloodhounds that are let loose in the garden every night'. The hapless fellow spent an uncomfortable night in the branches of a tree, until daylight came and he found his way back over the wall.

Beckford built his 300-foot tower on sugar, meaning that the money came from his vast sugar plantation in Jamaica, but he might have done so literally to much the same effect, because he was in such a hurry to finish it that the foundations were totally inadequate, the materials were too flimsy for such a lofty structure, and he supplied so much ale to his workforce to try to make them work faster that most of them didn't know if they were wielding a trowel or a tankard. The result was

The 300-foot tower built by Beckford on his abbey at Fonthill. But the foundations were too flimsy, the materials too fragile, and the workmen were mostly too drunk; the whole lot collapsed.

inevitable. Just after the six-year project was completed, the whole lot fell down.

Like any true eccentric, Beckford was not discouraged. He built another one, this time allowing seven years for the job instead of six, laying better foundations and using more suitable materials. He lived on his own in the abbey beneath the tower, holding imaginary dinner parties with food prepared for twelve, twelve places laid at table, twelve footmen poised to serve – and twelve empty chairs. In spite of the lack of guests he still decided the kitchens were inadequate to cope, and embarked on rebuilding them.

Again he was in too much of a hurry. He insisted that his Christmas dinner should be produced in the new kitchens, and although the hastily-applied mortar was hardly dry by Christmas morning, the ovens were duly lit and the dinner was cooked on time. Just as it was being served there was a familiar rumble. The kitchens collapsed.

Beckford, still undeterred, built them again, but by now the sugar market, like his over-hasty building projects, was

BECKFORD'S TOWER AT FONTHILL TOOK SIX YEARS TO PUT UP, AND ONLY A FEW SECONDS TO FALL DOWN. IT FINISHED UP LOOKING LIKE THIS. SO HE BUILT ANOTHER ONE . . .

crumbling. He had to sell the abbey – tower, kitchens and all – to a man called John Farquhar who could hardly have known about his reputation as a builder. Soon after he moved in, a gale hit the tower and it all came down again.

However, with the £330,000 from the sale of the abbey, Beckford started building again, this time in Bath – but happily with less haste and more solidity. He still insisted on a tower, but this time he employed a proper architect, and the tower was less than half the height of Fonthill, a mere 130 feet. That was in 1822, and untypically for a Beckford building it stands there today.

BECKFORD'S FINAL EFFORT AT TOWER-BUILDING, AFTER HE MOVED TO BATH, AND THIS TIME IT STAYED UP. IT STILL STANDS THERE TODAY.

In the same year that Beckford had his ill-fated Christmas dinner, an heir was born to the fourth Duke of Portland who was to match his little idiosyncrasies in various respects. Like Beckford, WILLIAM JOHN CAVENDISH SCOTT BENTINCK had curious views about travel. For his journeys to London from the family seat in Nottinghamshire he used a nineteenth-century form of motorail – his coach was driven to the local station and loaded onto a flat railcar attached to the rear of the London train. At the other end a fresh pair of horses was attached to it, and he was driven to his town house in Cavendish Square. Unlike modern motorail travellers, however, he insisted on remaining inside the coach throughout the journey.

Like Beckford he shunned company at his home at Welbeck Abbey. Visitors were banned, the servants were ordered to ignore him – anyone who touched his cap was instantly dismissed – and he conveyed messages to them through letter-boxes in the doors of his rooms. If he needed medical care, the doctor had to advise him from outside the door.

But his greatest similarity to Beckford was his passion for building. He spent much of his life in a sea of rubble, surrounded by hundreds of workmen – who of course were not allowed to speak to him. However, while Beckford liked to build upwards, as high as he could go, Bentinck built downwards, to live the life of a wealthy but lonely mole.

The centrepiece of his underground home was an enormous subterranean ballroom, large enough to take 2,000 dancers, though I gather it never witnessed a quickstep, or even a slow one, unless the Duke did an occasional knees-up on his own. Down in Wiltshire Beckford had the biggest empty tower in England; here in Nottinghamshire Bentinck had the biggest empty ballroom – 174 feet long, lit by thousands of gas jets, the ceiling painted to represent a glowing sunset, and a series of skylights in the ground level roof.

The Duke dug fifteen miles of tunnels, the most spectacular of them running all the way to the outskirts of the estate. Different authorities give different reasons for this. Some say there was a right of way across the estate for the locals, and the Duke dug the tunnel so they could still use it without him having to see them; but the more popular theory is that he could remain out of sight himself as he drove in his carriage from the coach-house at the Abbey to the station. There is no doubt that the tunnel is wide enough to take a coach-and-four; he lined it with glazed whitebricks and lit it, like the ballroom, with gas jets and plate-glass skylights in the roof.

Elsewhere in his underground labyrinth he built libraries full of unread books, and a billiard-room large enough for twelve

THE ASTONISHING UNDERGROUND BALLROOM AT WELBECK ABBEY, PART OF THE LABYRINTH WHICH THE BURROWING DUKE OF PORTLAND CREATED UNDER HIS ANCESTRAL HOME.

full-size tables, none of which was used. An underground railway conveyed meals from the kitchen to the dining-room – which was quite useful really, since they were 150 yards apart. The Duke did build the stables and riding school above ground – perhaps he had not thought of pit ponies – but even the riding school had no windows, so the effect inside was subterranean too. Not that it made much difference to the Duke; he never rode any of his horses, and nor did anyone else.

FROM THE AIR WELBECK ABBEY MAY LOOK LIKE JUST ANOTHER ANCESTRAL HOME WITH A FEW BITS ADDED ON – BUT UNDERNEATH ALL THAT ARE FIFTEEN MILES OF TUNNELS, A BALLROOM, A BILLIARD-ROOM . . .

But his oddest touch was in the old house itself. He had stripped Welbeck Abbey of its furniture and treasures and left it largely unused. Every empty room was painted a rather daunting

The Duke of Portland's final eccentric touch — a very exposed lavatory basin in each of the pink-painted rooms at Welbeck Abbey.

shade of pink, and in each one of them he installed in full view, perhaps as a gesture of defiance to his critics, a lavatory basin . . .

To be fair to the Duke, in spite of all his foibles, he treated his workmen well; indeed there is a strong suspicion that he only undertook his burrowing activities to provide them with work. But even his system of bonus payments had its eccentric feature. Each of his workmen — 15,000 of them at one estimate — was given, in addition to his wages, a donkey and an umbrella. As most of the work was underground they must have found it difficult to use either during the day, but at least they knew that if they emerged into a rainstorm they could shelter under their umbrellas as they rode their donkeys home. Knocking-off time at Welbeck Abbey must have presented a fascinating spectacle; I am surprised there is no pub in the area called the Ass and Brolly . . .

There is one other theory about the Duke's burrowing which is very much in his favour, if it is true. It is suggested that he was modest as well as philanthropic, and he employed all those men underground in order not to appear ostentatious, since nobody could see the results of their work. This is a rare trait in eccentric builders; usually, like William Beckford, they like their creations to be as ostentatious as possible, even if only a favoured few are allowed to see them. This was much easier in the eighteenth and nineteenth centuries, when estates were big, labour was cheap, and planning restrictions did not exist. These days the estates are broken up and their owners crippled by death duties, workmen are not inclined to settle for the odd donkey and umbrella, and the planners have taken over.

This means that eccentric builders, on the whole, have had to build small in this century. A notable exception was Julius Drewe, who made a fortune founding the Home and Colonial Stores and spent a fair chunk of it on Castle Drogo, 900 feet above the village of Drewsteignton in Devon. Like Beckford, he built on sugar — and butter, and eggs, and tins of baked beans . . .

Mr Drewe believed that he was a descendant of Drogo de Teign, one of William the Conqueror's nobles. He also believed that this was the site of Drogo's castle, and it seemed a jolly good

idea to build another one. So he contacted Sir Edwin Lutyens, gave him £50,000 – a sizeable fortune in 1910 – and told him he wanted 'a medieval fortress to match the grandeur of the site'. Twenty years later the Drewes moved in.

CASTLE DROGO AND THE MEN WHO BUILT IT: JULIUS DREWE (LEFT), SIR EDWIN LUTYENS (CENTRE) AND DREWE'S AGENT JOHN WALKER (RIGHT).

Sir Edwin turned his hand to many impressive buildings in his time, from the Viceroy's house in New Delhi to the Deanery Gardens at Sonning, but Castle Drogo must rank as one of his most remarkable. I have been a little unkind about it in the past; I once suggested that its granite walls and small windows made it look less like a medieval fortress than a modern prison, and the general effect was about as romantic as one of Mr Drewe's biscuit tins. I still think that the illustration in the handbook of the National Trust, which now owns it, bears out that view. But my architect friends assure me it is a

Julius Drewe and his personal room at Castle Drogo. Alas he enjoyed it for a very short time — he died two months after the castle was completed.

fine example of Lutyens' work, and I agree that from other angles it presents a much mellower picture. Certainly its views across the River Teign and Dartmoor are quite staggering. It is not the castle itself which is so eccentric as the idea behind it – plus the way Julius Drewe launched the project. It is said that on a family picnic he pulled up a mangold and announced: 'This is where the driveway will begin'. Lutyens took it from there.

John Halstead was at the other end of the financial spectrum from Mr Drewe, but he was able to indulge his eccentric building ideas on a smaller scale. He did not start with a Devonshire hillside, Sir Edwin Lutyens and £50,000; he started with a cottage in Rochdale and a passion for sea shells and pottery, preferably broken in small pieces. He finished up, not with Castle Drogo but with Shell House, a bizarre concoction of deceased molluscs and shattered ceramics.

Mr Halstead was a retired salesman who moved to Rochdale from Yorkshire in 1936 and bought a house in Broad Lane. He spent the next four years, until his death in 1940, decorating the outside walls with shells, broken plates and saucers, even cows' horns and bits of old bedstead. A neighbour recalled: 'We would often hear Mr Halstead chopping up his pottery in the early hours of the morning. He always used to rise with the sun'.

The local children were encouraged to collect bits and pieces for his mosaic walls, and he cemented them into various patterns. In the centre he arranged pieces of blue and white pottery to form the words *Tempori Parendum*, meaning 'We move with the times', though in Mr Halstead's case its significance seems obscure. On his death, however, it became all too appropriate. His daughter sold the house for £25, and the new owners decided that his eccentric form of pargetry was not for them. Only the photographs remain.

Eccentric builders do not confine themselves to creating curious homes; their eccentricity has spread into the garden, or at grander establishments, into the park. These are the follies which used to bespatter the more up-market estates, from the Earl of Shrewsbury's cast iron Chinese pagoda at Alton Towers to George Messiter's assorted obelisks at Barwick Park in Somerset. Gothic temples, Roman arches, ruined castles, gazebos and grottos, all manner of architectural oddities were planted among the flowerbeds and the ornamental lakes, far too many to be listed here. It is worth taking a couple of these folly-philes as

John Halstead in front of his Shell House at Rochdale. The 'shells' included broken crockery and bits of old bedstead.

examples, one because of the variety and ingenuity of his creations, the other for actually devising one which, so far as I know, remains unique in England – though they may be ten-a-penny in the Alps.

Sir Frank Crisp was a leading solicitor at the turn of the century. He was also a botanist, a horticulturist, and a landscape gardener. Most important of all, he was rich. So he built himself a mansion at Friar Park, Henley-on-Thames, with a couple of impressive towers and assorted turrets, then concentrated on the garden, which he actually started before the house. The focal point was the Alpine Garden, created with 7,000 tons of millstone grit brought from Yorkshire; and the focal point of the Alpine Garden was an accurate scale-model of the Matterhorn, complete with mountain rivers and waterfalls, and topped by a piece of rock taken from the summit of the Matterhorn itself. Sir Frank marked the spot on the mountainside where four men in Edward Whymper's expedition fell to their deaths after reaching the summit for the first time.

The scale-model of the Matterhorn built by Sir Frank Crisp in his grounds at Henley-on-Thames. It is topped by a piece of rock from the summit of the real mountain.

Having broken new ground in the folly business Sir Frank lapsed back into the more traditional grotto routine, but his grotto was based on the ice grotto at Grindelwald in Switzerland. It was embellished with blue ice, and led to an ice cave complete with icicles and, unexpectedly, a Chinese stork drinking water from a vessel on its bill. It worked on a hydraulic principle which Sir Frank recalled from his school-days.

He was blessed with an uncommonly patient head gardener, a Mr P O Knowles, who had to reconstruct the Matterhorn several times to satisfy his master. One particular face of the mountain was remodelled four times – until it reached the stage where Mr Knowles, instead of using rocks, piled up boxes covered with matting which he could move about until Sir Frank approved, then replaced them with rocks. Mr Knowles, it seems, was uncomplaining throughout. One writer commented: 'Almost the whole of the work was pulled down and rebuilt several times over, and this was carried out without any open festation of the weariness of spirit which it might be supposed would be the result of finding love's labour so continually lost!'

The patience of Mr Knowles, compared with the other gardeners, is noted by Sir Frank himself in his typically unorthodox warning to what he called IVs – Ignorant Visitors – not to criticise the gardens in their hearing. 'Every care is taken to secure as gardeners men of placid temperament and not given to outbursts of feeling,' the notice read, 'but exceptions will sometimes creep in, and the owner cannot therefore always be responsible for consequences. Last year when a female IV visited the grounds and felt it necessary to criticise the owner with what was described by bystanders as "feline ferocity", it fortunately

COMPLICATED CHIMNEY DESIGNS AT EAST BARSHAM MANOR IN NORFOLK (LEFT) AND COMPTON WYNYATES IN NORTHAMPTONSHIRE (RIGHT).

There is something about chimneys which brings out the eccentric in the most level-headed of builders. They do fine until they get up to roof level, then they wonder what to stick on top and go quite chimney-potty. The Tudors were probably the most spectacular exponents of chimney-pottery; people like SIR HENRY FERMOR, who gave his manor at East Barsham in Norfolk an amazing assortment of fat ones and thin ones, tall ones and short ones, plain ones and decorated ones, and each one different from the next. THE EARL OF NORTHAMPTON did much the same thing at Compton Wynyates, including one circular chimney with a striking left-hand thread . . .

The Industrial Revolution brought a new kind of super-chimney to carry away fumes and gases, or merely for ventilation. In spite of their mundane purpose they had their share of eccentric designers, the ultimate exponents of 'build it extravagantly and build it big'. THE FIRST EARL OF LONSDALE, who built Whitehaven Castle, also designed the ventilation chimney for the Whitehaven mine. When the builder asked how he wanted it to look, it is said that the Earl pointed at a candlestick and said: 'Build it like that!' The mine has long since closed, but the Candlestick Chimney still stands.

However the Candlestick is fairly run-of-the-mine compared with JOHN WAINHOUSE's chimney in Halifax. He built it for his dye-works, but gave it a spiral staircase, a viewing balcony round the top, and a cupola on top of that. It could not have been very practical as a chimney, nor indeed as a viewing point, since the parapet round the balcony was too high for Mr Wainhouse to see over, but at least nobody in Halifax can miss the Wainhouse Tower.

Sir Frank Crisp's Ice Cave, complete with blue icicles and, unexpectedly, a Chinese stork.

happened that it was the head gardener who was in attendance, and as he is a man who has great control of himself, no untoward incident happened and she left the grounds unscathed. Such immunity, however, could not always be guaranteed in the case of under-gardeners, and hence the owner ventures to make this appeal in the interest of the IV.'

Sir Frank (left) and his head gardener, Mr Knowles, carrying an unlikely bunch of monster grapes. One suspects the grapes, like Sir Frank, were a little larger than life.

The Matterhorn was not the only unusual feature of Sir Frank's gardens. He was very taken with caves and, in addition to the Ice Cave, he built a Vine Cave with glass bunches of grapes containing electric lamps, a Wishing Well cave in the water of which one could see the reflection of one's desired amour, and a Skeleton Cave which displayed a skeleton in mirrors 'in an apparently inexplicable manner', according to a 1910 guide. There was also an Illusion Cave, as if visitors had not suffered enough illusions already, which displayed a friar undergoing an unpleasant electrical experience, and a Gnome Cave in which the little chaps were depicted taking snuff, examining a fly, opening a champagne bottle, and generally behaving in very un-gnome-like fashion — not a fishing-rod between them. But it is the Matterhorn which looms over all these and puts Sir Frank's other eccentricities in the shade.

The Gnome Cave at Friar Park, where the gnomes took snuff, examined flies, opened champagne bottles, and other pursuits as unorthodox as their creator.

The Matterhorn may have been the largest folly in a private garden, but for the largest in a public one, my award would go to Sir Joseph Paxton, one of the most remarkable self-made men of the Victorian era, who started as an under-gardener at the Royal Horticultural Society's premises in Chiswick, and finished up as a newspaper proprietor, a director of many railway companies, an MP, and the manager of the Duke of Devonshire's vast estates at Chatsworth, Chiswick, Devonshire House, Bolton Abbey and elsewhere. He also designed and built what many considered at the time to be the most eccentric structure in England; it was called the Crystal Palace.

Joseph Paxton had the knack of being in the right place to meet the right people at the right time. During the course of his career they ranged from Lord Wellington, the retired hero of Waterloo, to George Stephenson, inventor of the *Rocket*, both of whom helped him on his way. But it started when, as a gardener at Chiswick, he regularly opened the gate for the Duke of Devonshire, whose estate adjoined the Society's gardens. They got into conversation, the Duke liked Paxton's novel ideas on garden development, and took him on as head gardener at Chatsworth when he was only twenty-three. The young man transformed the pleasure gardens, creating an entirely new landscape, and introducing eccentric little touches which, in later years, achieved a much larger scale. For instance, he installed a Victorian successor

JOSEPH PAXTON'S COPPER WILLOW TREE AT CHATSWORTH, AND (BELOW) COTTAGES IN HIS NEW VILLAGE OF EDENSOR.

to a copper willow tree dating back to the first Duke, which was fitted with water jets to spray unsuspecting strollers.

When he started designing garden buildings, he began with fairly modest glasshouses, but these got bigger and bigger until he built the Great Conservatory, an acre in extent with a carriage drive running through the middle. His most unusual creation was the lily house he constructed to accommodate a giant water lily, which had leaves six feet across and flower buds the size of footballs. Paxton noticed that the leaves were strong enough for his five-year-old daughter to sit on, and he based the design of the lily house on the radial ribs of the leaves. He made the ribs out of delicate cast iron, and gave the glasshouse a strength combined with apparent fragility which he used on a much larger scale in the Crystal Palace, many years later.

Meanwhile he had more work to do at Chatsworth. He moved an entire hamlet out of the park to improve the view, rebuilding it well out of sight of the house. Edensor was reckoned to be a model village, but again a little eccentricity crept in. The entrance lodge was built to look like a small fort, one Victorian house has Tudor chimneys while another has Italian windows, some of the cottages are eight-sided, and he threw in a Swiss chalet for good measure.

In 1843 Paxton staged an amazing outdoor entertainment at Chatsworth in honour of the Queen, involving powerful fountains and dramatic waterfalls, illuminated by fairy lights, gas flares and various other devices. It made a great impression on the spectators, not least the Duke of Wellington, who was determined to find out how the lighting worked and got up early next morning to investigate. He found not a trace of a candle-end or a scorched blade of grass; Paxton had used a small army of workmen during the night to dig up and returf the trampled lawns, rake the gravelled walks and, in fact, spring-clean the entire gardens.

'I would have liked that man of yours for one of my generals,' Wellington told the Duke, and this stood Paxton in good stead years later, when he proposed building an enormous glass-house in Hyde Park to hold the Great Exhibition of 1851; it just so happened that the Duke of Wellington was Ranger of the park, and his approval was essential.

JOSEPH PAXTON HIMSELF, PONDERING OVER HIS NEXT GREAT CREATION — OR IS HE PASSING ROUND THE HAT TO PAY FOR IT?

By that time, although Paxton always maintained his connection with Chatsworth, his interests had broadened into railways, newspapers and parliament. It was through another useful contact, an MP he met in the House called Ellis, that he became involved in the Great Exhibition. Ellis was bemoaning the shortcomings of the new Chamber, where the ventilation system failed to ventilate and the acoustics ensured that nobody heard a word, when Paxton mentioned he had an idea for the Great Exhibition building which would remove such problems. There was already a design in existence, very traditional and very boring, but Ellis dropped a word in the right ears and Paxton found himself with nine days to produce drawings for an alternative.

Paxton had no architectural training, and started off with a sketch he doodled on a piece of blotting paper during a meeting of one of his railway committees. Working night and day for a week, he transformed the sketch into more formal drawings and took them to London by train from Derbyshire. On the way he had another serendipitous encounter, this time with Robert Stephenson, who was on the Royal Commission which was staging the Great Exhibition. By the time they got to London he had convinced him that his drawings would work.

INSIDE THE ENORMOUS GLASSHOUSE WHICH PAXTON BUILT TO HOUSE THE GREAT EXHIBITION OF 1851. 'PUNCH' COINED A NAME FOR IT: THE CRYSTAL PALACE.

It took six more weeks of negotiation, but with Stephenson now on his side, Paxton's design was adopted. Essentially it was an enormous glasshouse covering eighteen acres, the walls and roof made of glass held together by bands of cast iron. When it was still touch and go, Paxton leaked the design to the *Illustrated London News*, pointing out that when the exhibition was over it could be dismantled quickly and easily to provide valuable scrap or be used elsewhere, thus recouping some of the expense. Public opinion swung behind him, *Punch* coined the title 'The Crystal Palace', and Paxton's most eccentric creation took its place in history.

However, my favourite folly-phile must be 'MAD JACK' FULLER, who was quite as sane as the rest of us and a lot saner than some of his critics, but he did have some very odd ideas. There are a couple of parallels between 'Mad Jack' and that other eccentric builder of the nineteenth century, William Bentinck, Duke of Portland.

Both of them were, for a time, Members of Parliament. The Duke, before he succeeded to the title, was MP for King's Lynn from 1824 to 1826; Jack Fuller was MP for his area of Sussex from 1801 to 1812. Both of them were reluctant to accept honours, though for very different reasons; the Duke twice declined the Order of the Bath because he did not fancy the journey to London, Fuller turned down a peerage because 'I was born Jack Fuller, and Jack Fuller I'll die'. I am not sure whether they were both born eccentric, or whether their years in Parliament made them that way, but Jack Fuller was already a very outspoken character and made a lasting impact on the House when he referred to the Speaker as 'the insignificant little fellow in the wig'; the Duke of Portland, on the other hand, seems to have said nothing much at all.

Fuller was in fact a hearty, twenty-two-stone extrovert, while the Duke was an aristocratic recluse, but one quality they did share, if stories are to be believed – they were both philanthropic as well as eccentric. The Duke is said to have undertaken his excavations at Welbeck Abbey to give work to the locals, while Fuller is supposed to have built the massive stone wall around his estate for the same reason, and he may have built some of his follies with that in mind too. It could certainly be true of the Brightling Needle, the sixty-five-foot obelisk he erected on Brightling Down, which serves as a landmark but not much else, and of the gloomy tower from which he is supposed to have watched the construction of the railway line to Hastings – except that he died before it was built. But there was sound reasoning as well as philanthropy behind two of his best known follies, the cone-shaped Sugar Loaf at Dallington, and the pyramid in Brightling churchyard.

The Sugar Loaf was built because of a bet with a neighbour. Fuller maintained that he could see the spire of Dallington church from his home at Rose Hill. In fact the church lay in a valley and was quite out of sight – so 'Mad Jack' had the forty-foot cone hastily erected to look like a church spire just peeping over the hill. The records differ as to whether the neighbour was taken in, but I rather hope so. It would be nice to think of somebody being fooled by a folly.

The twenty-five-foot pyramid in the churchyard is Fuller's mausoleum. He had it designed by Sir Robert Smirke, who built the British Museum, but to the layman it looks like just another pyramid, somewhat out of place in such a very English setting, as it looms rather ominously over the tombstones. But Jack Fuller wanted it big enough for him to be buried in it sitting upright at a table, wearing a top hat and holding a bottle of claret, with a roast chicken in front of him on the table. It was a typical pose for the genial squire, and I wish we could be certain that the corpse was duly installed in this fashion, but it was recorded in Alec Parks' book, *The Fullers Progress*, that 'folk with nothing better to do finally arranged to open his burial place, hoping to find a skeleton with an unopened bottle before it. I am quite glad they were disappointed'. I can't agree with Mr Parks – it rather spoils

THE BRIGHTLING NEEDLE, ONE OF 'MAD JACK' FULLER'S LITTLE WHIMSIES – SIXTY-FIVE FEET OF POINTED POINTLESSNESS.

the story. I hope that at least 'the folk with nothing better to do' cut their feet on the broken glass which Jack Fuller wanted to have strewn around him, to keep away the Devil . . .

There is another popular story that, in order to get permission from the rector to erect the pyramid, 'Mad Jack' agreed to move the pub opposite the church to another site half a mile away. There is indeed a Fuller's Arms some way from the church, but according to the parish records he got the rector's approval for the pyramid by paying for a new stone wall round the churchyard with a smart new gate between stone pillars.

Jack Fuller's final folly, his pyramid mausoleum in Brightling churchyard.

The Freston Tower, a vertical one-pupil academy

However it may have happened, and whatever was put inside it, the pyramid is undoubtedly there, and I trust that Jack Fuller is enjoying a bottle of heavenly claret somewhere above us, safe from the much more dangerous follies of twentieth-century mankind.

Finally there is the eccentric builder who erected, not exactly a folly, not exactly living accommodation, but something which combined the two. In 1549 **William Latimer** built a six-storey brick tower on his estate in Suffolk, overlooking the Orwell estuary, for the educational benefit of his daughter Ellen. In this one-pupil vertical academy she was taught a different subject on a different floor each day. She spent Mondays on the ground floor pondering the virtues of charity. Or could it have been chastity? On such an isolated site that would seem more appropriate. Tuesday was tapestry on the first floor, Wednesday was music on the second, Thursday was classics on the third, Friday was English literature on the fourth, Saturday was more relaxing with a little painting on the fifth, and finally on Sunday she studied astronomy on the roof.

We know very little about William Latimer. The family left shields in the parish church, and that's about it. But he deserves a place in the history of eccentric builders, because according to those who ought to know, he created the earliest English folly. In my view it is not a genuine folly because there was actually a practical use for it, albeit a rather odd one, but it could well have been that his Freston Tower gave everyone else the idea, in which case Mr Latimer has a lot to answer for. I hope 'Mad Jack' Fuller is not sharing his claret with him.

IN ECCENTRIUM MEMORIAM

and it's goodbye from him

Death, or the imminent prospect of it, not only concentrates the mind wonderfully, it can also bring out the hidden eccentric in us. A surprising number of people who led fairly normal lives have managed to surprise their friends and relatives after their deaths. Sometimes it was the manner in which they wished to be buried, (as in the case of 'Mad Jack' Fuller in the previous chapter), sometimes it was a bequest in their will, sometimes it was the epitaph they wrote for their tombstones. Always they made sure they had the last laugh.

Epitaphs written in the first person are not necessarily written *by* the first person. Manifestly, for example, the two engine drivers who died in a train accident at Bromsgrove were not responsible for the metaphorical masterpiece which began:

My engine now is cold and still, No water does my boiler fill,
My coke affords its flames no more, My days of usefulness are o'er.

And can one really believe that any hearty eater, however hearty, could compose this cheerful farewell on a tombstone in Cambridge:

Here lies my corpse, who was the man
That loved a sop in the dripping pan,
But now believe me I am dead,
See here the pan stands at my head.

A little more believable, perhaps, is the gloomy comment in the churchyard at Lopham in Norfolk:

At three score winter's end I died, A cheerless being, sole and sad.
The nuptial knot I never tied – and wish my father never had.

Snuff buff Mrs Margaret Thompson asked for her coffin to be lined with her unwashed handkerchiefs, to remind her of happier, sneezier days. Her body was covered, not with flowers, but with the best Scotch snuff.

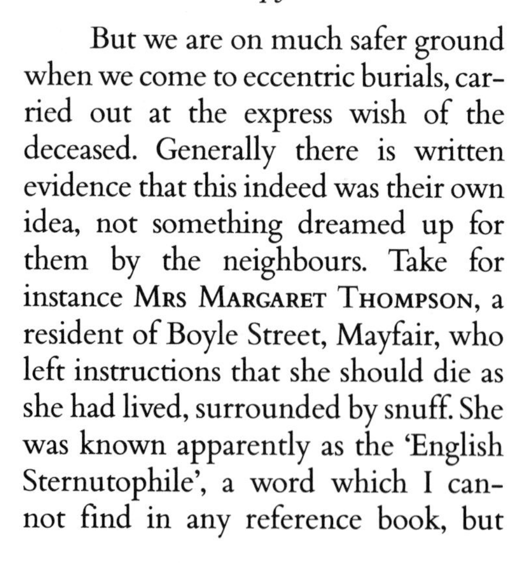

But we are on much safer ground when we come to eccentric burials, carried out at the express wish of the deceased. Generally there is written evidence that this indeed was their own idea, not something dreamed up for them by the neighbours. Take for instance **Mrs Margaret Thompson**, a resident of Boyle Street, Mayfair, who left instructions that she should die as she had lived, surrounded by snuff. She was known apparently as the 'English Sternutophile', a word which I cannot find in any reference book, but presumably refers to her passion for the sneezy stuff. The reference books also differ on dates. One says she died in 1776, another that she lived into the first half of the nineteenth century. But they are unanimous about the instructions she left for her funeral.

First her maid was instructed to line her coffin with all her unwashed handkerchiefs, either to surround her with memories of earlier sneezes, or for her use if she started sneezing again, because she also asked that, instead of flowers, her body be covered with the best Scotch snuff. While the body lay in the open casket there were instructions that no man should go near it – which perhaps was just as well, since the grieving mourners would probably have started sneezing too.

Mrs Thompson had thought of every detail for the funeral procession; it was going to be snuff, snuff and more snuff all the way. 'Six men to be my bearers, who are known to be the greatest snuff-takers in the parish of St James's, Westminster; instead of mourning, each to wear a snuff-coloured beaver hat which I desire to be bought for that purpose and given to them. Six maidens of my old acquaintance to bear my pall, each to wear a proper hood and to carry a box filled with the best Scotch snuff to take for their refreshment as they go along.

'Before my corpse, I desire the minister may be invited to walk and to take a certain quantity of the said snuff, not exceeding one pound, to whom also I bequeath five guineas on condition of his so doing. And I also desire my old and faithful servant Sarah Stuart to walk before the corpse, to distribute every twenty yards a large handful of Scotch snuff to the ground and upon the crowd who may possibly follow me to the burial place.'

For anyone who could not attend the actual funeral, she instructed that at least two bushels of snuff – could she really mean two sackfuls? – should be distributed outside her front door. After all that, I would like to think that Mrs Thompson's tombstone bore just one valedictory tribute: 'Atishoo!'

Miss Hannah Beswick of Cheetwood Hall, Manchester, did not depart this life so spectacularly or with such resounding finality. She was very wary about departing it at all, and when she did die in 1758 her body was preserved, on her instructions, for one hundred years; it became known as the Manchester Mummy.

According to old newspaper cuttings there were various theories about her long-delayed interment. One story was that her brother had displeased her by cutting down her favourite willow tree, and she thought that, so long as she remained unburied, he could not benefit from her will. Another suggested that

'THE MANCHESTER MUMMY', FIRST EMBALMED INSIDE A GRANDFATHER CLOCK-CASE, CONTINUED TO FEATURE IN THE MEDIA MANY YEARS LATER.

her doctor owed her a large sum of money which would have to be repaid once she was buried, so it was he who decided to embalm her instead. The generally accepted reason, however, was that another of her brothers had been mistakenly declared dead, and only showed signs of life as the coffin lid was being screwed down – he eventually recovered from what had been a deep trance. Miss Beswick was terrified that she might suffer a similar trance and not recover in time to escape from her coffin, so she wished to remain unburied, just in case.

She left her doctor a great deal of money – one report quoted £25,000, another said it was her entire estate – so long as he visited her regularly to see if she had revived. He cut down on travelling time by installing her embalmed body in his own house, concealed inside the case of a grandfather clock with a velvet curtain across the front, and for the next forty-five years, until he died himself, he dutifully drew aside the curtain each year on the anniversary of her death to make sure she was still well and truly dead.

Again the reports differ as to the precise location of his charge. One says it was placed outdoors on a flat leaded section of the roof, another that it stood at the top of the stairs. Wherever it was, the mummy could not have been too pretty a sight – apparently the body was embalmed with tar and swathed with bandages except for the face, which was left exposed so there was no impediment if it started breathing again. Nevertheless, after the doctor died it continued to be preserved in the Manchester Museum of Natural History, where according to a contemporary report 'it has long been an object of much popular interest'. In 1868 it was generally agreed, at long last, that Miss Beswick was definitely dead, and the Manchester Mummy was given a decent burial.

Not every eccentric embalmment takes place on the instructions of the deceased. During the time that Miss Beswick was occupying her doctor's clock-case, a MRS MARTIN VAN BUTCHELL was embalmed on the instructions of her husband.

THE BESWICK FAMILY AND THE MANCHESTER MUMMY.

(Query No. 431, August 8.)

[481] "Stalybridge" will find many particulars respecting the Manchester mummy and the Beswick family in the *Umpire* a few weeks ago.

L.

... ...

In briefly replying to the above query, I may inform "Stalybridge" that the matter is of deep interest to me, in that it refers to the Beswick family, to which I claim to belong. The Manchester mummy, which was exhibited in the Museum, Peter-street, Manchester, was Miss Beswick, a niece of my grandfather, Thomas Beswick, who died in Salford, November 28, 1866. With regard to the property, I may say that it is in dispute. I shall be pleased to correspond with any interested party regarding the above. I may say a gentleman in Manchester would be most willing to show the plans of the estate.

GEORGE BESWICK (late of Manchester).

Liverpool.

[Mr. J. Davenport, Bank Villas, Prestwich, and a correspondent from 4, Victoria Square, Newton Wood, would also be pleased to give to "Stalybridge" the information desired. EDITOR, N. & Q.]

Mr van Butchell was a London dentist with peculiar habits. He rode a white pony daubed with purple spots, and he had his name carved in foot-high marble letters over his surgery door, which these days might be thought a little unethical. He married twice, and each wife was told that all her clothes must be either white or black.

His first wife chose black, which perhaps was appropriate, since she died quite early. It would seem she had not been too happy about eccentricities like purple-spotted ponies, large

The Valley of the Shadow of Death does not normally feature in an ornamental garden, but JONATHAN TYERS chose this theme to create a most depressing stroll for his house guests at Denbies, his splendid country house near Dorking. What made it all the more unexpected was that Tyers was the plump and genial owner of one of London's most famous eighteenth-century pleasure gardens, the Spring Gardens at Vauxhall, where he had installed so many entertainments for the public that he became known as 'the master builder of delight'.

There was not much to delight in, however, when you entered the iron gates to his garden at Denbies. The gateposts gave you the first hint; they were in the shape of coffins, each surmounted by a human skull. One was supposed to be that of a famous highwayman, the other of a well-known courtesan. Tyers explained that they pointed a moral: man is all vanity and females are part vanity, part deceit. I am not sure I quite follow, but it *was* his garden. Once inside it you passed statues of a Christian and an unbeliever, both meeting particularly unpleasant deaths. The centrepiece of the garden was a small temple bearing an assortment of inscriptions, each one more depressing than the next.

Jonathan Tyers died in 1767, not in his Valley of Death but in his own bed. Denbies was sold, and the purchaser apparently took one look at the grisly gateposts, the macabre statues and the doom-laden temple, and did away with the lot. He is supposed to have described them as 'grave conceits'; I hope the pun was intentional.

marble name plaques and having to wear permanent mourning, because in her will she left her fortune to a distant relative, who was to receive it 'the moment I am dead and buried'. That phrase was seized upon by Mr van Butchell, who decided that although she was dead, she would never be buried, and he arranged for Dr Hunter, of Hunterian Museum fame, to embalm her corpse.

Then eccentricity took over. He fitted the embalmed body with glass eyes, dressed it in his wife's best clothes – black, of course – installed her in his drawing-room, and put her on show to the public for four hours every morning, six days a week. However long you may have had to wait at your dentist's, you can hardly have waited as long as Mrs van Butchell . . .

This went on until he remarried, when the second Mrs van Butchell – who incidentally chose to wear white – quite reasonably took exception to the continued presence of her predecessor and persuaded her husband to present the embalmed corpse to Dr Hunter for his museum. It remained there for 150 years and, unlike Miss Beswick, it never received a proper burial. The museum was bombed during the last war and Mrs van Butchell's remains were destroyed without trace.

Had she been more careful over the wording of her will, she might have made a speedier and more dignified departure. ERNEST DIGWEED, a retired Portsmouth schoolmaster, allowed no misinterpretation of the bequest he left in 1976, eccentric though it might be. He left £26,000 with the instruction: 'If during these eighty years the Lord Jesus Christ shall come to reign on earth, then the Public Trustees upon obtaining proof which shall satisfy them of His identity shall pay to the Lord Jesus Christ all the property which they hold on His behalf'. So far there has been no successful applicant for Mr Digweed's bequest; if none turns up by 2056, the money goes to the Exchequer.

Even when there is no delay in disposing of the deceased, as there was in Mrs van Butchell's case, there can be complications over what to do with the remains. Once cremation became popular the complications were greatly reduced; scattering ashes is a lot easier than coping with coffins, and it is fairly straightforward to dispose of the occasional urnful at sea, or on a favourite mountainside, or even in the herbaceous border. The brother of an old friend of mine asked that his ashes be consigned to the garden of his local pub and there was a moving, but not at all morbid, little ceremony at which his fellow regulars bade him an affectionate farewell.

When a coffin is involved, however, a distinct element of the macabre can creep in. There is for instance the last resting-place of one Henry Trigg, who was a grocer at Stevenage when it was still a pleasant little country town, long before the days of new-town developments, inter-city trains and the A1(M). Mr Trigg had a great fear of body-snatchers, a not uncommon hazard in eighteenth-century churchyards, and while some cautious folk merely asked for stout iron cages to be constructed over their graves to deter the robbers, Mr Trigg decided that the only safe place for his remains was in his barn — not buried in it, where they might be dug up, but wedged in the roof, so that it would take a full range of ladders, ropes and pulleys to steal them.

The coffin of Henry Trigg, perched in the rafters of his barn at Stevenage. It no longer contains Mr Trigg, but the National Westminster Bank, which now owns the barn, must regard it as one of their odder deposits.

To make sure his instructions were observed he warned his brother, who was his nearest relative, that he would not inherit the estate unless he was given this aerial resting-place, and when he died in 1724 his coffin was duly hauled up to the rafters. Sure enough, no grave-robber got anywhere near it, and a century later it was still perched there. However, the wooden coffin was beginning to rot away and there seemed a distinct danger that gravity would succeed where the grave-robbers had failed, and the remains of Mr Trigg would re-emerge. The coffin was therefore brought down to earth and replaced by a new one — which can still be seen in the barn roof — but it no longer contains the remains of Mr Trigg; I trust these have found a more orthodox resting-place elsewhere. The barn, incidentally, is now owned by the National Westminster Bank, which must consider the coffin to be one of its more eccentric deposits – though not without interest.

The Revd Langton Freeman, for some years Rector of Bilton in Warwickshire, left equally explicit instructions about the disposal of his remains. He had already established a reputation for eccentricity, mostly connected with his meanness. Having cadged a free night's lodging with a parishioner, he is said to have removed threads from the blankets to mend his clothes, and on a visit to his brother he stole a piece of ribbon to give to a lady friend, which his brother later spotted in her hair. His final directions about the disposal of his body, however, were not so much mean as just odd.

He died in 1783 at Whilton in Northamptonshire, where he had inherited the family estate and, presumably, no longer needed to unthread his host's blankets or pocket his brother's ribbons. He requested that for the first four or five days after his death, 'till my body grow offensive', it should remain in his bed. Then it should be carried into the garden – still on the bed – and put in the summer-house. The body was to be wrapped in a stout double winding-sheet 'as near as may be to the description we receive in Holy Scripture of our Saviour's burial' – but still on the bed. The door and windows of the summer-house were then to be locked and bolted, and surrounded first by evergreen trees, then by a fence made of iron or oak and painted dark blue.

The Revd Langton Freeman asked to be buried inside a summer-house in his garden – still lying on his bed.

The local paper, the *Northampton Mercury*, seems to have shown a curious lack of news judgment over this. It recorded all the charitable bequests in Mr Freeman's will but quite ignored this extraordinary clause, and there is no mention of his bizarre interment in any subsequent issue, but according to reliable local witnesses the instructions were obeyed to the letter, and Mr Freeman and his bed duly finished up in the summer-house. One hundred years later it was recorded that 'the fence and even the trees have now disappeared, and the summer-house is in ruins'. It added, however, that 'some years ago an entrance was effected through the roof, and the deceased was found completely mummified, without any wrappers, one arm lying down by the side, the other across the chest'. The bed, presumably, had disintegrated.

More recently the official records of Daventry Rural District Council confirmed the strange story of the body and the bed. They state that the summer-house still exists 'in which is buried the Revd Langton Freeman in his bed . . . He left thirty acres of land for the maintenance of himself in his bed in his summer-house'.

Eccentric last wishes are not always observed so meticulously. There is even a case where a whimsical epitaph written by the deceased was amended many years after his death because it offended the local Lady of the Manor. It can be found in the delightfully named Maggoty's Wood at Gawsworth, a few miles south of Macclesfield. The wood is named after Maggoty Johnson, who was born SAMUEL JOHNSON in 1691, but was a very different character from his pontificating namesake. He claimed to be one of the last paid jesters in England, providing entertainment for the Lord of the Manor of Gawsworth, Lord Harrington, and other country houses in the neighbourhood.

A SELF-PORTRAIT OF SAMUEL 'MAGGOTY' JOHNSON, PROBABLY THE LAST OF ENGLAND'S PROFESSIONAL JESTERS TO THE ARISTOCRACY. HE LIKED TO PLAY AT BEING AN ARISTOCRAT HIMSELF, AND ASSUMED THE TITLE OF LORD FLAME — EVEN ON HIS TOMBSTONE.

Johnson's official title was dancing-master, but his activities went a lot further than that. He was an accomplished singer and violinist, and a writer of satirical plays which he performed himself. His eccentricities came through in these plays, not least in their titles. His best-known, commissioned by the Duke of Montague as something of a practical joke, had the baffling title, *Hurlothrumbo*. It was quite fairly described by one critic as 'perhaps unrivalled in the English language for absurd bombast and turgid nonsense', but the Duke cracked it up as 'the most sublime effort of human genius', and it ran for fifty nights at the Haymarket Theatre in London before it dawned on the audiences that they were being had.

One of the characters in *Hurlothrumbo*, played by Johnson, was Lord Flame. He insisted on retaining the title in real life, and always behaved as if he merited the respect of a peer of the realm.

LORD FLAME'S TOMBSTONE IN MAGGOTY WOOD WITH THE EXTRA EPITAPH, ADDED ON THE INSTRUCTIONS OF A LATER LADY OF THE MANOR, WHO OBJECTED TO HIS ORIGINAL INSCRIPTION.

'MAGGOTY' JOHNSON ENJOYED PLAYING THE FIDDLE — IN MORE WAYS THAN ONE!

He did it so wittily that it all formed part of his stock-in-trade as a jester, and nobody seems to have objected – at least, not until after his death, when his final jest was to have 'Lord Flame' on his tombstone.

When he died in 1773 at the ripe age of eighty-two, he asked to be buried alone in the wood which was named after him. His remains were put in a simple brick tomb and covered with a stone slab, on which his farewell words were carved:

*Under this Stone rest the Remains of Mr Samuel Johnson,
Afterwards ennobled with the grander title of LORD FLAME
Who after being in his life distinct from other Men by the
Eccentricities of his Genius, Chose to retain the same
character after his Death.*

There followed a verse which contained a flowery tribute to his own brilliance, but it did explain why he wanted to be buried away from other people:

*Here, undisturbed, and hid from vulgar eyes, A wit, musician,
poet, player lies. A dancing-master, too, in grace he shone,
And all the arts of opera were his own. In comedy
well-skilled, he drew Lord Flame, Acted the part, and gave
himself the name. Averse to strife, how oft he'd gravely say,
These peaceful groves should shade his breathless clay; That
when he rose again, laid here alone, No friend and he
should quarrel for a bone; Thinking that were some old
lame gossip nigh, She possibly might take his leg or thigh.*

Those who knew him forgave this final extravagance, but it seems to have rankled over the years up at Gawsworth Hall. More than eighty years later the then Lady Harrington asked the curate to do something about it. Rather than obliterate the offending verse he added some extra lines on another stone, calculated to wipe the smile off anyone who might be amused by Maggoty Johnson's light-hearted farewell:

*If chance hath brought thee here, or curious eyes, To see a
spot where this poor jester lies, A thoughtless jester even in
his death, Uttering jibes beyond his latest breath, Look on
that stone and this: and ponder well; Then choose 'twixt
Life and Death, 'twixt Heaven and Hell.*

Having looked on that stone and this, I must say that if I had to choose 'twixt Maggoty Johnson and the curate, I'd go for Maggoty every time . . .

TECHNICENTRICS

mad inventors
or genuine geniuses?

'Inventors,' wrote Dostoevsky with his usual gloominess, 'have almost always been regarded as fools at the beginning of their careers – and very often at the end of them.' For once, he is putting it mildly. They have just as often been considered quite mad, or at the very least, highly eccentric. And so they should be; it takes a special kind of mind to invent things, and it is not surprising that inventors should be a little odd. I have been looking for some whose own life-styles were as unusual as their inventions.

Ever since Icarus tried to fly across the Aegean Sea, and the sun melted the wax that held his wings together, inventors have been trying to find a foolproof way to fly. Judging by the number of air accidents that still occur, they have yet to succeed, but at least their modern devices stay in the air for most of the time. In the days of THOMAS THORNEYCROFT they were still at the stage of strapping on wings and jumping off roofs, and 'Colonel Tom', as he was known around Wolverhampton in the last century, was into the wings routine too. Very wisely, however, he arranged that it was not he but his butler who did the jumping. The butler made a crash landing in the rhododendron bushes and Colonel Tom turned his attention to more grandiose inventions.

At his splendid mansion, Tettenhall Towers, he built a theatre-cum-ballroom for which he devised a sprung floor, a fireplace with a mechanically induced draught that produced flames ten feet high, a stage with a waterfall, a fountain and a

TETTENHALL TOWERS, PALATIAL HOME OF 'COLONEL TOM' THORNEYCROFT, WHO INVENTED A PAIR OF WINGS TO FLY OFF THE ROOF WITH, BUT WISELY TRIED THEM OUT FIRST ON THE BUTLER. THE BUTLER SURVIVED A CRASH LANDING IN THE RHODODENDRON BUSHES, AND COLONEL TOM TURNED HIS INVENTIVE TALENTS ELSEWHERE.

Colonel Tom's ballroom at Tettenhall Towers, equipped with a grandiose fireplace he designed himself. A mechanically-induced draught was able to produce flames ten feet high (above).

running stream, and 'a movable mechanical panorama of the American Civil War'. He rigged up a telegraphic link between the dining-room on the ground floor and his smoking-room up in one of the towers, to communicate more easily with his no-longer-airborne butler, and on top of the tower he installed 'a flashing apparatus, like the one used in Zululand' – though I have no idea what good this was to the Zulus, or indeed to Colonel Tom.

Many of his inventions were for domestic use, like the heated shoe-case for drying out footwear, and the douche-bath for treating sluggish livers – a sort of early jacuzzi. He also argued that kitchens should be situated above the dining-room, so the cooking smells did not reach the diners. That idea never caught on, but his method of linking the two by rope-lift did develop into the 'dumb-waiter', which became popular in many Victorian homes where the kitchen was not sited above the dining-room but below it.

Colonel Tom was a great believer in the benefits of fresh air. Tettenhall Towers had about sixty ventilators of assorted designs, but his ideas went far beyond that. He had a plan for piping fresh air to London from the coast and delivering it to every home. It

The stage in Colonel Tom's ballroom was equipped with a waterfall, a fountain and a running stream. When the house became a boys' school it was thought wise to remove them.

How to make the most of your hot bath water — a must in any dressing room. Colonel Tom made use of his boot, shoe and sock dryer for more than twenty years.

would be measured by fresh air meters, on the same principle as gas meters. He actually tried to form a Fresh Air Joint Stock Company in 1866, and was probably quite surprised when nobody bought shares.

He also failed to convince the city fathers of Shrewsbury that they should dam the River Severn to create 'the Henley of the Midlands', but he had slightly better luck with an idea for equipping battleships with steam jets to repel unwanted callers. It was tried out by the navy at Shoeburyness, but they must have decided it would be simpler just to shoot people instead. It was left to later generations to develop the water-cannon, which used the same principle as Colonel Tom's steam jets, without needing a boiler.

As well as producing inventions he also produced children, nine altogether — 'thirty feet of boys and quite twenty-one feet of girls' — as he put it. He used his theatre-ballroom for spectacular parties at which he staged his own plays and recited his own poetry. The parties were a great success; the plays and poems, one gathers, rather less so. But that was only one of his recreations. He took up ballooning when he was sixty, he was riding to hounds when he was eighty, and shortly before his death in 1903 he was still driving his coach-and-four around the streets of Wolverhampton.

His ballooning led to one more unlikely invention. During one flight he found himself being drawn down into his own iron-smelting furnace. With great difficulty he manoeuvred the balloon to safety, then went off and invented a special kind of fan which could steer the balloon away from such hazards in the future. It may be a measure of its success that no balloonist is known to have fallen into a smelting furnace ever since.

It turned out that 1822 was a vintage year for eccentric inventors. It saw the birth of Colonel Tom and also of SIR FRANCIS GALTON, distinguished scientist, enthusiastic statistician, founder of intelligence tests, fingerprinting and the science of eugenics, and regarded almost as highly by the other Fellows of the Royal Society as his cousin, Charles Darwin; yet he was also the man who invented a pocket counting device for recording the number of pretty women he met in the streets, who carried a brick wrapped in brown paper on the end of a rope so that he could lower it to the ground and stand on it to see over crowds, and who installed a warning signal in his house to let his guests know when the lavatory was engaged. 'It saves a futile climb upstairs,' he explained, 'and the occupant is not subjected to the embarrassment of having the door handle rattled.'

COLONEL TOM'S BALLOON WAS NEARLY SUCKED DOWN INTO THE FURNACE AT HIS OWN IRONWORKS — SO HE INVENTED A SPECIAL FAN TO STEER IT MORE ACCURATELY.

His reason for counting pretty women was rather more obscure. He wanted to draw up what he called a 'Beauty Map of Britain', and after many weeks of research in various towns throughout the country he produced the information that London had the highest proportion of beautiful women, and Aberdeen the lowest. It is difficult to see what this achieved, apart from making him very unpopular in Aberdeen, but with Sir Francis it was presumably the statistics that mattered, rather than what they might be used for.

Similarly he made surveys with his pocket counter of the number of people with blue eyes or fair hair, or both, long before the Nazis developed their theory of an Aryan master race. From studying reports of legal proceedings in different countries he worked out which of them had the highest level of honesty; he concluded that the most reliable witnesses were British, while 'the centry of gravity for lying,' as he put it, was situated in Greece. This no doubt made him as popular with the Greeks as he already was with the Aberdonians.

But his most eccentric survey involved measuring the size of African ladies' bottoms. His motives were entirely scientific; he wanted to find out the genetic reasons why Hottentot women had the biggest backsides. Nevertheless even Sir Francis appreciated that if he tried to place a tape-measure round this area of their anatomies it might be misconstrued, so he had the ingenious idea of surveying them from a distance with a sextant, and working out their measurements from that. This apparently proved perfectly acceptable to the ladies concerned – they no doubt considered him dotty, but inoffensive.

Sir Francis' passion for statistics led him down strange paths and produced some more odd inventions. He decided, for instance, to work out the boredom factor in lectures by measuring the movements of the audience's heads. He had noted that when a person was paying attention his head remained still, but when he was bored he let his head droop or even roll about. So Sir Francis invented an inclination-gauge to record the drooping and rolling about. Unfortunately this proved impractical, because the audience took more interest in the gauge than the lecture, and remained permanently rigid. Undeterred, Sir Francis made use of his faithful pocket counter again to record how many times they fidgetted, timed not by the hour or the minute but by the number of his own heartbeats – another example of his discretion, since he did not want to be seen studying his watch.

Sir Francis Galton (below) carried out a survey of African ladies' bottoms to find out why Hottentots had the biggest backsides – but he did it from a safe distance, with the help of a sextant.

Much more ingenious was his method of judging his guests' reactions to each other at dinner parties. He worked on the assumption that, if people were inclined towards one another, then they literally inclined - they leaned together. If they were indifferent they remained upright, and if they positively disliked each other then they leaned away. So he fitted pressure drums underneath the legs of their chairs, and was able to work out afterwards who got along best with whom. Most hosts, I imagine, could discover this more simply by looking round the dinner table and seeing who was chatting, who was dozing, and who was just plain bored, but Sir Francis liked to be scientific about his guest lists, as in everything else.

Like Colonel Tom, he made an attempt at winged flight; he invented a steam flying machine when he was only eleven, but one gathers he fared no better than the colonel's butler. Again like

Colonel Tom he was keen on proper ventilations, and applied the principle to his hat. After working hard for his degree at Cambridge he decided he had 'sprained his brain' by overheating it, so he inserted tiny shutters in his hat to cool it down. The shutters were operated by pressing a bulb on the end of a rubber tube. With his customary discretion he no doubt kept the bulb out of sight in his pocket, but passers-by could hardly miss the tube hanging down from his hat, nor the opening and closing of the shutters. It might well have been appropriate if tiny cuckoos had emerged . . .

Sir Francis wrote many learned treatises as the result of his unorthodox research, most of which could only be digested by his fellow scientists, but he did produce a bestseller which ran to five editions and was nearly adopted by the British Army as a standard manual. It was his *Art of Travel*, which was packed with useful tips on how to survive in unfriendly territory – hence the Army's interest. But the tips were in many cases so bizarre that not even the Army could take them too seriously.

His recipe for avoiding blisters, for instance, was to break a raw egg into each boot to soften the leather, and fill one's socks with soapsuds for additional lubrication. To avoid lice, you should make little beads out of mercury, old tea leaves and spit, and string them in a necklace round your neck. Treacle and lime juice spread on the gums would stop your teeth falling out if you caught scurvy, and he had a very simple solution for keeping your clothes dry in a rainstorm – you take them off and sit on them. His most useful tip, perhaps, was how to persuade a horse to cross a river if it objects to entering the water. You lead it along the river bank until it thinks you have given up the idea, and while it is congratulating

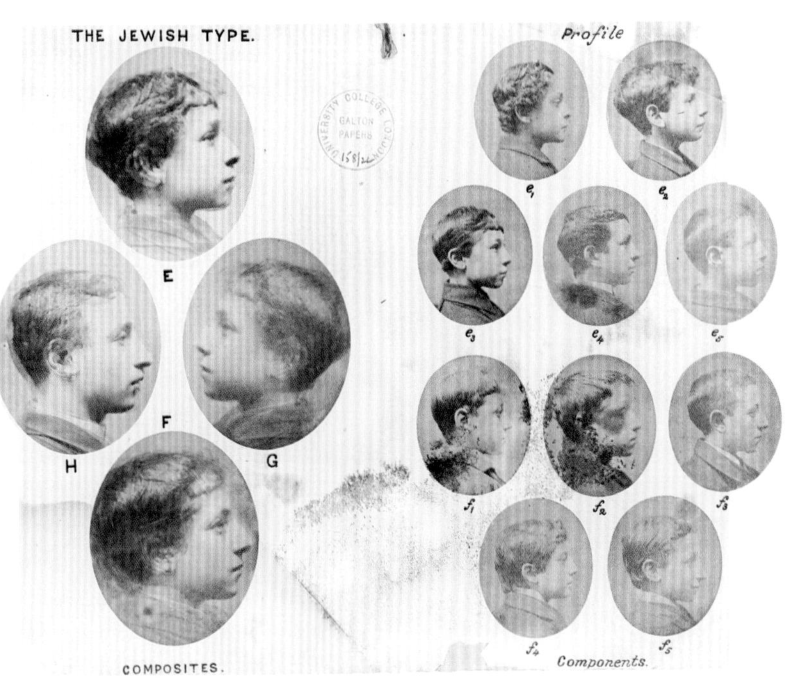

NOT ALL OF SIR FRANCIS' EXPERIMENTS WERE AS BIZARRE AS MEASURING BOTTOMS OR DRAWING UP A 'BEAUTY MAP OF BRITAIN'. HE WAS A PIONEER OF IDENTIFYING FINGERPRINTS AND CREATING COMPOSITE PHOTOGRAPHS.

itself you take it unawares amidships and shove it in. Then leap in after it, grab it by the tail, and keep splashing water in its face until it goes in the right direction . . .

Sir Francis made a variety of enemies in the course of his unorthodox investigations. He fell out with Gladstone, for instance, over his research into the size and shape of human heads. The Prime Minister was very proud of the nobility of his skull, and challenged him to find a nobler one. Sir Francis, having duly measured it, advised him there was nothing exceptional about it at all, and indeed his own head was far superior to it. He also upset the authorities at London Zoo when he tried out an ultrasonic whistle he had invented to test the limits of hearing among different species – he nearly started a stampede. But most of all he antagonised the Church with his statistical analysis of the power of prayer. If clergy really believed what they preached, he argued, they would not put lightning conductors on their churches; and he pointed out that, although the well-being and continued good health of monarchs was constantly prayed for by their loyal subjects, on average they died earlier than other folk for whom nobody prayed at all.

He eventually demonstrated this last point himself. He lived until he was eighty-nine, seven years longer than that most long-lived of monarchs, Queen Victoria, whose reign he saw commence and close.

JOHN GAINSBOROUGH, WHO WAS NOT AS GOOD AT INVENTING AS HIS BROTHER THOMAS WAS AT PAINTING, DID MANAGE TO PRODUCE A SELF-ROCKING CRADLE AND A MECHANICAL SINGING CUCKOO.

JOHN GAINSBOROUGH was experimenting with wings a century ahead of Sir Francis and Colonel Tom, and he too had little success. In fact he was probably the most unsuccessful inventor ever to get into the reference books, but this was because he was the elder brother of Thomas Gainsborough, and the artist's biographers gave John a mention just to provide an unkind comparison. John was bursting with good ideas for inventions, but never got around to finishing one before another took his fancy. 'Curse it,' he once explained, 'some little thing was wrong with it. If I had but gone on with it I am sure I should have succeeded, but a new scheme came across me.'

One can sympathise with his failure to fly – much cleverer men than he were still failing, long after he had gained his wings, one hopes, in the hereafter. But it is sad that his only inventions which actually worked were a self-rocking cradle and a mechanical singing cuckoo.

When John Gainsborough's unsuccessful attempts as an inventor got him into debt he took a leaf out of brother Thomas' book and did a spot of painting, in this case on the wall of the White Hart at Nayland. He also tried his hand as a watchmaker, but that business failed too, leaving only the shop sign which hung over the door.

John was trying his hand at mechanical gadgets when he was still at Sudbury Grammar School in the 1720s, and it seemed logical that when he left he would go into the watchmaking business. But he fared no better at watchmaking than at making anything else. In 1743 an announcement appeared in the *Ipswich Journal*: 'Whereas John Gainsborough junior, late of Sudbury, watchmaker, did lately set up the watchmaking business at Beccles, but has greatly abused the interest of his friends, and carried off goods and effects given him in trust; these are to apprise all persons to whom he may offer any watch to sale or pawn, to stop the watch and give notice of the same to Mr Tho Utting, watchmaker, in Yarmouth, or to Mr Thomas Tingey of Beccles, and they shall be paid for their trouble'.

Perhaps it was this unfortunate situation which earned John the nickname of 'Scheming Jack', or it may have been because of his constant efforts to raise money to finance his inventions. It did not help that he liked to work in brass, not the cheapest of materials, and Thomas Gainsborough's first biographer, Philip Thicknesse, records how he

John Gainsborough's much earlier equivalent of Richard Dimbleby's bogus 'spaghetti forest' — an apple-dumpling tree. He managed to cook the apples while they were still hanging on the branches.

was invited to visit brother John, who tried to borrow two guineas off him to buy more brass for his latest gadget. 'I told him I had not capacity to conceive the genius of his unfinish'd work,' wrote Thicknesse coldly, 'and I took my leave of this very eccentric and unfortunate man without giving him the two guineas he solicited.'

So the hapless Scheming Jack was the black sheep of the Gainsborough family. The third brother, Humphrey, also liked inventing things, but went into the ministry and made a much better go of that. But I can't help feeling a certain affinity with John, if only for an early idea he had which did actually work, though it hardly qualified as an invention in the usual sense. As an April fool jape, however, it was in the same league as Richard Dimbleby's famous spaghetti forest. As a boy, young John went into a local orchard, selected an apple tree and coated every apple on it with dough. Then he managed to cook each apple as it hung on the tree by holding a saucepan of water so the apple floated in it, and with his other hand holding a chafing dish underneath to heat the water.

When he had cooked all the apples in this way, he brought a neighbour to see the result. The neighbour, understandably, asked him what it was all about. 'This,' said young Gainsborough, 'is an apple-dumpling tree.'

Jeremy Bentham was another eccentric inventor who never seemed to finish an invention — at least not in his own lifetime, but one or two did materialise in a slightly different form many years later. He devised, for instance, a 'conversation tube' which could be laid between buildings on the same principle as a water-pipe, and it conveyed voices instead of water. Nobody could hear the voice at the other end, but 200 years later we got around to inventing the telephone.

He built a 'frigidarium' in his garden for storing food. It may not have been the first eighteenth-century ice-house, but it was certainly the first to bear that name which was to be taken up in due course by a fridge manufacturer two centuries later. And the most striking of his glimpses into the future was the 'panopticon', a design for a prison like the spokes of a wheel, with the control room at the hub. He was deeply interested in prison reform and spent many years trying to get the panopticon accepted by the authorities, but again it was long after his death that the idea at last caught on.

Bentham followed up his frigidarium and panopticon by inventing an entire new language, creating words to describe things more accurately. This time he had some success, though the words were not always attractive and can still grate on the purists. It was Bentham who devised 'codify' and 'maximise', which I am not too fond of, but I cannot quarrel with 'international'. However he was on a losing wicket with the word he invented as a collective noun for England, Scotland and Ireland. 'Brithibernia' never got off the ground . . .

Jeremy was an infant prodigy who taught himself to read before he was three, went to Oxford at twelve and got his degree when he was fifteen. He became a law student, and his father confidently expected him to become the youngest Lord Chancellor in history, but instead he became one of the great law reformers and thinkers of his time, and certainly the most prolific. He invariably wrote fifteen pages of philosophical thought every day, and when his thoughts came too fast to be set down in detail he would scribble notes and pin them to the curtains until he had time to expand them. Perhaps because of his speed of thought, his handwriting was quite appalling, and although eleven volumes of his work have been published, there remains a vast quantity of manuscripts which the experts are still struggling to decipher.

THE EMBALMED FIGURE OF JEREMY BENTHAM, WHO BELIEVED THIS WAS A BETTER WAY OF PRESERVING THE MEMORY OF THE DECEASED THAN PUTTING UP A STATUE.

All this mental effort did not detract from his physical fitness. He was still playing badminton when he was seventy-five, and his biographer says that he reversed the usual course of development – he was born old and grew young. But he did develop little eccentricities as the years went by. He conferred a knighthood on his cat, and let it be known that it should be addressed as 'Sir John Langborn'. In later years he ordained it as well, calling it 'The Revd Doctor Sir John Langborn', and when this distinguished feline died he gave it a full-scale funeral in his garden.

Bentham also devised names for his household equipment. His walking-stick was called 'Dapple', and he addressed the teapot as 'Dick'. But I suppose that these days, when otherwise quite sensible people give the most ridiculous names to their cars, this would not be regarded as odd at all.

His final eccentricity was put into effect after his death. He took the view that to preserve an illustrious person for posterity, it was not necessary to commission a statue; the person himself should be embalmed and put on display. Alternatively, instead of hanging a portrait on the wall as a reminder, the actual head of the deceased could be preserved on a shelf – 'many generations could be deposited on a few shelves, in a moderate-sized cupboard'. In larger establishments, where perhaps the squire would normally plant a row of trees alongside the drive, Bentham suggested planting embalmed members of the family instead. 'Varnish would protect the faces from the effects of rain.'

He directed that his own body should first be dissected by medical students as an aid to research, then the remnants should be embalmed, dressed in his old Quaker coat and his broad-brimmed yellow straw hat, and put in a glass case with his faithful walking-stick, 'Dapple', in his hand. These wishes were followed by his physician, Dr Southwood Smith, except that his head was replaced by a wax replica, as apparently the embalming process gave him a very peculiar expression.

The doctor kept the glass case containing Jeremy Bentham until he died in 1850, when it was left to University College, London, where Bentham had been a governor. For some years the deceased was a regular attender at meetings of the College Council; these days he only appears at the annual Bentham dinner.

One of his admirers in recent years was CHARLES KAY OGDEN, another brilliant linguist and philosopher, who followed up his ideas for a new language by inventing 'Basic English', a simplified version using only 850 words. It fared slightly better than Bentham's 'Brithibernia' and the like; Winston Churchill advocated Basic English as the international tongue when he spoke at Harvard in 1943, and the British Government backed it up with financial support after the war, but it finally succumbed in 1953.

Ogden showed all the right symptoms of an eccentric inventor. At Cambridge he smoked an imitation cigarette with a red bulb on the end. He considered fresh air was harmful and used an 'ozone machine' in his flat instead of opening the windows. As he grew older he kept a coffin handy in the front hall. He liked to collect almost anything; at one stage he had eighty-two family bibles, forty-two pairs of shoes and an assortment of mechanical birds, one of which burst into song if addressed in Basic English.

THE PREMISES OF THE CAMBRIDGE MAGAZINE, WHICH CHARLES KAY OGDEN EDITED DURING THE FIRST WORLD WAR. THE BUILDING IS NOW APPARENTLY A 'PERFECT SETTING' — EXCEPT FOR THAT AWFUL LAMP-POST . . .

He did not limit himself to this simplified language in the *Cambridge Magazine*, a controversial publication which he was editing at the outbreak of the First World War, and for which he obtained supplies of paper during the national shortage by purchasing large quantities of children's comics and pulping them. The magazine's views were distinctly anti-establishment. In a typical editorial he wrote: 'We hear there is a danger of undue pressure being brought to bear on Freshmen to join the Officers' Training Corps this term. We do not really believe that any college authorities would be so foolish as to jeopardise the chances of producing a really efficient body of officers by actions so illegal and unjustifiable'.

He still had unorthodox views about the Establishment thirty years later, when he fell out with officialdom over his Basic English proposals. He described his career in *Who's Who* at that time as '1946-48, bedevilled by officials'. Many of his sayings and writings have been lost, but two of his *bon mots* are well worth preserving. For the state of penury that he generally lived in, he invented the term, 'hand-to-mouth disease'; and he described a certain American university where sport took priority as 'a social and athletic institution, where opportunities of study are provided for the feeble-bodied'.

In spite of his failure to popularise his adaptation of the English language, Ogden did not forget his predecessor who helped to inspire it. It was at his suggestion that the embalmed figure of Jeremy Bentham, after one hundred years in its glass case, was given a clean set of underwear . . .

It is encouraging to find that, thanks to people like Charles Kay Ogden, the tradition of the eccentric inventor has continued into the twentieth century. Perhaps the finest example of the species in that period, in appearance and behaviour as well as inventiveness, was GEOFFREY NATHANIEL PYKE, the archetypal 'Professor Braynestawm' of the Second World War, whose ideas for defeating the enemy ranged from motorised sledges towing torpedoes to a battleship made of reinforced ice. Very few of them actually materialised, but his suggestions were a constant source of incredulity mixed with admiration and exasperation among the top brass in Combined Operations, headed by his friend Lord Mountbatten, who had him on his staff as a civilian adviser.

Lord Zuckerman was also on the staff at the time and described Pyke as 'not a scientist, but a man of a vivid and uncontrollable imagination, and a totally uninhibited tongue'. He disconcerted the generals by wearing a straggly beard, very shabby suits and no socks; and Lord Zuckerman records that this strange figure once met the Canadian Prime Minister, Mackenzie King, with his flies wide open, because he could not close the zip on the trousers he had just bought in Ottawa for the occasion. Before King could comment, Pyke told him sharply: 'Prime Minister, I would not have to present myself to you in this state were it not for the fact that Canadian engineers are totally inefficient!'

Geoffrey Pyke had quite a remarkable career, before he became involved in Combined Operations, dating back to the previous World War. When it started, he persuaded the *Daily Chronicle* that he had a plan for going to Berlin and sending back despatches for the paper. He somehow got there safely, but the Germans soon spotted him and nearly shot him as a spy. He managed to escape, and the *Daily Chronicle* built him into a public hero. He wrote a book and gave lectures, one of them at his old school, Wellington, where he had suffered more than his share of bullying as a youngster. He took some delight in telling the boys that, even during the worst moments of his imprisonment, he had never been as miserable as he was at school.

After the war he dabbled in the Stock Market, made an astonishing amount of money, and spent all of it on founding his own school, the complete antithesis of Wellington, where the pupils were never punished or reprimanded, or forced to learn any particular subjects; they were just encouraged to find things out for themselves. Surprisingly, it seemed to work, but Pyke lost his money as fast as he had made it, and the school had to close.

The Spanish Civil War first turned his inventive mind to matters martial. On behalf of the Spanish Loyalists he fitted motor cycles with side-cars which he designed both to carry hot food to the front, and to carry casualties back; and to save coal he invented a way of fitting bicycle pedals to shunting engines, though one imagines it took a powerful pair of legs to operate them. Perhaps the pedallers were the original 'Puffing Billies' . . .

The school founded by Geoffrey Pyke as the complete antithesis of Wellington, where he was utterly miserable. His pupils were never punished or reprimanded, or forced to learn; they were just encouraged to find things out for themselves. It seemed to work — until he ran out of money.

Just before the Second World War, Pyke decided he could discourage Hitler by taking a poll in Germany, to show him that most people wanted peace. Rightly assuming that Hitler might not approve, he persuaded a number of English students to go to Germany, equipped with a clipboard in one hand and a bag of golf clubs in the other, thinking this might baffle the secret police. His team of bogus golfers had hardly started their labours when the war started and they had to return hastily to England. This perhaps was just as well; the German secret police could hardly have missed them . . .

Once Pyke joined Combined Operations the ideas came thick and fast. To destroy the Romanian oilfields, for instance, he suggested sending in dogs carrying brandy, St Bernard-style, so the guards got drunk before the Commandos attacked. Or how about sending in women, to be even more distracting? When he

Heath Robinson started it, Rowland Emett continued it, and people like John Ward and Jake Mangol Wurzle have brought it up to date – the utterly dotty invention. Heath Robinson was a little before my time, but I remember an Emett machine which was commissioned by the General Post Office in 1962 to illustrate its various services. If you have never seen an Emett invention, this report I did for *Radio Newsreel* may give you the general idea:

'Emett sees the Post Office as a sort of magic carpet, a turtle-backed affair with waving wings and birdlike head, and at the rear, lying flat like a booster rocket, a fiery-tailed pillar box. Astride it a scientist bounces messages with a tennis raquet up to the satellites which circle overhead. One of these holds a little trainee satellite in a frilly skirt, preparing for her first orbit . . . Beneath the telegraph-pole which acts as a sort of mast, the captain of this craft has a telephone-box for a bridge. His crew are all manner of post office types, from a technician knitting an undersea cable (in cable stitch, no doubt) to a sub-postmistress selling a dog licence – to a dog.'

It would be difficult to beat this for inventive idiocy, but John Ward of Northamptonshire does his best. He calls himself a 'Junkist', and simply makes weird devices out of junk. His masterpiece is a kind of moon buggy made out of an old bed, some hair driers and vacuum cleaners, a linen basket, parts of a tumble-drier and a pram.

And Jake Mangol Wurzle? You will gather he invents silly names as well as silly machines, and his address is in the same mould: Wonderful Wurzle Lane, Peace Pond, Sally Nook, Huddersfield, Yorkshire Pudding. But what brings him into this chapter – and also brought him into court – was his motor bike, the Wonderful Wurzle Mark II. It had a fan on the front to repel pedestrians, a metal pole with an amber light on top to act as a lightning conductor, a line strung from it for his washing, and a basket on the back for his dog Manoyle. At St Alban's court a couple of years ago, Wurzle (aged fifty-two) pleaded not guilty to driving a dangerous vehicle on the M25. In defence he said the Wonderful Wurzle Mark II was perfectly road-worthy, and Manoyle was a safety-minded road user who always got out of his basket on the near side.

The magistrates must have had a soft spot for English eccentrics, or maybe they were a little eccentric themselves. The case was dismissed.

failed to get the dogs and brandy, let alone the women, he proposed the Commandos should dress up as Romanian firemen, and after the bombers had set fire to the oilwells they should turn out in replica fire-engines and spray the flames with water containing very small incendiary bombs. Combined Ops wouldn't buy that either.

Undeterred, Pyke turned his attention to the German occupying force in Norway. He invented a motorised sledge controlled by a man walking behind using long reins, so that if the sledge fell into a crevasse, the driver didn't – unless he forgot to let go of the reins. Unfortunately while walking behind the sledge the driver was completely exposed to enemy bullets, and most people preferred to ride in the sledge and take their chances with the crevasses . . .

Another of Pyke's sledges was designed to tow a torpedo. The plan was to drive the sledge up a slope with the torpedo tied behind, travelling slowly enough to tempt the Germans to give chase. Half-way up the slope the torpedo was released, so that it rolled back onto the Germans and blew them all up. As a further

Geoffrey Pyke's motorised sledge, controlled by long reins so that if it fell into a crevasse, the driver didn't – unless he failed to let go . . .

refinement, he suggested that to discourage the Germans from investigating the sledge when it was parked, a notice should be placed beside it saying: 'Officers' Latrine; for Colonels Only'.

Astonishingly, Pyke was authorised to go ahead, at least with the torpedo idea if not the latrine notice. He was sent to America to experiment with his sledges on the snow-covered slopes of the Rockies, thus providing a respite for his exhausted colleagues at Combined Ops. But their loss was the Americans' gain; it is difficult to know what amused them most, Pyke's torpedo-towing sledges or Pyke himself. But one gathers his disreputable appearance did not go down too well with the generals at the Pentagon, and maybe they failed to give his sledges a fair trial, but certainly not one of them was ever sent to Norway, with or without a latrine sign. But it was not the end of the motorised sledge; in due course the 'Weasel' played a vital part in polar exploration.

By far the most spectacular of Pyke's inventions was the good ship *Habbakuk*, an enormous aircraft-carrier half a mile long, with a hull thirty feet thick made entirely of reinforced ice. This material consisted of water mixed with wood shavings and frozen solid; it went under the name of 'Pykrete'. The idea was that *Habbakuk* would be fitted with freezing plants to keep it from melting, and although it would not break any speed records, its massive hull would be virtually impregnable.

THE GOOD ICE-SHIP 'HABBAKUK', HALF-A-MILE LONG WITH A HULL THIRTY FEET THICK, MADE ENTIRELY OF REINFORCED ICE. NOT EXACTLY SPEEDY, BUT VIRTUALLY UNSINKABLE.

Mountbatten loved it, so much so that it is said he rushed into Churchill's bathroom with a lump of Pykrete and dropped it into his hot bath water to prove it would not melt. He demonstrated its resistance to fire power in front of a group of generals by firing his revolver at it; the ricochet nearly hit him, and they needed no further convincing. A prototype *Habbakuk* was built on a Canadian lake, and Pyke's ice-ship might well have led the Allied troops across the Channel for the invasion of Europe – except that by the time it was ready they had already landed. The *Habbakuk* was never put to use, and like so many of Pykes' brainwaves, it sank without trace.

After the war he continued to dream up ideas for developing the Third World, for staffing the National Health Service, for reforming the education system, and for generally putting the world to rights. Still he could find nothing that seemed to work, and the years of mockery and frustration eventually became too much for him. As Lord Zuckerman put it: 'he was overwhelmed by the fantasies that he created'. In 1948, when he was still only fifty-four, he had his last eccentric idea. He shaved off his beard, bade farewell to an unappreciative world, and swallowed a bottle of sleeping pills.

And this time, it worked.

Anything further removed from the 'Professor Braynestawm' image of Geoffrey Pyke than the down-to-earth Yorkshireman PERCY SHAW it would be difficult to imagine, but Mr Shaw was also eccentric and he was also an inventor – not so prolific as Pyke, but spectacularly more successful. His early years were unremarkable; his father was a dyer's labourer in Halifax, and he started work when he was thirteen, carrying bobbins of wool in a blanket mill. He tried his hand at welding, boiler-making and constructing machine tools, inventing several little gadgets along the way which never came to much. He had his first success when he went into the road-making business and invented a mechanical pavement roller, incorporating an old car engine, two radiators, a steering column, and three solid-tyred lorry wheels. The idea soon caught on, but it was not a road roller that made him world-famous, it was what he put on the road itself.

THE SIMPLE INVENTION WHICH SAVED THOUSANDS OF LIVES AND MADE PERCY SHAW A MILLIONAIRE MANY TIMES OVER – THE CAT'S-EYE.

The story goes that Percy Shaw was driving from Bradford to Halifax one foggy night, along a road with a sheer drop on one side. Usually he had no difficulty in seeing his way, even in fog, because the steel tramlines shone in his headlights and he could follow them down the road. But on this night the lines had been

When Percy Shaw's workshop was developed into a sprawling factory he insisted that the sycamore tree he climbed as a boy should not be cut down. It still grows through the factory roof.

taken up for repair. He drove with great caution, knowing that a mistake could put him over the edge, but he was actually heading straight for the frail fence guarding the drop when his headlamps picked up two points of light; they were the eyes of a black cat sitting on a fence-post.

Mr Shaw survived, and so did the cat's eyes, millions and millions of them, in the form of reflectors sunk in the road surface. They are used now in virtually every country in the world, and they have saved untold thousands of lives.

Percy Shaw made his first cat's-eye in 1934; it was not long before he was turning out thirty thousand a week. It was estimated he made eleven million pounds in the process, and of course this wealth brought changes to the life of the former mill-lad – but in an unusual way. He continued to live in the same house all his life, refusing to have curtains in the windows because they obstructed the view, and with no carpets on the floor because they attracted tobacco ash. But with his millions he treated himself to three television sets, which were all kept on permanently, tuned to different channels.

His only real extravagance was a custom-built Rolls Royce with an electrically-operated petrol cap and seats, a fitted cocktail cabinet, and reading lamps at the back and front. But he never travelled very far in it, because he always maintained that he could find everything he wanted in his native Yorkshire. Probably the longest journey he made was to London to receive his OBE.

Percy Shaw was not only sentimental about Yorkshire, but also about his own early days in it. Next to his house was the old stable-workshop where he helped his father with odd jobs, and where he made his first cat's-eye, using tools he invented himself. When the business began to build up, the workshop had to expand, and in due course a substantial factory was built on the site. But next to the workshop was a sycamore tree which he used to climb as a lad, and he refused to let it be felled. The factory was actually built around it, and the sycamore continued to flourish, its upper branches poking out of the factory roof in the heart of a twenty-acre industrial site.

Percy Shaw died in 1976. His monument is not exactly all around you, but it lies ahead of you every time you get behind the wheel. If he had fancied having a sycamore tree growing through every factory roof in Halifax, a couple of dozen television sets to pick up every satellite channel, and a whole fleet of custom-built Rolls Royces, I reckon he deserved them all.

YUKKICENTRICS

if it moves, eat it

'I always maintained that the taste of mole was the most repulsive I knew – until I ate a bluebottle.' Thus stated Dr William Buckland, Dean of Westminster, first Professor of Geology at Oxford, and eccentric gourmet. He would eat almost anything that used to move. Dinner guests might find themselves confronted with a baked hedgehog or a crocodile steak; if they had a choice they were wise to plump for the hedgehog – crocodile is apparently very tough indeed.

The most gruesome story of his very catholic taste in food involved his friend Edward Harcourt, Archbishop of York, who had been in Paris during the French Revolution and acquired what was said to be the heart of Louis XIV, plundered from his tomb. The heart must have shrunk considerably since its operational days, because the Archbishop is reported to have kept it in a snuff-box. He was rash enough to show it to William Buckland, who exclaimed: 'I have eaten many things, but never the heart of a king' – and forthwith rectified the omission by swallowing it whole.

He used his unique knowledge of unlikely foodstuffs in all manner of equally unlikely ways. When he got lost on a nighttime journey to London he is reputed to have got off his horse, picked up a handful of earth, smelt it and tasted it, and announced calmly: 'Uxbridge'. And on a visit to a shrine where it was claimed that the fresh blood of a martyr could be found on

This drawing was sent to Frank Buckland as a valentine on February 14th, 1863. It portrays him sitting in the window of 'The Field' magazine, giving an illustrated lecture on salmon hatching to a bewildered gathering of passers-by. The snake being offered a frog on the left is, presumably, a reminder of Buckland's wider interests in the animal world. The winged imp with the knowing smile is more difficult to explain; as the drawing was intended as a valentine, could it be a wildlife version of Cupid?

the stone floor each day, Buckland dipped his fingers in the 'blood', gave them a lick, and immediately identified it as bat's urine . . .

He was a great advocate of bird droppings as fertiliser, and made his point very effectively at his Oxford college by using some of the stuff to write GUANO on the lawn. As the summer progressed the word stood out clearly, a much brighter green than the rest of the grass.

But William Buckland's experiments with food were modest compared with the activities of his son Frank, born in 1826 and, presumably, brought up on such weird dishes that he may well have thought roast beef and Yorkshire pudding was very eccentric indeed. **Frank Buckland** became a famous naturalist whose *Curiosities of Natural History* was a nineteenth-century bestseller, and launched a trend for compiling books of oddities and curiosities which, I am glad to say, continues today. Natural history, however, could offer nothing as curious as the average Buckland dinner menu.

There was a serious purpose behind it; he believed that as the population of Britain increased, it would need new and cheaper sources of meat, and he founded the Society for the Acclimatization of Animals in the United Kingdom, to encourage the production of home-grown exotic dishes. At the Society's dinner in 1862 the high spots were kangeroo stew, roast parrot and stewed sea slug. He apparently had high hopes of the sea slug – 'they are said to be the most succulent and pleasant food, not unlike the green fat of turtle'; but one disenchanted diner described it as a cross between calf's-head jelly and the contents of a glue-pot, and it never appeared on the menu again.

Plenty of other animals did, some successfully, some not. Elephant's trunk soup did not turn out too well, even though he boiled the trunk for several days, while a rhinoceros pie tasted, by his own admission, like very, very old beef. Similarly, when a panther died at London Zoo and Buckland persuaded the curator to send him a portion, he found that panther chop was 'not very good' – and if it was 'not very good' by Buckland's standards, it must have been absolutely awful. But this did not stop him

AS INSPECTOR OF SALMON FISHERIES, FRANK BUCKLAND WAS, PERHAPS, ALLOWED TO TAKE HOME THE ODD PERK. ONE WONDERS, THOUGH, IF IT EVER REACHED THE DINING-TABLE – FOR A MAN WHO LIKED TO SAMPLE PANTHER STEAKS AND ELEPHANT'S TRUNK SOUP, A POACHED SALMON MUST HAVE SEEMED A LITTLE MUNDANE.

applying to the curator again when several giraffes died in a fire at the giraffe house; he thought it was a great chance to acquire a giraffe steak, ready grilled . . .

Buckland, in fact, was always ready to sample any kind of meat; he was game for any animal, and to him, any animal was game. Roast ostrich was one favourite, mice fried in batter another. But he had no time at all for the more plebeian delights of horse-flesh, which some sections of the community resorted to in those days. He was once persuaded to attend a Horseflesh Dinner, which started with horse soup, followed by savoury horse tongue, and continued with a choice of boiled withers or roast baron of horse, stuffed with horse sausage. He worked his way through the lot, then announced that in his view 'hippophagy has not the slightest chance of success in this country'. He suggested that a dead horse could be put to better use by converting the hooves into inkstands and mounting the tail on a stick to swat flies.

Frank Buckland's interest in animals was not just culinary. At school and at college he kept an amazing assortment of pets – snakes, guinea-pigs, frogs, a monkey, a chameleon, and several mice. The mice were useful for feeding the snakes – and he ate quite a few himself. His pet slow-worms lived in his jacket pockets, emerging sometimes to cause confusion at tutorials. The larger animals were kept in a miniature zoo outside his students' quarters in Oxford. They included a bear called Tiglath-Pileser, named after an ancient Assyrian king. Frank was not a particular fan of the Assyrians, but the bear wandered into the college chapel while a student was reading the Bible passage which referred to King Tiglath-Pileser. The student had just got to his name when he saw the bear, and the words, we are told, 'froze on his lips'. Frank interpreted this as an informal christening ceremony, and the bear became Tiglath-Pileser, or more conveniently, 'Tig'.

Buckland originally hoped to be a surgeon, but his affinity for animals developed more strongly than for humans, and he concentrated on natural history. His wife Hannah fortunately shared his interest, and tolerated all manner of wildlife around the house after they were married. 'By the fire lived his monkeys,' wrote one chronicler, 'they did terrible damage and bit everyone in sight, but he loved them dearly, giving them beer every night and a drop of port on Sunday. A pet mongoose had the run of the house, pet rats scuttled over his desk, and a jackass let out a wild laugh every half-hour.'

Dining at the Bucklands' could be full of surprises — and not just the food. One evening Mrs Buckland's pet river hog got jammed under a chair, and when it headed for the door, the chair and the dinner guest went along too . . .

One of the pets, a South African red riverhog called Dick, was Mrs Buckland's particular responsibility. She had taken it in as an ailing piglet and nursed it through to health. Unfortunately, the pig not only got better, it got a lot bigger. One evening at dinner it crawled into its favourite hiding-place under one of the chairs, and became wedged. The unfortunate diner found himself suddenly being propelled away from the table and backwards towards the door . . .

Not all the animals in the Buckland household were alive. There were those awaiting consumption in the larder, of course, but others had been stuffed and placed around the house. One lady visitor, negotiating a dark stairway, went flying over an obstruction on the stairs, which turned out to be a dead hippopotamus. Far from sympathising, Buckland merely reprimanded her for her carelessness. Hippopotami, he told her sharply, did not grow on trees.

Travelling with Frank Buckland was almost as unnerving as visiting his house. He was generally conveying some small animals in his bags or his pockets, and he liked to allow them the maximum freedom to enjoy the journey. On one occasion, after dozing off in a railway carriage, he woke to see that several red slugs he had acquired were crawling over the bald head of his slumbering neighbour. There are various versions of what happened next, but the popular version is that, rather than waken his neighbour and face an embarrassing explanation, Buckland said goodbye to the slugs and got out at the next stop.

When he was in his forties Buckland was appointed Inspector of Salmon Fisheries, and here at last Mrs Buckland might have expected a few genuine delicacies for her dinner table. However, the only salmon to appear in her kitchen were the little ones that Buckland hatched out himself in his home-made hatchery. He once estimated there were 30,000 of them, which he took away and put in the rivers. He liked to warn his friends that, as salmon returned to the place of their birth, his kitchen sink was going to get very crowded as they came leaping out of the plug-hole . . .

Buckland spent much of his time now on the salmon rivers, catching fish eggs for the hatcheries, making sure the salmon could negotiate the weirs, and setting up 'ladders' to help them with the tricky ones. On one occasion he erected a temporary notice for their benefit while he was constructing the ladder:

> *No road at present over the weir. Go downstream, take the first turn to the right, and you will find good travelling water upstream and no jumping required.*

Frank Buckland died in 1880 at the age of fifty-four, as fascinated as ever by the natural life around him. He wrote in his will: 'I am going on a long journey where I think I shall see a great many curious animals. This journey I must go alone'.

WATER PLAYED A MAJOR PART IN LORD ROKEBY'S DIET. HE NOT ONLY DRANK A GREAT DEAL OF IT, BUT SPENT LONG PERIODS IMMERSED IN IT, IN WHAT MAY HAVE BEEN THE EARLIEST SOLAR-HEATED SWIMMING-POOL.

Buckland was by no means the first Englishman to worry about the adequacy of his country's food supplies, and devise an eccentric solution. In the eighteenth century LORD ROKEBY took quite the opposite approach to introducing new species into the English countryside. He maintained that, given sufficient encouragement, England was quite capable of living on existing home products, without importing any food at all. He demonstrated this with his own diet. 'Beef, over which boiled water had been poured, and eaten off a wooden platter, was a favourite dish,' we are told. 'Tea and coffee he would not touch, or sugar, for which he substituted honey. Wines and spirituous liquors he held in abhorrence – indeed, with exotics of every description he discouraged their consumption, from an idea that our own island was, by means of it productions, competent to the support of its inhabitants.'

He experimented with burnt peas and beans in place of imported coffee, and allowed himself no food containing wheat, which he considered an alien product. He always ate standing up at a little table just large enough to take one plate at a time – though how this encouraged home food production is not too clear. He had great faith in the beneficial qualities of water, which he not only drank in large quantities but bathed in constantly. He built himself a glass-roofed bath-house – it must have been one of the earliest solar heated swimming-pools – and was frequently to be found there, floating happily in the water, his long white beard spread out on the surface around him.

On his estate at Monks Horton in Kent, Lord Rokeby's enthusiasm for home-produced food applied only to livestock. He stopped all cultivation of the fields and turned them over to cattle, sheep and horses. These were allowed to wander into the ornamental gardens, though one hopes they kept clear of the bath-house. Amazingly, this haphazard system of animal husbandry paid off. The cattle grew fat, the tenants prospered, and so did Lord Rokeby, who accumulated a sizeable fortune. He kept it all in the house in bags marked 'GG' – Good Guineas – because he believed the Bank of England could collapse at any time and he refused to trust it with his money. The Bank survived, and so did Lord Rokeby, until he reached the ripe old age of eighty-seven.

The pursuit of good health and long life through eccentric eating has gone on ever since, and these days the quickest way to achieve fame, fortune and a permanent place in the bestseller lists is to tell people either to eat what nobody has thought of eating before, or to stop eating anything that normal people eat all the time. There was not such a market for diet books in the nineteenth century, and the COMTESSE DE NOAILLES who, in spite of her French name, was as English as they come, inflicted her odd dietary regime on only one person apart from herself, her unfortunate adopted daughter Maria. 'Adopted' is not quite the word; the Comtesse actually bought her in Paris from her impecunious Spanish father when she was nine, in return for either a vineyard or two bags of gold, depending which book you consult. But all the biographers are unanimous that, from her earliest days in an English convent school until long after she was married, Maria had to observe some very odd health rules invented by 'Madame', as the Comtesse was universally known.

THE COMTESSE DE NOAILLES, WHO LIKED TO HAVE A HERD OF COWS TETHERED OUTSIDE HER WINDOWS. THIS WAS NOT ONLY TO ENSURE A HANDY SUPPLY OF MILK; SHE ALSO BELIEVED THAT THE GASES THEY PRODUCED WERE BENEFICIAL TO HER HEALTH.

At school Madame arranged for a special cow to be in residence in the grounds so that Maria could be certain of having only pure milk. This was an extension of her own practice of keeping a herd of cows tethered near her windows, not only to benefit from their milk, but also from the methane gas they produced, which she considered extremely healthy. Fortunately she did not insist on the school providing for Maria what she always demanded for herself in hotels – a string of onions hung outside the bedroom door to keep away infection. But she did make the nuns drain the pond in the school grounds in case any bugs emerged from the stagnant water, and Maria had to wear Grecian tunics and handmade sandals, instead of the school uniform, to allow air to circulate freely round the body.

MARIA PASQUA, ADOPTED DAUGHTER OF THE COMTESSE DE NOAILLES, PAINTED WEARING THE COSTUME OF 'A GREEK CAPTIVE'. IN ONE WAY SHE WAS. DURING HER SCHOOL-DAYS MADAME CONSIDERED THAT THE STANDARD SCHOOL UNIFORM WAS UNHEALTHY, AND DRESSED HER IN GRECIAN TUNICS AND SANDALS SO THE AIR COULD CIRCULATE FREELY ROUND HER BODY.

At home Madame wrapped socks stuffed with squirrel fur round her head at night, and covered her chest with the skin of a Norwegian wild cat. If any germs penetrated these unlikely defences and she caught bronchitis, she switched her diet to soft herring roes until she recovered – which, surprisingly, she always did.

When Maria married she still could not escape from Madame's curious health tips. During pregnancy she was supposed to drink only water which had been used to boil the tips of pine branches; and when Madame came to stay, she not only demanded that the statutory cows be tethered in the garden, but all the trees near the house had to be felled in case she caught something nasty from the bark. I imagine that Maria, and certainly her husband, must have prayed constantly for an east wind, because Madame refused to travel anywhere with the wind in that direction; she was quite liable to stop a train and terminate her journey if she noticed that the trees were blowing the wrong way.

Madame rarely lived in one place for any length of time, but she did establish herself in a house near Eastbourne for the best part of twenty years, just at the foot of the Downs. Part of the Downs went with the house, and as it was good grazing land for sheep she switched her main allegiance from milk to mutton. This became the household's staple diet; large quantities were stored in a meat safe hanging from a tree in the garden, which had to be raised and lowered by a pulley. Madame herself always ate at a separate table with a small screen round her plate, ostensibly because she did not wish people to see her picking the bones, but it was strongly suspected that she was enjoying special dishes while everyone else laboured through their mutton stew.

In her later years, no doubt to Maria's relief, Madame moved permanently to France, and milk came into its own again. When her grandchildren visited her, she would take them on a picnic alongside a cow. The cow was milked direct into glasses, Madame added a dash of brandy, and that was the picnic. During her final illness she lived entirely on milk and champagne, but the milk, however beneficial, could not keep her alive indefinitely, and she died in 1908 at the age of eighty-four. She left £100,000 and twelve different wills to dispose of it. But one

Abbots Hall, near Aylsham in Norfolk, where Maria lived after her marriage. Before Madame would visit her, she asked that cows be put by the windows and the nearby trees cut down. To Maria's relief, the visit never materialised.

clause was very clear – Maria could only benefit if she always wore white in summer and never put on lace-up shoes. Mercifully there was no mention of milk, mutton, boiled fir-trees or stagnant ponds.

Fads over food have been carried to ridiculous lengths. The novelist Ronald Firbank is reported to have dined at some of London's most fashionable restaurants on nothing more than a pea; 'the day he was persuaded to supplement this with a slice of toast was a day of general rejoicing'. When Lord Byron indulged in this sort of abstemiousness, however, one had to take it, as it were, with a pinch of salt. A friend of Byron's, Samuel Rogers, records how he invited him to dinner soon after they first met.

'I asked him if he would take soup? No, he never took soup. Would he have some fish? No, he never took fish. Presently I asked if he would eat some mutton. No, he never ate mutton. I then asked him if he would take a glass of wine? No, he never tasted wine.'

By this time even the courteous Mr Rogers was becoming a little exasperated. He asked him, rather snappily, what he did eat and drink. 'Nothing but hard biscuits and soda-water,' Byron replied. His host launched a search in the kitchen, but the cook was right out of both items. Byron eventually settled for an even more bizarre combination, mashed potatoes soaked in vinegar.

Some days later Samuel Rogers told a mutual friend the story. 'How long will Lord Byron persevere in his present diet?' he asked. 'Just as long as you continue to notice it,' the friend replied – and went on to tell him that Byron had gone straight from his house to a club in St James's and eaten a hearty four-course dinner . . .

Such flippancy over food would not have been tolerated by WILLIAM KITCHINER, founder and secretary of the Eta Beta Pi dining club ('Eat a Better Pie?' Surely not!) – and a very particular host. His invitations to dine with the 'Committee of Taste' allowed for no misunderstanding: 'The specimens will be placed upon the table at five o'clock precisely, when the business of the day will immediately commence'. Late comers were never admitted, no matter what the excuse. Kitchiner took the view that 'the perfection of several of the preparations is so exquisitely evanescent that the delay of one minute after their arrival at the meridian of concoction will render them no longer worthy of men of taste'. Many a dinner hostess, waiting by the oven while the menfolk have another gin and tonic, will know how he felt.

This eccentric epicure devised a 'portable magazine of taste'

A guest who combines verbosity with insomnia must qualify for the title of 'The Person You Would Least Like to Entertain To Dinner'. PROFESSOR RICHARD PORSON, distinguished Cambridge academic at the turn of the nineteenth century, had a third qualification which clinched it – he drank like a fish. He would stay on, drinking and talking, quite possibly all night, with his fellow guests long departed and his host fast asleep. Eventually his friends told him they would only invite him if he left at 11pm, to which he reluctantly agreed, but in the homes of more casual acquaintances who failed to make this proviso, there was no budging him.

One such acquaintance, a gentleman called John Horne Tooke, had been warned of Porson's tenacity, but having learned that he had not slept for three nights, thought it safe to ask him for dinner on the fourth. He was wrong. Porson talked through dinner, after dinner, and on through the night. He was still there at breakfast-time, and still talking. The only way to get rid of him, thought his host, was to invent a story about having to meet someone at a coffee house. 'Splendid,' said Porson, 'I'll come with you.' And he did. When Horne Tooke eventually escaped and returned home he told his servants never to admit Porson again. 'A man who could sit up for four successive nights,' he reasoned, 'could sit up for forty.'

He was probably right. His capacity for liquor of any sort seemed unlimited. John Hoppner, the artist who painted his portrait, knew this all too well, and when he had him in for dinner he told him his wife had gone out with the only keys to the wine cellar. Porson immediately insisted that Mrs Hoppner must keep a bottle somewhere for her own use and, in spite of his host's objections, he searched her bedroom and duly uncovered a bottle which he drained forthwith. When the lady returned after Porson had gone, her husband angrily accused her of secret drinking and showed her the empty bottle. 'Great heavens,' she cried, 'that was the paraffin for the lamp.'

Richard Porson, not surprisingly, died before he was fifty. In spite of his eccentricities he was greatly revered at Cambridge, and was buried in the chapel at Trinity.

He is remembered in the academic world for many learned expositions, but I prefer to remember him for the gently devastating way in which he once declined a dinner invitation which he didn't fancy – maybe the host was a teetotaller.

'No thank you,' he said, 'I dined yesterday.'

Maybe I'll use it myself . . .

which members could take out to dinner. This was not an early *Good Food Guide*, but a case containing all the equipment and condiments necessary to turn an average meal into a masterpiece. There were twenty-eight bottles of assorted sauces, not least Dr Kitchiner's own creation known as Wow-Wow sauce, a powerful combination of port, pickled cucumbers, capers and mustard. There were slices of lemon peel, pickled walnuts, essence of celery and other auxiliary delicacies; and to make sure the proportions were correct, the magazine contained scales, a set of weights and measures, a pestle and mortar, and a nutmeg grater. I am not sure how their hosts reacted when Kitchiner or his colleagues produced all this at the dinner-table, but I imagine they did not invite them twice. His tastes differed greatly from the frugal Comtesse de Noailles, but he did share her appreciation of fresh milk. He urged that travellers should ride on cows rather than horses, to ensure a constant supply throughout the journey. I am surprised that Madame never thought of that one herself.

Dr William Kitchiner, who refused to admit late arrivals to his dinners: 'The perfection of several of the preparations is so exquisitely evanescent that the delay of one minute after their arrival at the meridian of concoction will render them no longer worthy of men of taste'.

At the opposite extreme to the eccentric gourmets are the eccentric gluttons, those trenchermen of vast appetite, enormous girth, and incredible thickness of skin, who could tuck away tremendous quantities of food and drink at the drop of a salt-cellar. A modest example was Dr George Fordyce, an esteemed eighteenth-century physician, who did not allow his medical knowledge to get in the way of his appetite. To be fair, he only ate one meal a day, but that one meal, which never varied, would have lasted most of us a week. He would arrive at four o'clock precisely at an establishment at Paternoster Row in London called Dolly's Chop House. He put away half a chicken, or a plate of boned fish, as a starter before tackling the main course, a rump steak weighing one and a half pounds. This was washed down with a tankard of strong ale, a quarter-pint of brandy and a bottle of port. Then he strolled to three other coffee houses in the vicinity, taking a brandy and water at each. And thus fortified, he went off to see his patients.

This led to an interesting encounter with a titled lady who was languishing on her sick-bed when the doctor reeled happily through the doorway. The story goes something like this. They exchanged a few pleasantries and he attempted to feel her pulse, but at this stage he realised he was in no condition to do so. 'Drunk, by Jove,' he muttered to himself reproachfully. Whereupon his distinguished patient burst into tears.

'I know,' she cried, 'forgive me. I'll never touch another drop.'

INDEX

K

L

M

N

O

P

Q

R

S

T

W

Acknowledgments

Many of the photographs/illustrations in this book were specially commissioned, others supplied to us or requiring acknowledgment are listed below.

1 Brighton Central Reference Library. **2** *top left* The Savage Club, London *top right* Waterton Park Hotel *bottom* The Berners Estates Company. **3** *top* Derbyshire County Council – Local Studies Library, Derby *below* Dinton Hall. **5/6** Punch Publications. **7** Wakefield Museums, Galleries and Castles – The Waterton Collection: Wakefield Museum. **8/9** Leicestershire County Council – Thurrock Museum. **11** *top* The Marquess of Tavistock and the Trustees of the Bedford Estates *bottom* Ashridge Management College. **12** *top* Hertfordshire Local Studies Collection, Hertfordshire Library Service. **13** *top* Mary Evans Picture Library *bottom* Doran Dyble Photography. **15** *top* Waterton Park Hotel *bottom* National Portrait Gallery, London. **16** Wakefield Museums, Galleries and Castles – The Waterton Collection: Wakefield Museum. **19** Pictorial reference – Lord Mount Edgcumbe. **23** Mary Evans Picture Library. **25** The Mansell Collection. **29/30** Mary Evans Picture Library. **31** Leicestershire Museums, Arts and Records Service. **32** top Mary Evans Picture Library. **39** National Portrait Gallery, London. **44** Essex County Council, Chelmsford Library. **46** Suffolk Record Office, Ipswich Branch. **47** *bottom* Edward Reeves. **49** *top* National Portrait Gallery, London. **50** Morrison Photos Ltd. **51/53** The Manx Museum and National Trust. **52/53** Morrison Photos Ltd. **54** *bottom* Centre for Oxfordshire Studies, Photographic Archive. **62** Skegness Library. **63** *left* L Jackson. **64/66** *bottom* The Boston Collection. **67** London Borough of Harrow Libraries. **68** *bottom right* Painshill Park Trust Ltd. **70** *top* The Bodleian Library, Oxford. Gough Maps 30, fol 59b *bottom* The Duke of Abercorn. **71** London Borough of Harrow Libraries. **74** Reproduced by Courtesy of the Trustees of the British Museum. **78** Savage Club, London. **79** *top*/**80** North Hertfordshire District Council – Hitchin Museum. **79** *bottom* Mr and Mrs Michael Skeggs. **83** Mary Evans Picture Library. **84** The National Trust (Petworth). **86** Keith Fletcher. **87** Brighton Central Reference Library. **88/89** Mary Evans Picture Library. **90** By permission of the British Library. **91** Derbyshire County Council – Local Studies Library, Derby. **94** Brighton Central Reference Library. **95** Mary Evans Picture Library. **98** Guy Gravett. **100** National Portrait Gallery, London. **102** *top left and right* Dinton Hall. **103/104** Mary Evans Picture Library. **105/107** By permission of the British Library. **108** Avon County Library: Bath Central Library. **111** National Portrait Gallery, London. **115** Board of Trustees of the Chevening Estate/Centre for Kentish Studies. **117/118** *top*/**119** Sunday Times Magazine. **118** *bottom* Norfolk Museum Service, Castle Museum, Norwich. **120** Mary Evans Picture Library. **121** By permission of the British Library. **123/124** Sir Tatton Sykes. **122/127/128** National Portrait Gallery, London. **129/130/131** *top* The Berners Estates Company. **146** Tate Gallery, London. **141/148/149** *left* Beckwith Antiques. **149** *right* Hertfordshire County Record Office, The Gerish Collection. **152/153** National Trust. **158** Mary Evans Picture Library. **161/162/163/164/165** The Trustees of the Beckford Tower Trust. **167** Aerofilms. **169/170** National Trust. **171** Local Studies, Central Library, Rochdale. **172/174** Centre for Oxfordshire Studies, Photographic Archive. **176** *top left and right* Chatsworth House Trust. **177** Mary Evans Picture Library. **178** The Crystal Palace Museum. **184** *bottom* Manchester Public Libraries. **185** *left* Surrey Local Studies Library. **189/190** *bottom* Gawsworth Hall. **190** *top* National Trust. **193/194** *bottom*/**195** Reproduced from the collection of Wolverhampton Public Libraries. **196** *bottom*/**197** University College London Library. **198** Gainsborough Private Collection. **199** *top* White Hart, Nayland *bottom* Gainsborough's House, Sudbury, Suffolk. **201** University College London Library. **203** *top and bottom right* Cambridgeshire Collection, Cambridgeshire Libraries. **207** Crown copyright, Imperial War Museum. **208** The Illustrated London News Picture Library. **211/212/213** The Buckland Papers, Devon Record Office. Ref 138m/F811 and F843. **218** Tate Gallery, London. **221** Mary Evans Picture Library.

Every effort has been made to obtain the appropriate rights or permission to publish all copyright material. The publishers would be pleased to acknowledge any omission in future editions.

Bibliography

The following is a select listing of reference material consulted in the preparation of this title. The publishers wish to express their gratitude to the many individuals and organisations whose material and specialised knowledge was invaluable in the preparation of this book.

Anon. *Home Life with Herbert Spencer*, Arrowsmith, 1910.
Billington, S. *A Social History of the Fool*, Harvester, 1984.
Blunt, W. *John Christie of Glyndebourne*, Bles, 1968.
Boston, E. R. *Font to Footplate*, Line One, 1986.
Burgess, G. H. O. *The Curious World of Frank Buckland*, Baker, 1967.
Bushell, P. *Great Eccentrics*, Allen & Unwin, 1984.
Caufield, C. *The Emperor of the United States of America and Other Magnificent British Eccentrics*, Corgi, 1982.
Cecil, D. *The Cecils of Hatfield House*, Constable, 1973.
Colville, J. *Those Lambton's*, Hodder & Stoughton, 1988.
Cooke, O. and Smith, E. (eds.) *Collectors' Items from the Saturday Book*, Hutchinson, 1955.
Glendenning, V. *The Life of Victoria Sackville-West*, Weidenfeld & Nicholson, 1983.
Goffin, M. *Maria Pasqua*, Oxford University Press, 1979.
Hadfield, J. (ed.) *The Saturday Book Number 26*, Hutchinson, 1966.
Hebbert, A. (ed.) *Secret Britain*, AA, 1986.
Hobson, R. *Charles Waterton: His Home, Habits and Handiwork*, Whittaker, 1866.
Hughes, S. *Glyndebourne, A History of the Festival Opera*, David & Charles, 1981.
Johnston, S. *Collecting – The Passionate Pastime*, Viking, 1986.
Keay, J. *Eccentric Travellers*, Ariel Books (BBC), 1982.
Kennedy, C. *Eccentric Soldiers*, Mobrays, 1975.
Michell, J. *Eccentric Lives and Peculiar Notions*, Thames & Hudson, 1984.
Miller, J. *An Englishman's Home*, Countryside Books, 1985.
Murphy, S. *The Mitford Family Album*, Sidgwick & Jackson, 1985.
Newman, A. *The Stanhopes of Chevening*, Macmillan, 1969.
Nichols, M. *The World's Greatest Cranks and Crackpots*, Octopus, 1990.
Sitwell, E. *English Eccentrics*, Penguin, 1971.
Snelling, O. F. *Rare Books and Rarer People*, Werner Shaw, 1982.
Weeks, D. *Eccentrics – The Scientific Investigation*, Stirling University Press, 1988.
Whitmore, R. *Mad Lucas*, North Herts District Council, 1983.